W9-BHG-973

The Last Man Takes LSD

Foucault and the End of Revolution

Mitchell Dean and Daniel Zamora

VERSO
London • New York

First published by Verso 2021

1 3 5 7 9 10 8 6 4 2

Verso
UK: 6 Meard Street, London W1F 0EG
US: 20 Jay Street, Suite 1010, Brooklyn, NY 11201
versobooks.com

Verso is the imprint of New Left Books

ISBN-13: 978-1-83976-139-3
ISBN-13: 978-1-83976-141-6 (UK EBK)
ISBN-13: 978-1-83976-140-9 (US EBK)

British Library Cataloguing in Publication Data
A catalogue record for this book is available from the British Library

Library of Congress Cataloging-in-Publication Data
A catalog record for this book is available from the Library of Congress
Library of Congress Control Number: 2020948742

Typeset in Minion by Hewer Text UK Ltd, Edinburgh
Printed and bound by CPI Group (UK) Ltd, Croydon CR0 4YY

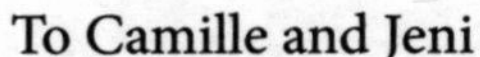

To Camille and Jeni

Contents

Acknowledgements

The true origins of our collaboration on this book go back to the invitation extended to both of us to debate each other on Foucault and neoliberalism at the University of Amsterdam by Daan Wierdsma on behalf of the student philosophy association, AmFiBi, under the guidance of their teacher, Dr Karen Vintges. If our debate did not generate the expected drama that night in December 2016, we offer this book as a belated compensation.

The book, of course, has other, more 'scattered', origins. We would like to thank Nicholas Brown, who invited one of us to speak on Foucault at the Marxist Literary Group conference on 17 June 2014 and Anne Barron who invited the other to speak a few days later at the British Library on 'Remembering Foucault' on the thirtieth anniversary of his death. We also thank Frédéric Panier, Vanessa De Greef, Roger Lancaster, Anwen Tormey, Serge Audier, Jamie Peck, Nik Theodore, Pedro Ramos Pinto, Emile Chabal, Jean-Yves Pranchère, Niklas Olsen, Solange Manche, David Priestland, Martin Conway, Corey Robin, Paul Henman, Sanford Schram, Melinda Cooper and Philip Mirowski, for their interest, warm invitations to speak and write, and invaluable advice and suggestions. We want to thank Stephen Sawyer and Daniel

Steinmetz-Jenkins for taking this debate seriously, Michael C. Behrent for opening up original and new ways to read Foucault's work, and Anton Jäger for his invaluable support and comments. Finally, our thanks go to Walter Benn Michaels, Jennifer Ashton, Adolph Reed and Todd Cronan, without whom this book would never have seen the light of day.

A version of Chapter 1 was originally published as Mitchell Dean, 'Foucault and the Neoliberalism Controversy', in Damien Cahill, Melinda Cooper, Martijn Konings and David Primrose (eds), *The Sage Handbook of Neoliberalism,* London: Sage, 2018, pp. 40–54. Parts of Chapter 2 were first published as Daniel Zamora, 'Finding a "Left Governmentality": Foucault's Last Decade' in Stephen W. Sawyer and Daniel Steinmetz-Jenkins (eds), *Foucault, Neoliberalism and Beyond*, London: Rowman and Littlefield, 2019, pp. 53–72. Chapter 3 draws upon Mitchell Dean and Daniel Zamora, 'Did Foucault Reinvent His History of Sexuality through the Prism of Neoliberalism?', *Los Angeles Review of Books*, 18 April 2018, and Daniel Zamora 'Governing the Soul, Governing the Text: Foucault, May 68, and the Fall of the Sovereign', *The Tocqueville Review* 41:1, 2020, pp. 141–59. Finally, an earlier version of Chapter 7 was originally published as Mitchell Dean, 'Rogue Neoliberalism, Liturgical Power and the Search for a Left Governmentality', *South Atlantic Quarterly* 118:2, 2019, pp. 325–42.

An earlier version of this book was published as *Le dernier homme et la fin de la révolution. Foucault après Mai 68,* Lux, Montréal, 2019. Chapters 4 and 6 are entirely new additions to that book. We gratefully thank Alexandre Sanchez for her support for that publication and Lux for allowing us to retain the English-language rights.

Finally, we wish to express our sincere gratitude to Henri-Paul Fruchaud, on behalf of Michel Foucault's heirs, for his kind permission to reproduce two previously unpublished letters by Michel Foucault to Simeon Wade.

Introduction: The Last Man Takes LSD

> The important question today . . . is the idea and theme of the revolution. European history has been dominated by this idea. It is exactly this idea that's in the process of disappearing at the moment.
>
> Michel Foucault, Japan, 1978[1]

In the spring of 1975, Michel Foucault was set to lay claim to being the last great French intellectual of the twentieth century. He was about to publish the first volume of the work that would clinch that title for him, the *History of Sexuality*. Yet, fed up with the conformist and closeted culture of France at that time, he would once again seek refuge elsewhere, continuing a pattern of his adult life that had taken him to Sweden, Poland and later to Tunisia, where he had lived during the events of May 1968. So taken was he by the atmosphere of liberation in San Francisco that he contemplated

1 Michel Foucault, 'Michel Foucault and Zen: A Stay in a Zen Temple', in Jeremy R. Carrette (ed.), *Religion and Culture: Michel Foucault*, New York: Routledge, 1999, p. 114.

emigrating and becoming a Californian. It seems then that Foucault fell in love with California. It was there that the austere anti-humanist thinker of the 1960s, who had proclaimed the 'death of man' in open hostility to Jean-Paul Sartre's philosophy of freedom, would experiment during the final decade of his life with new forms of relating to others and inventing oneself in the S/M clubs of San Francisco.

It was there also that he might be said to have become the 'last man' to take LSD. Foucault described the event as a 'great experience, one of the most important in my life'.[2] Yet the French philosopher came very late to the experiment with hallucinogenic drugs. While many others would later 'drop acid', as personal 'trips' of this kind were called, their cultural zenith was the late 1960s, and, in this sense, Foucault was the 'last man' of intellectual note to take LSD as a part of the first wave of its use as a consciousness-expanding drug. He had been preceded by Timothy Leary, Aldous Huxley, R.D. Laing, Allen Ginsberg, The Beatles and many others. Dropping acid was a headline experience of the youth counterculture of the late '60s in California. Between 1964 and 1966, the writer Ken Kesey and his gang of 'Merry Pranksters' travelled across the United States on a psychedelic bus, stopping regularly to throw LSD parties. These 'acid tests' would be one pathway from the Beat Generation to the hippie movement in the years to come.[3] No doubt LSD and other 'psychedelic' drugs would continue to be used, with varying and sometimes greater prevalence, but never again would LSD, and the experience it afforded, come to define culture, art, fashion and style in general as it did in the late 1960s.

The mind-altering qualities of the drug were conceived at the time as part deep self-analysis and psychotherapy and part intense religious experience. Timothy Leary would even found a church, the League for Spiritual Discovery, with LSD as its sacrament.

2 Michel Foucault, Letter to Simeon Wade, 14 May 1975.

3 This story is told in the book by Tom Wolfe, *The Electric Kool-Aid Acid Test*, published in August 1968.

Foucault himself would agree that the experience was 'mystical', offering him 'visions of a new life' and 'a fresh perspective' on himself.[4]

Some months later, in a letter to Simeon Wade, the young acolyte who had invited him to take the drug, Foucault wrote that the experience had led him to entirely rewrite the first volume of his *History of Sexuality*. He would set aside the hundreds of pages already completed, throw the completed second volume onto the fire and then abandon the prospectus for the multi-volume work. Except for the first volume, which became a manifesto for the emerging gay movement in California and elsewhere, none of the remaining volumes were ever published in their initial form.[5]

Foucault went to Claremont Graduate School in southern California during the first of several research visits to Berkeley. Given the relatively obscure nature of the institution, his presence can only be due to the persistence of Wade, the author of a self-produced fanzine entitled *Chez Foucault*. Foucault is pictured there in his white roll-neck sweater and white wide-rimmed sunglasses that made him look like a cross between Kojak and Elton John.

Accompanied by his lover and companion, the pianist Michael Stoneman, Wade would drive Foucault on a journey that culminated in the acid trip at Zabriskie Point in Death Valley, the desert remains of a lake that dried up 5 million years ago. But the trio were late even in this choice of place. The celebrated Italian film-maker, Michelangelo Antonioni, had begun filming his Californian classic, *Zabriskie Point*, there in 1968, against the backdrop of the student protests, the Black Panther movement, drug culture and sexual liberation. His film included an orgy at the location. By May

4 See James Miller, *The Passion of Michel Foucault*, London: HarperCollins, 1993/2019, pp. 245–51.

5 Heather Dundas, 'Foreword' to Simeon Wade, *Foucault in California*, Berkeley: Heyday, 1990/2019, p. xvii; Miller, *Passion*, pp. 252; Heather Dundas, 'Michel Foucault in Death Valley: A Boom Interview with Simeon Wade', *Boom California*, 10 September 2017.

1975, we might suppose it was less an avant-garde aesthetic event than a hippie cliché to drop acid there. At least the trio found a less plebeian soundtrack for their reveries than Antonioni, replacing Pink Floyd and The Grateful Dead with tapes of Richard Strauss, Stockhausen and Pierre Boulez.[6] Foucault took acid during the death throes of a period when LSD was considered as what his colleague, the historian of ancient thought Pierre Hadot, would call a 'spiritual exercise', soon to be replaced by the cocaine-fuelled entrepreneurialism of the discos and nightclubs of the late 1970s.

The effect on Foucault was profound. He would indeed radically alter the direction of his research in the following years.[7] When he finally published the second and third volumes of the *History of Sexuality* almost eight years later, the project put at its centre the 'techniques of the self' he had discovered in the ethics of classical Greece and ancient Rome. Rather than studying sexuality through the paradoxes of repression and avowal inherited from Christianity, he placed it in the long line of ways humans would view themselves, govern themselves, and seek to moderate, control or liberate, as the case may be, what they would regard as pleasures, desires or temptations of the flesh. What moderns call 'sexuality' was no longer to be viewed as a deep truth to be unlocked from within our unconscious, as Freud would have it. It was simply one more way in which we invent ourselves as human beings in relation to erotics, the household and family, daily life and ethics. Given its historical relativity, and its relation to the confessional culture of medieval Christianity, sexuality was something from which the ancients could help us escape, or, as Foucault would often put it, something about which we could at least 'think otherwise'. We should not liberate our sexuality but free ourselves from the whole confessional system that predicated liberation on sexuality.

6 Wade, *Foucault in California*, pp. 77, 79, 85.

7 The first edition of *La volonté de savoir* (The Will to Knowledge) advertised six volumes 'to appear'. Foucault had even collected a large amount of documentation to prepare the writing of each of them. See Stuart Elden, *Foucault's Last Decade*, Cambridge: Polity, 2016, pp. 62–4.

It would not be unfair to say that during the 1960s Foucault had shared in the obsession of a certain kind of French philosophy with doing away with the 'subject', a strange term that is both technical and obscure. Rejecting the subject, announcing its death or the death of the author, became a standard trope in the discourse and literary theory of Foucault, Barthes, Derrida and company. By the 1970s, the subject was explained not only as a kind of fiction of the pronouncements of the social and behavioural sciences, but as a result of the application of such pseudo-sciences within what Americans like Erving Goffman would call the 'total institutions' of the asylum, the hospital, the school and, above all, the prison. The scandal of Foucault's work on prisons, for example, was his replacement of the idea that they might deform and brutalize the human subject with the claim that in their search for greater humanism they would fabricate the very subjects that they dominated or subjected.

After his California experiences, and exposure to the 'Californian cult of the self', however, Foucault's subject becomes a free one, an active agent capable of making itself through spiritual and physical exercises, such as people in the West might seek through mediation and yoga, therapy and 'self-help', and with the potential for radical self-transformation through extreme experiences. 'To make the "*principe de plaisir*" a "*principe de réalité*"', he wrote to Wade, was 'an ethical and a political problem to be solved nowadays'.[8] Thus, engaging in erotic adventures, psychotropic drug experiments and the 'invention' of new lifestyles made possible the transgression of the normalized self that is produced by the institutions of the modern welfare state. To put this in the terms of the American neoliberals Foucault was reading at the time, the 'entrepreneur of the self' was willing to put their very identity at risk in the act of self-creation.

Foucault is, however, the last man to take LSD in another, more profound, sense, than that of simply being a cultural late-adopter.

8 Foucault, Letter to Simeon Wade, 14 May 1975.

He was a self-diagnosed last man in the sense that he had already announced the 'death of man' – in the form of *homo dialecticus* and the sovereign subject – as early as 1964,[9] and then, most famously, in *The Order of Things* two years later.[10] He would later expound a number of significant endings – of politics and the revolution, among others. At times, Foucault liked to present himself as an anti-Hegelian, placing himself in the positivist tradition in France that was opposed to German idealism and its philosophies of history.[11] But, even in the 1960s, the shards of the philosophy of history, with its teleologies and eschatologies, ripped through the fabric of the austere formalism of the archaeologist. In many ways, Foucault's thought bears the arcane visage of the French Hegel. This was the one taught at the Ecole Pratique des Hautes Etudes by Alexandre Kojève in the 1930s – later a key inspiration for Francis Fukuyama's book *The End of History and the Last Man*[12] – and, more directly, by Jean Hyppolite, through whom Foucault claimed to have 'heard something of Hegel's voice', and to whom, he claimed in his inaugural lecture at the Collège de France, he owed the 'greatest debt'.[13]

In his early twenties, Foucault wrote a thesis on Hegel's *Phenomenology of Spirit*, which had been translated into French by Hyppolite.[14] Taking up his chair at the Collège some twenty years later, Foucault will admit that the resources he mobilized against

9 Michel Foucault, 'Madness, the Absence of an Oeuvre', in *History of Madness*, London: Routledge, 2006, p. 543.

10 Michel Foucault, *The Order of Things: An Archaeology of the Human Sciences*, London: Tavistock, 1970, p. 387.

11 Michel Foucault, 'Georges Canguilhem, Philosopher of Error', *Ideology and Consciousness* 7, 1980, pp. 51–62.

12 Francis Fukuyama, *The End of History and the Last Man*, New York: Free Press, 1992.

13 Michel Foucault, 'The Order of Discourse', in Robert Young (ed.), *Untying the Text: A Post-Structuralist Reader*, Boston: Routledge and Kegan Paul, 1981, p. 74. See also Michel Foucault, 'Jean Hyppolite, 1907–1968', in *Dits et Écrits I, 1954–1975*, Paris: Gallimard, 2001, text no. 67, pp. 807–13.

14 David Macey, *The Lives of Michel Foucault*, New York: Penguin, 1995, p. 32.

Hegel may be but a ruse through which the German philosopher lies in wait for us.[15] As Foucault's biographer, David Macey, points out, it could hardly have escaped his notice that it was the Hegelian Kojève who first ensured that the 'death of man' entered into the public lexicon in the late 1940s.[16] To be sure, this was not the figure of the human sciences who 'would be erased, like a face drawn in sand at the edge of the sea', but a being facing its own finitude – its own death.[17] Nonetheless, Foucault would share with Kojève the thesis of the 'end of the revolution', and the assumption that modern Islam had potential commonalities with the Greco-Latin Mediterranean heritage.[18]

Foucault also shared with Kojève trips of discovery to Japan. The latter found in the ritual life of the Japanese an alternative post-history to mankind's 'return to animality' exemplified by the United States but also followed by Soviet and Chinese communism and the developing Third World. Japanese culture – the tea ceremony, the Noh theatre, flower arrangements – appeared to Kojève as a kind of snobbery devoid of substantive human values.[19] Similarly, the enigma of Japan and the 'mysterious' nature of its inhabitants brought Foucault back there for his second trip in April 1978, informed by the texts of the great counter-cultural icons of the time, Alan Watts and D.T. Suzuki.[20] His trip included a stay at a Zen temple, and it was there, in discussion with Omori Sogen Roshi, one of the most important Zen masters of the twentieth century, that he argued that, 'since 1789, Europe has changed according to the idea of revolution. European history has been dominated by this idea. That's exactly the idea that's disappearing

15 Foucault, 'The Order of Discourse', p. 32.

16 Macey, *Lives*, p. 90.

17 Foucault, *The Order of Things*, p. 387.

18 Alexandre Kojève, 'Outline of a Doctrine of French Policy (August 27, 1945)', *Policy Review*, August–September, 2004, p. 19.

19 Alexandre Kojève, *Introduction to the Reading of Hegel*, Ithaca NY: Cornell University Press, 1980, pp. 161–2n.

20 Macey, *Lives*, p. 400. See Alan Watts, *The Way of Zen*, New York: Pantheon, 1957; D.T. Suzuki, *Zen and Japanese Culture*, New York: Pantheon, 1959.

right now.'[21] He was announcing nothing less than 'the end of politics', and in doing so placed himself within an Hegelian intellectual lineage apparently at odds with his own self-understanding.

At the time of the demise of the Soviet Union and the fall of the Berlin Wall, Fukuyama argued that a global aspiration for liberal democracy would satisfy the human desire for recognition, honour, status and achievement. No longer would humankind disagree over the mode of social organization. The struggle between socialism and capitalism would be replaced by 'the endless solving of technical problems' and 'the satisfaction of sophisticated consumer demands'.[22] We had all become, from now on, more or less partisans of liberal democratic capitalism.

Fukuyama called this world 'post-historical'. 'What people believe' was now replaced by 'what they desire', putting the subject at the centre of politics. If in class conflict what counted was what 'side' we were on, all that counted in the era of the end of history was knowing 'what' or 'who' we were. As Walter Benn Michaels has noted, in the post-historic era, rather than seeking to 'change the world', the last man – and the last woman – seek to change themselves, replacing devotion to a cause with a commitment to experimentations with the self.[23]

It might be objected that to call Foucault the 'last man' is to reduce him to the conformist, disciplinary individual he diagnosed in *Discipline and Punish*, or at best to the seeker of the pleasurable but trivial satisfactions of consumer society. This would be the contemptible 'last man' of Nietzsche's Zarathustra:

21 Michel Foucault, 'M. Foucault to Zen: zendera taizai-ki', *Umi* 197, August–September, 1978, in *Dits et Écrits II, 1976–1988*, Paris: Gallimard, 2001, text no. 236, p. 623. English version in Foucault, 'Michel Foucault and Zen', p. 114.

22 Francis Fukuyama, 'The End of History?', *The National Interest*, Summer 1989, p. 25.

23 Walter Benn Michaels, *The Shape of the Signifier*, Princeton: Princeton University Press, 2004, p. 156.

> One still works, for work is a form of entertainment. But one is careful lest the entertainment be too harrowing. One no longer becomes poor or rich: both require too much exertion. Who still wants to rule? Who obey? Both require too much exertion.
>
> No shepherd and one herd! Everybody wants the same, everybody is the same: whoever feels different goes voluntarily into a madhouse.[24]

These words remind us so much of what Foucault would write and talk about in the years following his own 'acid test'. He would reject the welfare state as rooted in the Christian pastoral relation of commanding shepherd and obedient flock. He would seek to avoid the problem of inequality by new negative income tax measures, what today we call universal basic income. And, in the idea of human capital, he would be fascinated with work not as production but as a form of choice and self-consumption. Yet, as Foucault never ceased to insist, all this was but part of an investigation of who we have become in our present, a diagnosis of our limits and capabilities that portends a possible transcendence. He foresaw that the end of politics and the revolution did not mean a passive contentment but that the last men would 'deliberately seek out struggle, danger, risk and daring . . . unfulfilled by peace and prosperity', as Fukuyama would put it a few years later.[25]

Rather than the mediocre, passive and conformist Nietzschean 'last man', Foucault's last man would increasingly come to exercise autonomy, governing himself and turning life into an 'aesthetics of existence'. Foucault is anti-Hegelian in that he rejects the struggle for 'recognition' rooted in the Master–Slave dialectic. He does not, however, replace it with the class struggle of Marxism, but with the fight for self-creation, for maximizing self-government and

24 Friedrich Nietzsche, 'Thus Spoke Zarathustra: A Book for All and None', in *The Portable Nietzsche*, ed. and trans. by Walter Kaufmann, New York: Viking Press, 1954, p.130. Passage cited by Fukuyama, *The End of History and the Last Man*, p. 305.

25 Fukuyama, *End of History and the Last Man*, p. xxii.

autonomy against the heteronomy of 'subjectification' (*assujettissement*). Foucault's last man realizes that not only is the revolution over but so too the dull, and potentially authoritarian, politics of progressive social reform in the welfare state, with its therapeutics of the soul. Taking LSD would be one, if not the first, of many experiments that the last man would undertake to become something other than a given identity. Foucault's visits to a Zen monastery or to Taoist communes were doubtless another kind of experiment, and, on a collective level, his two trips to Iran would help him observe a 'political spirituality' long forgotten in the West but alive in a kind of liturgy of sacrificial self-transformation as a counter-conduct against the West, its state and its modernization.

Most dramatically, while under the influence of drugs, Foucault would later be run over by a car in Rue Vaugirard where he lived. He had 'the impression that [he] was dying' and experienced 'a very intense pleasure' that would be 'one of his best memories'.[26] Here the philosopher of the 'death of man' would experience, for a moment, Kojève's Hegelian 'death of man' as a self-overcoming, which is 'truly *his* death – that is, something that is proper to him and belongs to him as his own, and which can consequently be known by him, wanted or negated by him'.[27] Foucault would often use the term *épreuve* to refer to the use of the body in 'limit experiences' such as the intensification of pleasure in the rituals of sadomasochism, experiences that would far transcend the everyday contentment of Nietzsche's last man. In his use of this term, akin to the idea of an ordeal or a test, we are a reminded of the Merry Pranksters' 'acid test'. As Foucault would argue in his celebrated text, 'What is Enlightenment?', 'the historical-critical attitude must also be an experimental one' that would be a 'test' of and transcend

26 See Michel Foucault, 'Une interview de Michel Foucault par Stephen Riggins', 1983, in *Dits et Écrits II, 1976–1988*, text no. 336, p. 1353. For the English version, see Michel Foucault, 'An interview with Stephen Riggins', in Michel Foucault, *Ethics, Subjectivity and Truth: The Essential Works*, vol. 1, ed. Paul Rabinow, New York: The New Press, 1997, p. 129.

27 Kojève, *Introduction*, p. 245.

the limits of one's given identity.[28] As François Ewald, Foucault's assistant at the Collège de France, wrote for the twentieth anniversary of the philosopher's death:

> it is with Foucault that we find the first great elaboration of the mode of existence of the contemporary individual, freed from the 'grand narratives' and alienations in the mass movements that marked the twentieth century, assigned to construct and to value its existence through the invention of arts of life and lifestyles.[29]

This is the incredible story of our book: of the greatest mind in France, of his meeting with a California he adored as a place of warmth and tolerance and thought of as disconnected even from the rest of the United States, of his rejection of the terms of political discourse and search for a new left 'governmentality' in place of socialism, and of his replacement of the sovereign subject with new powers and new forms of autonomous self-creation akin to those he discovered in Greco-Roman Antiquity and which today survived in clandestine form in the Orient. But it will be the surprising encounter with a new and increasingly influential form of political thought, neoliberalism, that will be decisive among all these shifts. It will be in its *épreuves* of too much governing, according to the modes of truth-telling that arose from the market, that Foucault will find the space for a last man that could escape the conformity of the sovereign subject and its disciplinary normalization without returning to the submission to sovereign rule.

In this account, Foucault not only reshaped his *History of Sexuality* as a genealogy of the modern subject in order to envision alternative ways to constitute the self, he also rethought the

28 Michel Foucault, 'What is Enlightenment?', in *The Foucault Reader*, ed. Paul Rabinow, New York: Pantheon, 1984, p. 46.

29 François Ewald, 'Le philosophe comme acte', *Le magazine littéraire* 435, October 2004, p. 30.

Enlightenment as a critique of how we are governed *and* deployed neoliberalism as a framework within which to invent a left governmentality that would create a less normative way of exercising power. These several projects should not be seen as separate enquiries but as multiple *épreuves* forming a single enterprise: the 'problematization' of *the* present, and of who we take ourselves to be in that present, or, to be more precise, of Foucault's present.

All of this might simply be an incredible story that gives yet more context to the development of Foucault's thought and to what Americans would persist in calling 'French theory' in the decades that followed. Yet, for us, this story is also crucial to the history of our present, one that is today again enacted on the streets, in which those rendered obsolete by this 'left governmentality' and declared intolerant and backward by the Foucauldian last man resort to a brutal and politically dangerous violence in order to be heard.

1

The Birth of a Controversy

> What I am trying to do is provoke an interference between our reality and the knowledge of our past history. If I succeed, this will have real effects in our present history. My hope is my books become true after they have been written – not before.
>
> Michel Foucault, 1980[1]

Understanding Foucault's relationship to neoliberalism is far from a straightforward matter. His lectures on neoliberalism, *The Birth of Biopolitics*, delivered in early 1979, would be published in 2004 and appear in English only in the fateful year 2008. As a result, destiny has tied these lectures – which were concluded a month prior to the election of the Thatcher government in the United Kingdom and almost two years before the Reagan administration took office in the United States – to a wholly different context. That context was the worst economic crisis in the North Atlantic world

1 Michel Foucault, 'Truth Is in the Future', in *Foucault Live: Collected Interviews, 1961–1984*, ed. Sylvère Lotringer, New York: Semiotext(e), 1996, p. 301.

since the Great Depression and the subsequent revaluation of the legacy of neoliberalism and its poster children. It was a financial crisis that continues to define our present, from the recurrent debt and budget crises of the countries of the European Union to the political traumas of the United States, the United Kingdom and France.

A second complication is that these very lectures are made available under the general editorship of his former student and assistant, François Ewald, thus making him perhaps Foucault's most influential follower and arbiter of what constitutes his oeuvre. The apparent irony here is that Ewald, in his work with the employers' association, MEDEF, has promoted what Maurizio Lazzarato describes as the 'policies and mechanisms for . . . reconstructing society according to neoliberal principles' that were first revealed to him in Foucault's lectures of 1979.[2] By the end of the millennium, Ewald had become the most important intellectual advocate of the boycott by employers of French corporatist arrangements in the name of the vitality of civil society. While the case of Ewald's neoliberalism has been raised for some time by Mauricio Lazzarato, Antonio Negri and Jacques Donzelot, among others,[3] the question of Foucault's own relationship to neoliberalism has been put on the agenda by none other than Ewald himself. In 2012 at the University of Chicago, in conversation with the economist, Gary Becker, Ewald suggested that Foucault had offered an 'apology of

2 Michael C. Behrent, 'Accidents Happen: François Ewald, the "Antirevolutionary Foucault", and the Intellectual Politics of the French Welfare State', *Journal of Modern History* 82:3, 2010, pp. 585–624.

3 Maurizio Lazzarato, 'Neoliberalism in Action: Inequality, Insecurity and the Reconstitution of the Social', *Theory, Culture and Society* 29:6, 2009, p. 110. Antonio Negri, 'Interview', *Le Monde*, 3 October 2001. Jacques Donzelot and Colin Gordon, 'Governing Liberal Societies: The Foucault Effect in the English-speaking World', *Foucault Studies* 5, 2008, p. 55. See also Jean-Yves Grenier and André Orléan, speaking in 2007 of 'Foucault's liberal temptation', in 'Michel Foucault, l'économie politique et le libéralisme', *Annales. Histoire, Sciences Sociales* 5, 2007, pp. 1155–82.

neoliberalism'.[4] Indeed, both major branches of neoliberalism have now endorsed Foucault's presentation of the thought of their schools. Representatives of the Ordoliberals have lauded Foucault's lectures on their school,[5] and Gary Becker himself admitted to being hard pressed to find anything critical of his own work or that of his colleagues, emphasizing to a somewhat confused Foucauldian interlocutor after reading the lectures, 'I don't *disagree* with much.'[6]

The questions surrounding Foucault's relationship to neoliberalism are, if anything, intensifying. Recently, several books have appeared in French suggesting some degree of endorsement of neoliberalism by Foucault, although drawing the opposite political conclusions. Among them, there is Geoffroy de Lagasnerie's *La dernière leçon de Michel Foucault*, which depicts Foucault's lectures as an exercise in 'mental hygiene' for the Left, by using neoliberalism to 'rethink the conditions of elaboration of an emancipatory practice'.[7] His book is a brief, polemical essay rather than a scholarly monograph, and perhaps should be addressed as such. It adopts a breezy and accessible style and runs through a range of affinities between Foucault and neoliberalism. These include a common rejection of the juridical-political vocabulary and orientation of state and sovereignty; an embrace of plurality (or multiplicity), immanence and heterogeneity; a suspicion of the concept of society, totalizing knowledge and theory more generally,

---

4 Gary S. Becker, François Ewald and Bernard E. Harcourt, 'Becker on Ewald on Foucault on Becker: American Neoliberalism and Michel Foucault's 1979 "Birth of Biopolitics" Lectures', *Coase-Sandor Institute for Law & Economics Working Paper* 614, 2012, p. 4; Mitchell Dean, 'Michel Foucault's "Apology" for Neoliberalism', *Journal of Political Power* 7:3, 2014, pp. 433–42.

5 Niels Goldschmidt and Hermann Rauchenschwandtner, 'The Philosophy of the Social Market Economy: Michel Foucault's Analysis of Ordoliberalism', Freiburg Discussion Papers on Constitutional Economics, 07/4, Freiburg, Walter Eucken Institute, 2007.

6 Becker, Ewald and Harcourt, 'Becker on Ewald', p. 3.

7 Geoffroy de Lagasnerie, *La dernière leçon de Michel Foucault*, Paris: Fayard, 2012, p. 156.

including the social and behavioural sciences; and an anti-totalitarianism asserting a fundamental ungovernability that vitiates state planning and the normative focus on order.

Foucault, Lagasnerie argues, attempted to read neoliberalism affirmatively and used it to develop a critical approach. In doing so, he 'transgressed a boundary deeply inscribed within our intellectual space'.[8] The 'great audacity' of Foucault is that he was not content simply to follow neoliberalism's dogmas but adopted the far subtler idea of 'using neoliberalism as a test, as an instrument of critique of both thought and reality'. By reading neoliberalism in its own terms rather than as a foil for his own position, Foucault moves to engage neoliberalism as a 'kind of experimental dispositive',[9] as a form of critique and as 'the instrument of the renewal of theory itself'.[10] Lagasnerie claims, then, to read Foucault from the Left as someone seeking to unlock the possibilities of neoliberalism for leftist thought. Foucault's engagement with neoliberalism, for him, thus points the way to a new critical theory and a 'project of renewing what Pierre Bourdieu called "the libertarian tradition of the Left"'.[11]

While Lagasnerie's book does offer a trenchant argument, it suffers from a number of striking deficiencies. First of all, it ignores all of those works that have raised this relationship in a more contextual perspective and situated Foucault's interest in neoliberalism in relation to an increasing affinity with the 'Second Left' exemplified by figures such as Pierre Rosanvallon.[12] In this sense, Lagasnerie's work is completely decontextualized and largely

8 Ibid., p. 19.

9 Ibid., pp. 28–9.

10 Ibid., p. 35.

11 Ibid., p. 16.

12 See in particular Michael C. Behrent, 'Liberalism without Humanism: Michel Foucault and the Free-Market Creed, 1976–1979', in Daniel Zamora and Michael C. Behrent (eds), *Foucault and Neoliberalism*, Cambridge: Polity, 2015, pp. 24–62 (originally published in *Modern Intellectual History* 6:3, 2009); Isabelle Garo, *Foucault, Deleuze, Althusser & Marx*, Paris: Démopolis, 2011; José Luis Moreno Pestaña, *Foucault, la gauche et la politique*, Paris: Textuel, 2011.

ignores Foucault's relationship with the CFDT,[13] the 'New Philosophers', or the role of neoliberal rationalities and left politics in the years since Foucault wrote. It is as if the Third Way, New Labour and Bill Clinton's administration had never happened.

Further, the essayistic and polemical character of the text means that it engages insufficiently with Foucault's work itself. English-language readers familiar with Foucault's work on governmentality and the large secondary literature on neoliberalism may find themselves dissatisfied at many points. For example, the book fails to distinguish between the various schools of neoliberalism or between neoliberalism and classical economic liberalism (after Adam Smith). In this way, it is consistent with how neoliberals themselves presented their ideas. It takes some contortionist talent not to see the chasms that separate Hayek not only from John Stuart Mill but even from Becker. These distinctions are, however, key to Foucault's analyses.

Basically, Lagasnerie is only very superficially interested in the intellectual history of neoliberalism. Although he regrets that the political affinities displayed by the neoliberals have generally 'obscured the perception of their work',[14] he nonetheless reproduces a very complacent reading of their ideas. He does not, for example, seem to perceive that if neoliberalism is apparently 'on the side of disorder', it was, in its Austrian version, extremely attentive to the desire to build a 'constitutionalized' economic order sheltered from the vagaries of democracy. One of its great successes was precisely not to oppose the 'authoritarian impulses' of the Keynesian order but to 'insulate' the economic system from democratic spaces by a legal system that, in Hayek's words, would 'dethrone politics'.[15] The 'sovereignty of the consumer' aimed from the outset to constitute a space freed from democracy rather than

13 The Confédération française démocratique du travail (French Democratic Confederation of Labour) is one of the five major confederations of trade unions.

14 Lagasnerie, *La dernière leçon*, p. 27.

15 See Quinn Slobodian, *Globalists: The End of Empire and the Birth of Neoliberalism*, Cambridge, MA: Harvard University Press, 2018.

to 'renew' it. It reconceptualized the *demos* as a simple variation of the competition of individual interests in a market, the impersonal system of prices being substituted for any other form of collective political deliberation.

The biggest howler in this sense occurs when Lagasnerie claims, amid his exegesis of Foucault's lectures, that '*Homo oeconomicus* thus appears, in a proper sense, as an ungovernable being'.[16] Yet, Foucault's point concerning neoliberalism and its difference from classical liberalism is precisely the opposite: '*Homo oeconomicus* is someone who is eminently governable. From being the intangible partner of laissez-faire, *homo oeconomicus* now becomes the correlate of a governmentality which will act on the environment and systematically modify its variables.'[17] In other words, Foucault contrasts the quasi-naturalistic and ungovernable status of the economic subject in classical economic liberalism with the constructed and manipulable status of the economic subject in neoliberalism, the case in point being that of Gary Becker. The specificity of neoliberalism will therefore rather reside, as we show in this book, in the *environmental* relation it has with subjects. At the least, Foucault's interest in neoliberalism is partially driven by the idea that the economic subject opens the way for new forms of power and regulation, and hence in some respects reverses its place in classical economic liberalism.

There is indeed a strange discord between the temporalities of French and English receptions of Foucault's neoliberalism lectures. Anglophone readers, schooled in the governmentality literature starting with Colin Gordon's seminal introduction, and a massive literature on governmentality studies,[18] would thus find Lagasnerie's

---

16 Lagasnerie, *La dernière leçon*, p. 155.

17 Michel Foucault, *The Birth of Biopolitics: Lectures at the Collège de France, 1978–1979*, trans. Graham Burchell, London: Palgrave Macmillan, 2008, pp. 270–1.

18 See Colin Gordon, 'Introduction', in Graham Burchell, Colin Gordon and Peter Miller (eds), *The Foucault Effect: Studies in Governmentality*, London: Harvester Wheatsheaf, 1991, pp. 1–51; Mitchell Dean, *Governmentality: Power and Rule in Modern Society*, London: Sage, 1999.

arguments deficient from a simple scholarly perspective, whatever the merits of the overall intervention he seeks to make.

But it is only two years later, with the publication of more contextual books, that the debate really started. *Foucault and Neoliberalism* in particular assembled various perspectives that, beyond their differences, largely registered Foucault's affinities with neoliberalism as a matter of concern for the intellectual history of the Left and an occasion to reflect on its recent theoretical trajectories.[19] Needless to say, the ensuing debate, stirred by an interview published in *Jacobin* with one of the current authors (Zamora),[20] has added both heat and light. That interview in particular made the point that Foucault barely raised problems of economic and social inequality, recasting the main social question away from 'exploitation' to matters of personal conduct.

Finally, it is important to mention Serge Audier's book, *Penser le 'néolibéralisme'*, with its well-documented and detailed account of the context in which Foucault gave his lectures and of the intimate link between his interest in neoliberalism and the French 'crisis of socialism'. The key Second Left intellectual, Pierre Rosanvallon, recently described this book as the 'indispensable' reference on the topic, one that fully captures Foucault's late trajectory and places it in the context of the struggles within the French Left between its statist and anti-statist components.[21] It is 'the absence of historical training and concerns', argues Audier, that has shaped the complacent and uncritical reception and readings of Foucault's lectures.[22]

From this perspective, there is a healthy debate to be had about Foucault's relationship to neoliberalism given the central position he still occupies in critical thought. However, before exploring this

19 Daniel Zamora and Michael C. Behrent (eds), *Foucault and Neoliberalism*, Cambridge: Polity, 2015.

20 Daniel Zamora, 'Can we Criticize Foucault?', *Jacobin*, 10 October 2014.

21 Pierre Rosanvallon, *Notre histoire intellectuelle et politique, 1968–2018*, Paris: Seuil, 2018, p. 386.

22 Serge Audier, *Penser le 'néolibéralisme': le moment néolibéral, Foucault et la crise du socialisme*, Paris: Le bord de l'eau, 2015, p. 26.

relationship further, and in particular how it fits into the last decade of the philosopher's work, we need to reposition Foucault's intellectual enterprise in a little more detail.

Foucault and the liberal arts of government

Foucault's analysis alerts us to the plurality of forms of neoliberalism, and to their emergence within, but movement across, national borders and temporal contexts. He demonstrates the worth of an intellectual-historical study of the variants of neoliberalism and even the biographies of its key figures.[23] This brings neoliberalism down to earth as something that is identifiable and study-able, something more plural, contingent and historically rooted than a narrative of 'neoliberalization' might indicate.

With the recent publication of excellent intellectual-historical studies of neoliberalism by Mirowski and Plehwe, Jamie Peck, Angus Burgin, Niklas Olsen, Quinn Slobodian and, more recently, Jessica Whyte,[24] this point might seem redundant. But, if we allow Foucault the status of a thinker of the Left, then this project was almost unique at the time of his lectures. In the United Kingdom, there was Andrew Gamble's paper in *The Socialist Register* in 1979,[25] and Stuart Hall's pieces on Thatcherism in *Marxism Today*,[26]

23 Foucault, *The Birth of Biopolitics*, p. 10.

24 See, notably, Philip Mirowski and Dieter Plehwe (eds), *The Road from Mont Pèlerin: The Making of the Neoliberal Thought Collective*, Cambridge, MA: Harvard University Press, 2009; Jamie Peck, *Constructions of Neoliberal Reason*, Oxford: Oxford University Press, 2011; Angus Burgin, *The Great Persuasion: Reinventing Free Markets since the Depression*, Cambridge, MA: Harvard University Press, 2012; Slobodian, *Globalists*; Niklas Olsen, *The Sovereign Consumer: A New Intellectual History of Neoliberalism*, Basingstoke: Palgrave Macmillan, 2018; Jessica Whyte, *The Morals of the Market: Human Rights and the Rise of Neoliberalism*, London: Verso, 2019.

25 Andrew Gamble, 'Free Economy and the Strong State', *The Socialist Register* 16, 1979, pp. 1–25.

26 Stuart Hall, 'The Great Moving Right Show', *Marxism Today*, January 1979, pp. 14–20, and 'Thatcherism: A New Stage', *Marxism Today*, February 1980, pp. 26–8.

published in 1979 and 1980. But it is interesting that, despite Laclau and Mouffe's 1985 recognition that neoliberalism was a 'new hegemonic project',[27] there was little engagement on the Left with the sources of this project. This was despite the fact that, as Foucault's lectures would report, the neoliberal project had been a practical doctrine of government since the very beginning of the Federal Republic of Germany, almost forty years earlier. For Foucault, this neglect was due to mistaking neoliberalism as a mere revival of classical liberalism or simply another ideology of market capitalism. The Left, still in thrall to a complex version of the base–superstructure model of ideology, was not able to develop a project to try to grasp neoliberalism 'in its singularity'. As Foucault puts it: 'Neo-liberalism is not Adam Smith; neo-liberalism is not market society; neo-liberalism is not the Gulag on the insidious scale of capitalism.'[28]

In paying serious attention to the intellectual-historical sources of neoliberalism, Foucault anticipated those who would regard neoliberalism as a 'thought collective',[29] that is, as an empirically and historically identifiable group of thinkers pursuing a common intellectual project and political ambition, but within a certain space of conversation and dissension. The neoliberal thought collective proved to be one of the most successful, if not *the* most successful, political movements of the second half of the twentieth century, in its influence, capture and appropriation of the powers of national states and other governmental organizations above and below the nation-state.

Yet, almost contrary to this careful intellectual-historical approach, with its emphasis on the plurality and historical

---

27 Ernesto Laclau and Chantal Mouffe, *Hegemony and Socialist Strategy: Towards a Radical Democratic Politics*, London: Verso, 1985, p. 175.

28 Foucault, *The Birth of Biopolitics*, p. 131.

29 Philip Mirowski, 'Postface: Defining Neoliberalism', in Mirowski and Plehwe, *The Road from Mont Pèlerin*, p. 428; Philip Mirowski, *Never Let a Crisis Go to Waste: How Neoliberalism Survived the Financial Meltdown*, Verso: London, 2013.

contingency of the various strands of the neoliberal thought collective, was another of Foucault's bold masterstrokes: the identification of neoliberalism – and indeed classical liberalism – as an 'art of government', something he announced at the very beginning of his lectures. Citing Benjamin Franklin's notion of 'frugal government', Foucault defined liberalism as neither a philosophy nor an ideology but as an art of government animated by the suspicion that 'one always governs too much'.[30] This general framework allowed him to distinguish between classical economic liberalism (that of Adam Smith in particular) and neoliberalism and between varieties of the latter. Whereas classical liberalism seeks the limitation of the state in the face of the necessary and natural processes of the economy, neoliberalism will either attempt to found the legitimacy of the state on the market, as the Ordoliberals would in reconstructionist West Germany, or to extend the market and its rationality to all forms of social existence and to test and evaluate every single act of government, as in the case of American neoliberalism. To regard neoliberalism as an art of government, however, is to shift the frame decisively from the theory of ideology to the practical orientation of neoliberalism as a form of governmentality. In other words, neoliberalism becomes a form of *statecraft*. The importance of this move is that it displaces the tendency to view neoliberalism as something merely superstructural in relation to the capitalist economy, and forces us to look at it as a practical and technical exercise concerned with governing states. Neoliberalism is not simply a philosophy of freedom and the market that happens to have implications for governing states. It is all about governing states – or about governing states and other organizations.[31] It is a doctrine, or set of doctrines, concerned with a practice centred first and foremost on the exercise of political sovereignty.[32]

30 Foucault, *The Birth of Biopolitics*, pp. 322, 319.
31 See Slobodian, *Globalists*.
32 Foucault, *The Birth of Biopolitics*, p. 3.

Foucault made a third set of distinctive contributions concerning the critical ethos of neoliberalism. Here, we find that at least one part of his orientation to neoliberalism is the identification of what it criticizes or, more bluntly, what it problematizes. These problematizations are of course national-context dependent – the Ordoliberals, for example, oppose ideas of national economy derived from Friedrich List in the 1840s, Bismarckian state socialism, and the wartime planned economy, while Friedrich Hayek displays a particular animus toward the US New Deal and the welfare state programmes of Beveridge in the UK.[33] The American school opposes both the latter and the economic and social programmes of the post-war federal administrations in the United States, particularly Democratic ones.[34] However, their common enemies are even more interesting – in particular the economics and policy prescriptions of John Maynard Keynes. This approach to neoliberalism underlines its political nature and the relations of antagonism that animated it, against all those who would reduce its concerns to economic, technical or even ethical issues.

These three points derived from Foucault emphasize the political character of neoliberalism as a diverse movement or network, one no doubt with differences of opinion, but united by common enemies and the goal of instituting a specific regime of government in various organizations, but particularly in national states and their agencies. Beyond these important aspects of Foucault's analysis, however, it is imperative to grasp which neoliberalism Foucault was referring to, which 'present' he was challenging.

Foucault in his present

'When I say something', Foucault would argue, 'I am speaking to the present. What I say is not intended to speak to the future, at

33 Ibid., pp. 107–10.
34 Ibid., p. 217.

least in the sense that it will necessarily apply to the future.'[35] If he indeed liked to define himself as a 'historian of the present', it is especially ironic that the majority of the literature about his work completely ignores his present.

In a brief interview he gave in 1980 in a small review in America, Foucault went so far as to claim that 'I am not merely an historian . . . What I do is a kind of historical fiction . . . what I have done from a historical point of view is single-minded, exaggerated.' He even confessed that perhaps 'I dropped out some contradictory factors'.[36] To his friend Claude Mauriac, Foucault would admit that, if he never thought of writing fiction, he nevertheless 'likes to make a fictive use of the materials he assembles, puts together, builds, doing with purpose, with authentic elements, fictitious constructions'.[37] These constructions were then, as Judith Revel argues, attempts to 'interrupt' the 'permanence' and the historic 'stability' of the present.[38] History thus becomes a tool to subvert present configurations. This attitude – questioning the problems of his present – shaped Foucault's work from the very start. We cannot, for example, understand his *History of Madness* without placing it in the wider discussion that French psychiatry went through in the years immediately following the Second World War. Foucault's extraordinary book was in part a direct reaction to the attempts to reform the institution by French psychiatrists like Henri Ey, Georges Daumézon and Lucien Bonnafé.[39] In the same vein, it would be difficult to explain the enormous success and traction that *The Order of Things* received in 1966 without understanding the importance of the theme of 'humanism' in post-war

35 Wade, *Foucault in California*, p. 117.

36 Foucault, 'Truth is in the Future', p. 301.

37 Claude Mauriac, *Le temps immobile tome 9. Mauriac et fils*, Paris: Grasset, 1988, p. 244.

38 Judith Revel, *Foucault avec Merleau-Ponty. Ontologie politique, présentisme et histoire*, Paris: Vrin, 2015, p. 77.

39 See in particular Michael C. Behrent, '"There are still many chains to be removed": Foucault and the postwar movement for psychiatric reform', unpublished manuscript.

French philosophy. Similarly, it would not be possible to understand the significance of Foucault's *Discipline and Punish* without having in mind his involvement in the Prisons Information Group (GIP), his visit to Attica prison in 1972, and the incarceration during the early 1970s of many militants of the Maoist group, the Gauche prolétarienne (GP).[40]

From this perspective, Michael Behrent's work on Foucault's last decade has lucidly forced into focus not only the world that Foucault worked in but also his forms of action within it. Grasping that world is somewhat like peeling the layers of an onion. The outer layers include the end of the *trente glorieuses* (France's 'Long Boom') in the early 1970s, the ensuing economic and fiscal crises, and the beginnings of the breakdown of the state-led settlement that followed the Second World War. This is accompanied by the reception of American economic ideas and policies in France. Domestically, there is the long-delayed coming to power of the Left and the programme of the Union of the Left between the socialists and communists. Internationally, there is the Cold War, the division of Europe, and the Soviet Union's interventions in Eastern European politics, from Hungary and Czechoslovakia to Poland.

A further inner layer would be the history of French militancy from May '68 to Maoism, the worker experiments with self-management such as at the Lip factory at Besançon,[41] and the critique of Soviet totalitarianism condensed by the figure of the Gulag with the publication of Aleksandr Solzhenitsyn's *The Gulag Archipelago* in 1974. Closer to the core, there are Foucault's own commitments and political actions: collaboration with the Maoists in prisoners' actions and through the GIP; activism for

40 See Perry Zurn and Andrew Dilts, *Active Intolerance: Michel Foucault, the Prisons Information Group and the Future of Abolition*, New York: Palgrave, 2016.

41 Foucault visited the Lip factory in July 1973 and commented: 'This isn't about an anti-authoritarian struggle, it's about unemployment.' Related in Daniel Defert, 'Chronologie', in Foucault, *Dits et Écrits I, 1954–1975*, p. 59.

immigrant's rights; support for Soviet dissidents; the Croissant Affair[42] and the Left terrorism of the Red Army Faction;[43] and his journalism on the Iranian revolution.[44]

At the core, then, we find Foucault the political activist pursuing his ideas and research in public, through his lectures, interviews and newspaper articles, and often with key interlocutors including his peers and colleagues, his audiences, his assistants and research students, and participants in his seminars. If the language in which this discussion took place is not immediately transparent to us today, this is not to say that it was deliberately obfuscatory. Rather, it is not possible to understand this idiom without understanding the kinds of action that were performed with words, what they were a response to, what reception they received and how they were interpreted. And yet it would be wrong to assume that all this was univocal. Even among politically mainstream or conservative interpreters of Foucault, there would be some disagreement. Consistent with Foucault's engagement with André Glucksmann and the *nouveaux philosophes*, Ewald would come to understand Foucault as replacing the Revolution/State couple with the question of power. This formed at least part of the story of Ewald's own long trajectory from Maoist militancy to his advocacy of a restructuring of the welfare state in the name of the forces of civil society.[45] In contrast, Blandine Kriegel, an earlier

---

42 Klaus Croissant was a lawyer for the 'Baader-Meinhoff Gang' (the Red Army Faction) who had sought asylum in France in July 1977, and who was later incarcerated in Santé prison and extradited on 16 November of that year. Foucault had supported his right to asylum and sustained a fractured rib as police dispersed a demonstration outside the prison. He would, however, refuse to sign a petition that described the West German state as 'fascist', a stance thought to be at the base of a breach with Gilles Deleuze. See Macey, *Lives*, pp. 392–6; and Didier Eribon, *Michel Foucault*, Cambridge, MA: Harvard University Press, 1991, p. 259–62.

43 Michel Sennelart, 'Course Context', in Michel Foucault, *Security, Territory, Population: Lectures at the Collège de France 1977–1978*, trans. Graham Burchell, London: Palgrave Macmillan, 2007, pp. 369–401.

44 Janet Afary and Kevin B. Anderson, *Foucault and the Iranian Revolution: Gender and the Seductions of Islam*, Chicago: University of Chicago Press, 2005.

45 As told in Behrent, 'Accidents Happen'.

student and assistant of Foucault, would read his 1976 lectures as reasserting the importance of sovereignty and law, on her way to outlining a republican statist position.[46] More broadly, Foucault's lectures have been interpreted and used by French neoliberals and autonomist Marxists, by several varieties of anti-statists, and by those who would endorse and practise a state-focused politics as high-level public servants and political advisors.

We have already noted Foucault's animus toward official Marxism and communism as a recurring theme. We perhaps should be careful in specifying his relationship to Marxism and to Marx. Foucault engages with many Marxisms, and in different discussions and contexts.[47] From his early courses in 1952–53 in Lille,[48] when he had just left the French Communist Party, to the first volume of his *History of Sexuality*, Foucault was in constant discussion with Marxism and tried to link his power analyses to the accumulation of capital and the formation of capitalist production and class hegemonies. Christofferson describes a Marxist turn in the early 1970s, in which Marxist references begin to enter Foucault's vocabulary. His own relationship to Marx, however, was not consistent throughout his trajectory, perhaps taking a more overtly anti-Marxist inflection in the second half of the 1970s. Nonetheless, it is possible to distinguish between Foucault's consistent attitude to institutional and official forms of Marxism

---

46 Blandine Barret-Kriegel, 'Michel Foucault and the Police State', in T.J. Armstrong (ed.), *Michel Foucault Philosopher*, London: Harvester Wheatsheaf, 1992, pp. 192–7; Blandine Kriegel, *The State and the Rule of Law*, Princeton: Princeton University Press, 1996.

47 Michel Foucault, 'Considérations sur le marxisme, la phénoménologie et le pouvoir', *Cités* 4:52, 2012, pp. 101–26. English Version: Michel Foucault, Colin Gordon and Paul Patton, 'Considerations on Marxism, Phenomenology and Power: Interview with Michel Foucault', *Foucault Studies* 14, 2012, pp. 98–114; Michel Foucault, 'The Mesh of Power', *Viewpoint Magazine* 2, 2012.

48 See in particular Aner Barzilay, 'Foucault's Early Reading of Marx and the Two Meanings of Humanism', in Stephen W. Sawyer and Daniel Steinmetz-Jenkins (eds), *Foucault, Neoliberalism, and Beyond*, London: Rowman and Littlefield, 2019, pp. 73–95.

and his engagement with the various intellectual currents aligned with it.

While neither the affective and acting individual nor the political and intellectual context allow us to explain anything, including his relation to liberalism, they do circumscribe the space in which the emergence and reception of neoliberalism would occur for Foucault. His enduring hostility to communism and institutional forms of Marxism, and critique of its totalizing claims to scientificity, place him within the more general French anti-totalitarianism milieu. Related to this are his rejection of the Union of the Left and thus of the Mitterrand government, particularly at the time of its accusatory claims regarding a 'silence of the intellectuals' in the early 1980s[49] as well as the Polish Solidarity uprising. The latter led to several critical interventions against the government in which Foucault took an active part, along with the French physician and founder of Médecins Sans Frontières (MSF), Bernard Kouchner.[50] More fundamentally perhaps, there is his continued scepticism toward socialism as a body of thought: for its inherent racism when it stresses the problem of struggle in 1976,[51] and its presumed inability to generate an autonomous governmentality in 1978.[52] This is the background against which the question of the renovation and revival of liberalism came to be posed and the framework of governmentality developed.

49 This was a discussion of why intellectuals remained silent in relation to the Socialist government and its policies during the early years of Mitterrand's presidency, mainly conducted in the columns of *Le Monde*. The accusatory nature of it raised Foucault's ire. See Eribon, *Michel Foucault* (English version), pp. 305–6.

50 Ibid., p. 299.

51 'Socialism was', Foucault argued, 'a racism from the outset, even in the nineteenth century.' See Michel Foucault, *Society Must Be Defended: Lectures at the Collège de France 1975–1976*, trans. David Macey, New York: Picador, 2003, p. 261. He goes on to qualify this generalization in the next two pages to argue that racism is manifest in socialism when it is concerned 'to stress the problem of struggle', and that socialist racism was only 'liquidated' with the domination of social democracy and processes such as those around the Dreyfus affair.

52 Foucault, *The Birth of Biopolitics*, p. 92.

Neoliberalism

Michael Behrent's discussion of neoliberalism and the Second Left is perhaps the most instructive recent addition to our knowledge of these contexts of Foucault's thought.[53] The early moves toward eliminating longstanding price controls under Prime Minister Raymond Barre, the academic and publishing inroads made by economic liberalism during the crisis of the 1970s, and the popularization of quite a bit of the American neoliberal canon by Henri Lepage in his 1978 essay, *Demain le capitalisme* (a key source for *The Birth of Biopolitics*), all form part of a broad picture. However, Foucault's active engagement with these themes and literatures comes via another trajectory, more firmly located on the Left and descended from the legacy of '68. The Second Left, as Behrent and Audier tell us,[54] was a faction of socialists and trade unionists (centred on the CFDT), under Michel Rocard, that sought a new approach to socialist politics based on the decomposition and distribution of the state into a voluntary association according to the principle of 'self-management', *autogestion*. Their main concern was to free the Socialist Party, on the verge of forming a government for the first time, from its 'social-statism'. But the key here for Foucault's relation to neoliberalism is that *autogestion* was not a movement of the economically liberalizing Right attacking the welfare state, but of a Left interested in a post-individualistic, collective autonomy.

According to the testimony of Daniel Defert, it was from a 'leftist perspective' that Foucault read Hayek in the mid-1970s.[55] The notion of 'self-management' had its lineage in the cultural elements of '68, the struggles against social institutions and the state of post-'68 Maoism and militancy (such as in the prisoners' movement),

53 Behrent, 'Liberalism without Humanism'.

54 Ibid., pp. 35–7, and Audier, *Penser le 'néolibéralisme'*.

55 Quoted by Audier, 'Quand Foucault découvre le néolibéralisme. Prophétie géniale ou symptôme d'une crise de la gauche?', in Daniel Zamora and Michael C. Behrent (eds), *Foucault et le néolibéralisme*, Brussels: Aden, forthcoming.

and the themes of a politics of everyday life posed by the women's and gay movements. Most directly, the term emerged from the workers' occupation and collective takeover of workplaces such as occurred at the Lip factory in 1973–74.

Foucault participated in Second Left conferences and mobilizations and praised the work of its major theorist, Pierre Rosanvallon, who would later join his seminars. In the Course Summary of *The Birth of Biopolitics*, Foucault credited Rosanvallon with the discovery of liberalism as critique of government that deploys the market as a site of truth production or 'veridiction'.[56] Rosanvallon thus suggested the core of Foucault's approach to liberalism as an art of government in which the market functions as a 'test' and a 'privileged site of experiment'. The Second Left would have concurred with Foucault's astonishing claim that there was no autonomous socialist governmentality and that the only alternatives were to latch socialism onto a liberal governmentality or ones akin to those of a police state.[57] In this sense, Foucault's engagement with, and at times affirmative reading of, aspects of American neoliberalism in his lectures is not a simple case of seduction by neoliberalism. It is about how certain currents on the Left, immersed in anti-totalitarianism, defining themselves in opposition to the mainstream 'social-statism' of the large socialist and communist parties, and consciously adopting an experimental ethos, came to appreciate the opportunities provided by new ways of governing associated with market rationalities.

One objection to this argument would be that not all anti-statisms are equivalent and that an economic-liberal critique of the state is different from anarchist or other workerist anti-statisms, and from the French Maoist combination of hyper-populism, voluntarism and spontaneism. This should again qualify any over-identification of Foucault with neoliberalism. What, we might ask, was the nature of his anti-statism? Did his persistent analytical

56 Foucault, *The Birth of Biopolitics*, p. 320.
57 Ibid., p. 92.

anti-statism translate into a normative and political anti-statism? And what are we to make of his theme of 'state phobia' and his attempt to defuse it by tracing its genealogy?[58] Foucault's critique of the discourse of the state tried not simply to pose the problem of how to limit the Leviathan but to remove the state altogether from the centre of political analysis and discourse, repurposing the concept as 'nothing but the mobile effect of a regime of multiple governmentalities'.[59] Perhaps we have to find a way to describe a certain affinity that obtained between Foucault's own political-intellectual trajectory and neoliberalism. Behrent's suggestion of a 'strategic endorsement' implies an affirmative relation but within a political field. By contrast, Andrew Dilts's formula of 'sympathetic critique and indebtedness'[60] might appear at first sight more nuanced. If one accepts Dilts's argument that Becker and his colleagues' theory of human capital formed a key pathway to Foucault's later work on the care of the self, however, then neoliberalism enters the very core of Foucault's intellectual trajectory. While Lagasnerie seems to indicate a position close to that which Behrent identifies, Dilts would thus appear to confirm Ewald's own diagnosis of this shift in Foucault's work, when he claimed that Foucault's reading of Becker and his conception of *homo oeconomicus* was 'like a step between his earlier theory of power and the later lectures about subjectivity and so on'.[61]

58 Mitchell Dean and Kaspar Villadsen, *State Phobia and Civil Society: The Political Legacy of Michel Foucault*, Stanford: Stanford University Press, 2016.

59 Foucault, *The Birth of Biopolitics*, p. 77.

60 Andrew Dilts, 'From "Entrepreneur of the Self" to "Care of the Self": Neo-Liberal Governmentality and Foucault's Ethics', *Foucault Studies* 12, 2011, p. 133n.

61 Becker, Ewald and Harcourt, 'Becker on Ewald', p. 7.

The intellectual

Beyond this context, to which we will return in more detail, we must also understand Foucault's intervention as that of an intellectual, with the constraints and specificities that this implies. How should we think about the lives of intellectuals, and particularly those who gain fame and recognition for their work and ideas both in and beyond academic circles? Some will say that this is a profoundly un-Foucauldian question, but we should note that, unlike some of his followers, he was not bound dogmatically to a method when it came to his own account of neoliberalism and its progenitors, announcing that he would 'break a bit from my habits and give a few biographical details'.[62] Of course, there is the question of how should we maintain the correct distance between an intellectual's life and their work. If we propose to read their contribution in terms of biography, then we are in danger of missing the contribution itself. If we divorce them too far, then we are in danger of universalizing a thought that was specific to particular debates, and of mistaking local insight for global truth. Both extremes also miss the problem of intellectuals themselves, of what might be called their persona or habitus, a feature of which is precisely a form of this universalization even if, as in Foucault's case, they theorize the 'specific intellectual'.

Michael Scott Christofferson[63] approaches this latter problem when analysing the unqualified endorsement Foucault gave of André Glucksmann's *The Master Thinkers* in his review of the book.[64] Glucksmann's identification of critical theory (Hegel, Fichte, Marx and Nietzsche) with Reason, and of Reason with domination located in the binary logic of State and Revolution,

62 Foucault, *The Birth of Biopolitics*, p. 102.

63 Michael Scott Christofferson, 'Foucault and New Philosophy: Why Foucault Endorsed André Glucksmann's *The Master Thinkers*', in Zamora and Behrent, *Foucault and Neoliberalism*, pp. 6–23.

64 Michel Foucault, 'The Great Rage of Facts', in Zamora and Behrent, *Foucault and Neoliberalism*, pp. 171–5.

acknowledged neither the dispersed character of power relations uncovered by Foucault nor the specificities of forms of rationality and science in his genealogies. Why, then, was Foucault moved to write so laudatory a review of a writer who would only offer a vulgar interpretation of his own work and who gave so bombastic a view of the Enlightenment in which 'to think is to dominate'? Christofferson indicates the cultural celebrity at stake and 'Foucault's use of the mass media in his strategy of intellectual consecration'.[65] This analysis reminds us that academic and intellectual activity is firmly rooted in matters of status or honour and the desire for recognition, as Max Weber would have pointed out. In a relatively short time, Foucault was able to parlay his cultural celebrity in France – along with his training and capacities, of course – into formal academic status (a Chair at the Collège de France), and via the United States to achieve global fame by the time of his death at the age of fifty-seven. Even he, we suspect, would not have guessed at the extent of that fame today.

Status-seeking is neither a positive nor negative feature of the habitus of the intellectual. Rather, it defines it. While an intellectual and academic career might lead to material rewards, its main attraction is the gaining of access to the very outward symbols of status – prestigious posts, awards and honours, high-level fellowships and invitations, and so forth – and the personal, emotional and even erotic benefits that accrue from fame and hosts of followers. The other side of the coin to status-seeking is a resentment at all those who represent obstacles to this recognition and honour.

A prestigious persona is not merely a matter of perception or attributions of status or honour to an individual. Particularly for the intellectual it is something cultivated and forged through training, intense competition and rivalry, and rigorous examination. As David Macey has shown, this was precisely the male-only culture of the École Normale Supérieure at the time of Foucault's entry into it in 1946. This was no doubt intensified by its existence as a

65 Christofferson, 'Foucault and New Philosophy', p. 11.

boarding school, with its influential live-in tutors known as *caïmans*, such as Louis Althusser, then in transition from Catholic to communist. At the pinnacle of France's educational structure, the ENS was further stratified with its clear division between the arts and sciences, the arts students 'considering themselves vastly superior to the relatively uncivilized scientists', and with philosophy being seen among the former 'as the noblest of disciplines'.[66] In this respect, the final goal, the *agrégation*, which consisted of three written papers on the entire history of philosophy, and progression to an oral defence before a board of august academics, was less a technical examination of a distinct syllabus and more a test of the 'mastery of a culture' required for entry into a highly privileged caste. Such mastery qualified one as a distinctive type of spiritual-intellectual being. In this closed, monastic environment of hierarchical division and small communal groups, 'great importance attached to the verb *briller* – "to shine", "to be brilliant" '.[67]

It was in this environment at the ENS that Foucault, like many *normaliens* under the influence of Louis Althusser, would become a member of the PCF, the French Communist Party, in 1950. In later life, however, he would display a remarkable and persistent hostility toward the PCF, many of its intellectuals and certain forms of Marxism. He speaks in an interview from April 1978, made available only recently, of the absence of a Marxist review or reaction to his *History of Madness*, almost two decades previously.[68] Later that year, in conversations with an Italian journalist, there is a more nuanced account of this reception: here the Marxist psychiatrist Lucien Bonnafé and the *Evolution psychiatrique* group are said to have shown initial interest before deciding to 'excommunicate' the book after 1968, placing 'it on the "index", as though it were the gospel of the devil'.[69] This self-narrative of the failure of

66 Macey, *Lives*, p. 26.

67 Ibid.

68 Foucault et al., 'Considerations on Marxism', p. 103.

69 Michel Foucault, *Remarks on Marx: Conversations with Duccio Trombadori*, New York: Semiotext(e), 1991, p. 80–1.

Marxist psychiatry to welcome his work, and then to violently reject it, perhaps explains little except a sense of status injury. It does, however, indicate an important site of inquiry into Foucault's relation to a movement he claims had some potential to pose the problems later associated with 'antipsychiatry', but which reached an 'impasse' due to the 'Marxist climate'.[70] It also fits in with a larger personal narrative he often gave. In the same conversations, he recounts his three-year membership of the Communist Party in the early 1950s, and the discovery that the so-called 'doctors' plot' against Stalin was a fraud that French apparatchiks refused to explain or condemn, leading him to leave the party. In France, the Communist Party also had a long history of homophobia, generally describing homosexuality as an 'illness'. In the early 1970s, the communist trade union CGT would even notoriously refuse the participation of the gay revolutionary group FHAR (Homosexual Front of Revolutionary Action) in the May Day demos because homosexuality was 'a tradition foreign to the working class'.

A stronger version of the same feeling about communism is captured by Foucault's biographer, Didier Eribon, who suggests that 'since he quit the Communist Party and especially since he lived in Poland, Foucault developed a ferocious hatred of everything that evokes communism, directly or indirectly'.[71] Where Foucault seems most hostile is in relation to Marxism's 'totalizing' theoretical tendencies, manifest in its claims to scientificity and, most particularly, in its institutionalization and effects on intellectual culture. He speaks, for example, of the 'odious character' of the diffusion of a 'Soviet model' of denunciation and enmity throughout French political groups and intellectual life.[72] In the language he uses here we can detect the bitter experience of successful *normaliens* in the 1960s, when Althusser would adopt a

70 Michael Behrent provided a detailed account of Foucault's relationship to Marxist psychiatry of the 1950s in a PhD seminar, 'Foucault, Governmentality, Context', Copenhagen Business School, 27–29 October 2014.

71 Didier Eribon, *Michel Foucault*, Paris: Fayard, 2011, p. 237.

72 Foucault et al., 'Considerations on Marxism', p. 107.

militant anti-humanist Marxism opposed to the humanism then avowed by the PCF. Members of the secret 'Groupe Spinoza' Althusser founded sought to co-opt 'neo-structuralists' like Foucault, Lacan and Derrida in the theoretical struggle against the 'humanist front', at the same time as they clandestinely investigated and interrogated their theoretical worth in that struggle and their degree of political infidelity.[73] Not without insight, the minutes of their meetings showed that they judged Foucault's greatest danger to be his 'political adventurism'.[74]

Status-seeking is closely related to distinction, and one way of gaining that distinction is through avant-gardism. As Christofferson again notes, Foucault was something of a master at participating in the avant-garde without acceding to its ideologies or trying to offer a philosophical justification for them.[75] Witness his use of *marxisant* vocabulary and sympathy for the revolutionary Left in the early 1970s, at the time of his association with the Maoist Gauche prolétarienne in the prisoners' action group, the GIP. We can perhaps gloss this as a canny philosophical approach. Rather than looking for a practice that was consistent with his own theoretical position, Foucault adopted an 'experimental attitude',[76] which consisted of participating in a practice – or starting with an 'experience' as he would put it, often one that appears on the horizon – and then working out its conceptual, theoretical and philosophical implications. He was thus able to participate in and explore the new and interesting without identifying himself wholly with it. His deliberate withholding of normative judgements in his presentation of arguments – about, for instance, neoliberalism – was in the service of this experimental attitude rather than an attempt at a value-free social science. 'In this sense', he avowed, 'I consider

73 Edward Baring, *The Young Derrida and French Philosophy, 1945–1968*, Cambridge: Cambridge University Press, 2011, p. 273n.

74 Ibid., p. 276.

75 Christofferson, 'Foucault and New Philosophy', pp. 12–13.

76 Foucault, *Remarks on Marx*, p. 27.

myself more an experimenter than a theorist.'[77] Foucault has been described in an article by Colin Gordon as a 'man of action in a world of thought'.[78]

There are costs and benefits of this adventurous and experimental ethos. In the same period as his lectures on neoliberalism, Foucault would undertake his quite extensive journalism on the Iranian revolution based on two journeys to Iran. His observations here would yield early insight into the global ramifications of political Islam, and produce new concepts of a revolutionary action animated by 'political spirituality'. At least initially, however, he underestimated the repressive impact of the mullahs' regime for women, religious and ethnic minorities, and homosexuals.[79] Not unlike in the case of Foucault's relation to neoliberalism, the willingness to embrace and experiment with the new in the political field, and to derive new intelligibilities and theoretical positions and concepts from it, often has a downside in the form of a reluctance or slowness to recognize the kinds of domination it installs and the violence it engenders. Foucault's anti-communism and his experimental attitude are lenses through which to view his relation to neoliberalism and his limitations in recognizing its dangers. It is in this context that we must grasp his ambition to use neoliberalism to invent a left governmentality.

77 Ibid.

78 Colin Gordon, 'Man of Action in a World of Thought', *Times Literary Supplement*, 21 June 1996, pp. 9–10.

79 Michel Foucault, 'What are the Iranians Dreaming About?', in Afary and Anderson, *Foucault and the Iranian Revolution*, pp. 203–7. We discuss this in detail in Chapter 4.

2
Searching for a Left Governmentality

> We are perhaps living at the end of politics. For it's true that politics is a field which has been opened by the existence of the revolution, and if the question of the revolution can no longer be raised in these terms, then politics risks disappearing.
>
> Michel Foucault, 1977[1]

In his 1977 movie, *A Grin Without a Cat*, the French filmmaker Chris Marker gives his own account of the struggles that took place between 1967 and 1977 and, more generally, of the hopes of an entire generation in the aftermath of May 1968. Marker's movie was an attempt to understand the birth of a French 'new left' and how it reshaped conceptions of politics and contestation. He suggested that May '68, rather than reproducing the classic oppositions of post-war politics, transformed the terms through which one could think about politics. A new 'kind of problematic' emerged, he wrote, giving 'staggering blows in every field of the

1 Foucault, 'The End of the Monarchy of Sex', in *Foucault Live*, p. 223.

orthodoxy, right or left'.[2] As the movie puts it: 'There was the police blockade – this was an order – and there were unions' security services – that was another order. In between there was a space to be taken. This meant a new kind of struggle.' The first order obviously represented the Gaullist power and its repressive state and culture. But another kind of order was also increasingly seen as an obstacle to real social transformation: the post-war Left and its state-centred understanding of politics and social transformation. From this perspective, for many intellectuals after '68, the communist opposition, the unions and, later, the Union of the Left (the coalition of the French Communist Party, the Radical Party and the Socialist Party under the Common Programme) were no less problematic than the Gaullist power. To a certain extent, both Left and Right were seen as functioning within the same logic and replacing certain masters with others (what do we win by replacing 'the employers' arbitrary will with a bureaucratic arbitrary will?' asked the Marxist and ecological thinker André Gorz[3]). This centrality of the state in the political parties of both Left and Right was qualified by members of the 'Second Left' like Pierre Rosanvallon and Patrick Viveret as the dominant 'political culture'. A culture either 'from the left or the right . . . and for which the central element is the state, considered at the same time as the object of the struggle and the space of social transformation',[4] that had become, since the war, the underlying framework for all political discussion. For Rosanvallon and Viveret, May '68 marked the birth of a 'new political culture' that sought to transform not only the Left, but also a general understanding of what politics could be about.

It was precisely this task – reshaping our understanding of politics and the Left – that became central in Foucault's last

2 Chris Marker, 'Sixties', *Critical Quarterly* 50:3, 2008, pp. 26–32.

3 Michel Bosquet, 'Occupons le terrain', *Le Nouvel Observateur* 116, August 1976, p. 23. Bosquet is a nom de plume of André Gorz.

4 Pierre Rosanvallon and Patrick Viveret, *Pour une nouvelle culture politique*, Paris: Seuil, 1977, p. 7.

decade, a task he thought his generation had failed to achieve. As his friend Claude Mauriac explained in 1978, 'Foucault condemned his generation who had proved unable to bring a new hope to humanity, after Marxism, either to continue or replace it.'[5] And it is precisely from this perspective that he would be interested in neoliberalism, as a stimulating kind of governmentality that could offer alternatives to a socialist Left, which he rejected for its intellectual framework, its strategy and its programme. To understand Foucault's last political decade it is thus essential to inscribe his work both within a general opposition to the post-war Left and within the promotion, in the intellectual and political field, of a 'new political culture' whose aim was to get rid of a certain conception of the Left and of social transformation. For this new 'culture', neoliberalism was not exactly the enemy, but what Foucault called a true 'utopian focus' opening up new perspectives for a Left that should be delivered from the socialist project as it was formulated in the nineteenth century. These two developments, far from being foreign to Foucault's project, constituted its core elements after the mid-1970s. As the philosopher Isabelle Garo argues, for Foucault 'it is clear that the neoliberals were looking for an alternative that cuts across his own concerns'.[6] Neoliberalism offered him a means to rethink resistance, to imagine an intellectual framework that could create a space for minority practices, and to fulfil a key ambition of his last decade: finding a way to be 'less governed'. In the early 1980s it was not Man, but Marxism and its political project that would be erased, 'like a face drawn in sand on the edge of the sea'.

---

5 Claude Mauriac, *Le temps immobile VII. Signes, rencontres et rendez-vous*, Paris: Grasset, 1983, ebook.

6 Garo, *Foucault, Deleuze, Althusser & Marx*, p. 173.

Foucault against the post-war Left

Foucault's last decade was marked by an increasing hostility to the post-war Left and its ideas. What Sartre once called 'the unsurpassable horizon' of his time was now put on trial. Marxism, and what it represented in intellectual life (a strong state, universal social rights, centralized economy and investment, the idea of revolution, etc.), became a target for Foucault and many other intellectuals. 'Do not talk to me about Marx any more! I never want to hear anything about that man again . . . Me, I've had enough with Marx', Foucault would respond to a young student in September 1975.[7] With the French publication in 1974 of Aleksandr Solzhenitsyn's *The Gulag Archipelago*, and, by the summer of 1975, with rising concerns among the French Left about the radicalization of the Portuguese revolution, the intellectual debate had taken a rabidly anti-Marxist turn.[8] Foucault's work itself would become more openly anti-Marxist, as his activism slowly shifted away from its Maoist connections towards the struggle for Eastern dissidents.

It is therefore not surprising that, in an unpublished interview in 1977 between Foucault and militants of the French Communist Revolutionary League (LCR), he responded that he 'wouldn't mind' if they described his thought as a 'war machine against Marxism'.[9] In a 1978 interview entitled 'How to Get Rid of Marxism', published in a Japanese journal, he described Marxism as nothing more than 'a modality of power in an elementary sense'. He then explained that 'there is one clear determining factor: the fact that Marxism has contributed to and still contributes to the impoverishment of the political imaginary, this is our starting

---

7 Eribon, *Michel Foucault* (English version), p. 266.

8 See Michael Scott Christofferson, *French Intellectuals Against the Left: The Antitotalitarian Moment of the 1970s*, New York: Berghahn Books, 2004.

9 'Entretien inédit entre Michel Foucault et quatre militants de la LCR, membres de la rubrique culturelle du journal quotidien Rouge (juillet 1977)', at 1libertaire.free.fr.

point'.[10] While Foucault scholars are right when they suggest that he was obviously not a Marxist or a supporter of any existing model of revolutionary socialism, they rarely acknowledge that he was not only opposed to Marxism, but also to the 'political imaginary' that could be derived from it. The issue was therefore not merely about Marxism as a political doctrine, but, more generally, about its role as a symbol of the political project of the post-war Left. What Foucault and many intellectuals at the time were struggling against was not only socialism abroad, but also a certain kind of socialism and its legacy in France. More fundamentally, after 1968, it is the very notion and entire conceptual structure of revolution that Foucault would reject.

Against the Union of the Left

The period in which Foucault's attacks against Marxism were most violent – between 1975 and 1978 – was, in general, also a moment of intense debate on the relations between totalitarianism and the French Left. During this period, the possibility of a Union of the Left winning elections after its impressive results in 1974 – and the possibility of communists returning to government for the first time since 1947 – worried many post-'68 Left intellectuals. As Foucault's companion Daniel Defert recalls, it was well known that 'the leftists did not have a great enthusiasm for the Union of the Left . . . Fantasies of arrests of leftists had even circulated!'[11] Foucault himself explained to his close friend Claude Mauriac in 1978 that he 'never had particular sympathy for the Union of the Left'.[12]

Founded in 1972, the Union of the Left united under the 'Common Programme' the PCF (French Communist Party), the PS (Socialist Party), and the MRG (Movement of the Radicals of the

10 Michel Foucault, 'La méthodologie pour la connaissance du monde: comment se débarrasser du marxisme', July 1978, in *Dits et Écrits II*, text no. 235, p. 599.

11 Daniel Defert, *Une vie politique*, Paris: Seuil, 2014, ebook.

12 Mauriac, *Le temps immobile VII*.

Left). This ambitious programme proposed the nationalization of the banking system, increases in wages, a reduction of working hours, an expansion of social security, the 'democratization' of the workplace, and even the dissolution of NATO and the Warsaw Pact. This alliance, as Marc Lazar writes, marked 'the victory of those who defended a strong interventionism of the state' on the Left.[13] The programme – described by the French historian François Furet as 'the last neo-Bolshevik program of universal history'[14] – was therefore seen by the coalition as a first step toward socialism.

At the same time, however, the alliance deepened tensions within the Left. Indeed, as Pierre Grémion noted, since May '68 an important wing of the Union had seen the state 'as an obstacle rather than a useful tool'[15] for social transformation. This division was particularly strong within the Socialist Party, where a minority current, called the Second Left ('la deuxième gauche'), led by Michel Rocard and figures such as Patrick Viveret and Pierre Rosanvallon, defended an anti-statist Left that advocated abandoning any project of radical social transformation. This necessary evolution constituted for them the guarantee of a political thought and project of social transformation that did not carry 'the totalitarian germ'.[16] From this perspective, these critics played an important role in crafting the more general argument that any triumph of the Common Programme could lead to a 'totalitarian temptation'[17] in France.

---

13 Marc Lazar, 'La gauche et l'État: le "moment programme commun", 1974–1978', in Danielle Tartakowsky and Alain Bergounioux (eds), *L'union sans unité. Le programme commun de la gauche (1963–1978)*, Rennes: Presses Universitaires de Rennes, 2012, p. 109.

14 François Furet, *Le passé d'une illusion. Essai sur l'idée communiste au XXe siècle*, Paris: Calmann-Lévy, 1995, p. 563.

15 Pierre Grémion, *Modernisation et progressisme. Fin d'une époque 1968–1981*, Paris: Esprit, 2005, p. 8.

16 Rosanvallon and Viveret, *Pour une nouvelle culture politique*, p. 25.

17 The phrase is the title of a book by centre-left editorialist, Jean-François Revel, published in January 1976. See Christofferson, *French Intellectuals Against the Left*, pp. 142–7.

This idea of a risk to liberty in the case of a Socialist victory in France was also mentioned in an interview Foucault gave in 1976, where he discussed the problems of socialism and argued that it was necessary 'to invent an exercise of power that is not scary'.[18] What is interesting here is that he thought not only that the socialist project was potentially 'scary', but that what socialism needed was not 'another freedom convention or another bill of rights: that is easy and so useless', but a change in the conception of 'power and its exercise'.[19] Foucault here clearly references the transformation of the French Communist Party's concerns about civil liberties. By taking its distance from the USSR with the intervention in Czechoslovakia in 1968, and then abandoning the concept of the 'dictatorship of the proletariat' in 1976, the party had moved its stance on the Soviet conception of democracy in a more liberal direction. From this perspective, Foucault's declarations show that he rejected the PCF's claims to respect liberty and democracy, though the problem was less the party's programme than its conception of social change and power itself. The danger was not so much the supposedly 'hidden totalitarian intentions' of the Common Programme, but the socialist project itself. Socialism and revolution themselves now became a risk for liberty.

This helps explain Foucault's strong misgivings about the Common Programme (what he called the 'common imposture'[20]), the 'hatred'[21] he had for Mitterrand and for the whole project of the Left since the war: an interventionist state, social rights based on universal policies, public service, etc. This was the one of the reasons why Foucault, as Claude Mauriac wrote in his memoirs,

---

18 Michel Foucault, 'Crimes et châtiments en U.R.S.S. et ailleurs', February 1976, in *Dits et Écrits II*, text no. 172, p. 74.

19 Ibid.

20 Cited in Mauriac, *Le temps immobile VII*.

21 Paul Veyne quoted in Roger Pol Droit, 'Paul Veyne: "Foucault ne rêvait pas à la revolution"', *Le Monde*, 20 March 2008.

did not want the Left to win the elections of 1978,[22] even though had he voted for Mitterrand in 1974,[23] and why, as his close friend the historian Paul Veyne recounts, he did not vote for Mitterrand in 1981.[24] Remarking that Foucault 'couldn't stop being angry about the arrival of the Socialists in power', Veyne thought that 'he preferred Rocard to Mitterrand'.[25] Even in 1982, when Foucault was invited to the Elysée with Jean Daniel, Pierre Vidal-Naquet, Simone de Beauvoir and Alain Finkielkraut, he described the president's socialist economic policy as evidently 'incompetent'.[26] This was a policy that Mitterrand would finally abandon the following year in favour of his 'austerity turn', with the active support of central members of the Second Left.

Revolution as a totalitarian project

Foucault's strong opposition to both the Union of the Left as well as a certain kind of institutional politics should be understood as part of a more general opposition to the idea of revolution itself. His statements must be placed within the context of the huge campaign around Eastern European dissidents and against 'totalitarianism' that took place between 1975 and 1978, amplified by the diffusion of *The Gulag Archipelago* under the aegis of the 'New Philosophers'. Foucault himself began to be drawn to the problem of Eastern dissidents especially after the publication, in September 1976, of the transcript of the fake trial of the doctor Mikhaïl Stern in the Soviet Union.[27] He even paused the promotion of his newly published *The Will to Knowledge* (volume one of the *History of*

22 Mauriac writes: 'Michel Foucault acknowledges that he does not wish for a victory of the left', *Le temps immobile VII*.

23 Wade, *Foucault in California*, p. 58.

24 Paul Veyne, *Et dans l'éternité je ne m'ennuierai pas: Souvenirs*, Paris: Albin Michel, 2014, p. 209.

25 Paul Veyne, *Foucault, sa pensée sa personne*, Paris: Albin Michel, 2008, p. 195.

26 David Macey, *Michel Foucault*, Paris: Gallimard, 1993, p. 449.

27 August Stern, *Un procès ordinaire en U.R.S.S*, Paris: Gallimard, 1976.

Sexuality) to promote the cause of the Soviet dissident on the TV show *Apostrophes*. In the following years, this concern would take on an increasing importance in Foucault's public activity, as he participated in numerous events that drew him closer to the 'New Philosophers' like André Glucksmann and Bernard-Henri Lévy, and even travelled with Bernard Kouchner and the French film actress Simone Signoret to Poland in 1982.

What is less frequently mentioned, however, is that these campaigns were not only about repression in communist countries but also about the project of French socialism. As Christofferson puts it, the anti-totalitarian intellectuals 'focused on totalitarianism's ideological origins, arguing that political projects inspired by Marxist or revolutionary ideology inevitably result in totalitarianism.'[28] In so doing, they openly associated their critique of totalitarianism with the entire project of the post-war Left, suggesting that the 'French Left's roots in this revolutionary tradition (especially Jacobinism) made it particularly susceptible to totalitarianism.' As the historian Hervé Chauvin argues, within the anti-totalitarian Left, 'a certain amalgamation was cultivated between the situation in Eastern Europe and the potential risks related to the arrival of a Socialist government in France.'[29] In this way, a significant number of former leftists and members of the anti-statist Left cast doubt on the possibility that the socialist project could be democratic. As Michael Behrent writes, they portrayed the Union as 'crypto-totalitarian.'[30] Claude Mauriac, in an article in *Le Monde*, strongly criticized this new 'anti-totalitarian Left', arguing that its 'insidious, pernicious logic . . . abusively [linked] the Gulag to Marxism, Marxism to communism,

28 Michael Scott Christofferson, 'An Antitotalitarian History of the French Revolution: Francois Furet's *Penser la Revolution Francaise* in the Intellectual Politics of the Late 1970s', *French Historical Studies* 22:4, 1999, p. 568. The next quote is on p. 569.

29 Hervé Chauvin, 'L'union de la gauche et la problématique des droits de l'homme en URSS', in Tartakowsky and Bergounioux, *L'union sans unité*, p. 88.

30 Behrent, 'Liberalism without Humanism', p. 48.

communism to the Common Programme and the Common Programme to the Gulag'.[31] It is therefore interesting to note that Mauriac, who had been a close friend of Foucault, felt that something had been broken and would speak of a 'rupture' between him and the philosopher after writing that article.[32]

Foucault's views on this movement are well known and pretty clear in his writings of the period. Even if his own position was more careful, he still endorsed some of the most important interventions within the debate. There was, of course, his known admiration for the work of the French historian François Furet on the French Revolution – especially *La Révolution française* (1965) and *Penser la Révolution française* (1977)[33] – books that, far from just revisiting the history of the Revolution, also attacked the relevance of its ideals. Furet's critiques of French Revolution historiography deeply resonated with his own past 'illusions' about communism and the possibility of radical transformation.[34] It was 1789 itself that had 'opened a period where History drifted', one that had to end with the idea of radical social transformation itself.[35] The publication of *Penser la Révolution française* in 1977 was therefore seen by many as a critique of the French Left's fascination with Jacobinism and revolutionary ideas. In this sense, as Christofferson has convincingly shown, Furet's fears that the French 'passion for equality' was a threat to liberty also fed into the debate among French intellectuals on the legitimacy of the Union of the Left.[36]

Alongside his praise of Furet's work, Foucault supported strong attacks on the ideas of revolution and egalitarianism

31 Claude Mauriac, 'Il ne faut pas tuer l'espérance', *Le Monde*, 7 July 1977.

32 Mauriac, *Le temps immobile VII*.

33 See among others, Foucault, 'The Great Rage of Facts'. He will also describe *Penser la Révolution française* as a 'very clever book', in Foucault, 'L'esprit d'un monde sans esprit', in *Dits et Écrits II*, text no. 259, p. 745.

34 François Furet was a member of the French Communist Party until 1959 before becoming strongly anti-communist.

35 François Furet, *Penser la Révolution française*, Paris: Gallimard, 1977, p. 80.

36 Christofferson, 'An Antitotalitarian History'.

through his endorsement of the French 'New Philosophers'.[37] This media-oriented movement, initially launched by Bernard-Henri Lévy in an issue of *Nouvelles Littéraires* in June 1976, had a strong public and political impact in the spring of 1977. Presenting themselves as repentant former leftists after the French publication of *The Gulag Archipelago* in 1974, the main figures in this movement reached the general public with works such as *The Angel* (1976) by Guy Landreau and Christian Jambet, *Barbarism with a Human Face* (1977) by Lévy, and *The Master Thinkers* (1977) by André Glucksmann. Openly admiring Foucault, their bestsellers mobilized his writings and were strewn with references to the *History of Madness* or the 'great confinement', striving, as Lévy wrote, to pave the way for a 'Foucauldian analysis of Soviet society'.[38] The movement then launched into a radical denunciation of totalitarianism, popularizing the idea that it was the direct consequence of Reason, of the modern state, or of Marxism itself. The millions of deaths due to communism, wrote Glucksmann, were 'the logical application of Marxism'. In his book, which sold more than 100,000 copies, this former activist of the Proletarian Left argued that Auschwitz was a product of 'Western reason' and that 'to think, to conceive, is to dominate'. In support of their political enterprise, Foucault had frequent exchanges with the New Philosophers, addressing, as in a 1977 interview with Lévy, the question of revolution:

> the return of the revolution, that's our problem . . . There is no doubt that, without it, the question of Stalinism would be no more than a textbook case – a simple problem of the organization of the societies, or of the validity of the Marxist theory.

37 On Foucault and the New Philosophers see Peter Dews, 'The Nouvelle Philosophie and Foucault', *Economy and Society* 8:2, 1979, pp. 127–71; Audier, *Penser le 'néolibéralisme'*, pp. 178–94.

38 Bernard-Henri Lévy, 'Le système Foucault', *Le Magazine Littéraire* 101, 1975, p. 9.

> But, with Stalinism, it's about something else. You know as well as I: it's the desire for revolution itself that is a problem.[39]

Against the idea that Stalinism was a 'deformation' of Marxism, or the Gulag a 'misreading' of Marxism, Foucault asked in a book where he preferred to remain anonymous, 'how far do we have to go in the socialist idea, in the socialist programme, to find the root of the Gulag? Is it enough to say: Stalin, Stalinist mistake, Stalinist economism, Stalin's paranoia?'[40] Foucault's own answer to that question would become very clear in his enthusiastic endorsement of Glucksmann's books, *La cuisinière et le mangeur d'hommes* (The Cook and the Man Eater) and *Les maîtres penseurs* (The Master Thinkers).[41] In his highly laudatory review of the latter work for *Le Nouvel Observateur*, Foucault would almost draw a direct line between Hegel, Marx and the Gulag: 'Reread Marx or Lenin, compare with Stalin, and you will see where the latter went wrong . . . With the gulag, one saw not the consequences of an unfortunate error, but the effects of the theories that were "truest" theories in the realm of politics', he wrote without qualification.[42] As he continues,

> All of our submissiveness finds its principles in this double invitation: make the revolution quickly, and it will give you the state that you need; hurry to make the state, and it will generously dispense the reasonable effects of the revolution. Having to think about revolution, its onset and end, the German thinkers have pegged it to the state, and they have sketched the state-revolution with all its final solutions. Thus the master thinkers

39 Michel Foucault, 'Non au sexe roi', March 1977, in *Dits et Écrits II*, text no. 200, p. 266. See Foucault, 'End of the Monarchy of Sex', p. 223.

40 Thierry Voeltzel and Michel Foucault, *Vingt ans et après?*, Paris: Verticales, 2014, p. 190.

41 See Christofferson, 'Foucault and New Philosophy', pp. 6–23.

42 Foucault, 'The Great Rage of Facts, pp. 171–2.

> put together an entire mental apparatus, that which underlies the systems of domination and obedient behaviours in our modern societies.[43]

Glucksmann's two books, which Foucault saw as crucial and brilliant contributions,[44] would explicitly make the state the main enemy of any left politics. Since statism explained the Gulag and the concentration camps – statism became the force behind all the genocides – we should refuse any left programme organized around it. Racism itself would be understood as a function of the rise of the state. As Glucksmann writes, 'the incidence between the emergence of modern states and the revival of racism is always to be found'.[45] It is interesting to note that Foucault himself had formulated a very similar idea when he described the relations between statism, mass violence and racism in his lectures at the Collège de France in 1976. But if Foucault's analysis there made sense for Nazism, it became much shakier when applied to socialism. 'Whenever you have these socialisms, these forms of socialism or these movements of socialism that stress the problem of the struggle you therefore have racism.' 'The most racist forms of socialism were', he added, 'Blanquism of course, and then the Commune, and then anarchism.'[46] In his view, all socialists before the Dreyfus affair 'were racists to the extent that . . . they did not re-evaluate – or accepted if you like as self-evident – the mechanisms of biopower that the development of society and the State had been establishing since the eighteenth century'.[47] From this perspective, it is not surprising that Glucksmann would indirectly attack the idea of the nationalizations proposed by the Common Programme. As he asks, 'what have we won in replacing a

43 Ibid., p. 174.

44 Ibid., p. 172.

45 André Glucksmann, *The Master Thinkers*, New York: Harper & Row, 1980, p. 117.

46 Foucault, *Society Must Be Defended*, p. 262.

47 Ibid., p. 263.

capitalist by a civil servant?' In his view, 'for a long time nationalization is domination'.[48]

Finally, in a 1977 interview titled 'Torture is Reason', Foucault was asked if he could think of an alternative to the 'police state' that he associated with socialism. His answer was as clear as it was radical:

> I would say that we are back at the year 1830, which means that we have to start all over again from the beginning. However, the year 1830 still had behind it the French Revolution and the whole European Enlightenment tradition; we have to start all over again from the beginning . . . In one word this important tradition of socialism may be called fundamentally into question because everything this socialist tradition has produced historically may be condemned.[49]

These positions and the lack of nuance that characterized them significantly affected Foucault's friendship with Gilles Deleuze, who openly denounced the media operation of the New Philosophers. For Deleuze, it was a 'null' thought, with 'concepts as big as hollow teeth', that responded only to a logic of 'marketing' feeding on 'martyrology' and 'corpses'. However, we must understand Foucault's endorsement less as an intellectual or conceptual validation of the New Philosophers than as offering some political support for their approach. Considering that he made the above-quoted statement in a context where almost half of the French population was ready to vote for a Socialist candidate and project, Foucault's radical critique of the socialist legacy may reasonably be interpreted as a strong dismissal of a socialist alternative. From this standpoint, it is clear that for Foucault, as for the Second Left, the discussion was no longer about the type of reform that would

48 Glucksmann, *Master Thinkers*, p. 141.

49 Michel Foucault, 'La torture, c'est la raison', December 1977, in *Dits et Écrits II*, text no. 215, p. 398.

be needed, but about the very definition of the Left. The study of neoliberalism he was undertaking at the same time would prove to be a fascinating opportunity to redefine a Left freed from socialism.

Neoliberalism beyond Right and Left

In this context of hostility towards the post-war Left, Foucault and many others set out in search of what could be called a 'left governmentality'. As he consistently stated, in his view the French Left did not have a 'problematic of government' but only 'a problematic of the State'.[50] This idea was explicit in his lectures on *The Birth of Biopolitics* given at the Collège de France, where he famously argued that there was no 'autonomous socialist governmentality' and that, therefore, 'in actual fact, and history has shown this, socialism may only be implemented, connected up to diverse types of governmentality'. A socialist governmentality was thus, for Foucault, still to be 'invented'.[51]

Neoliberalism with a Franco-German prism

From this perspective, it is interesting to note how much Foucault's lectures on biopolitics were marked by what Audier called the French 'crisis of socialism'. If we are used to reading these lectures as being about neoliberalism in general, they are nonetheless also strongly related to the French politics of the time. Foucault's focus is partially on Valéry Giscard d'Estaing and Raymond Barre's neoliberal policies[52] and on Germany – especially Helmut Schmidt's SPD (Social Democratic Party). This choice may seem a

50 See Defert, 'Chronologie', p. 87.

51 Foucault, *The Birth of Biopolitics*, p. 92.

52 On these economic policies see Serge Berstein and Jean-François Sirinelli, *Les années Giscard. La politique économique 1974–1981*, Paris: Armand Collin, 2009.

strange one for anyone interested in the rise of neoliberal governmentality in the late 1970s. Why, for instance, is there no reference to Pinochet's coup against Allende in Chile and the neoliberal experiment that followed? Or to Ronald Reagan's hyper-conservative governorship of California between 1967 and 1975?[53] Why was Foucault only interested in a very abstract reading of neoliberalism, with no regard for its potentially very conservative effects, already manifest in Barry Goldwater's extremely conservative 1964 US presidential campaign, conducted under Milton Friedman's economic counsel, and in Reagan's presidential bid in 1976? He does not even mention Friedrich Hayek's aristocratic conception of democracy, or the often reactionary opinions of Austrian neoliberals.

One of the reasons for this standpoint is elucidated by Audier, who highlights Foucault's interest in the very good relations – 'unique' as Giscard said himself[54] – between Giscard's neoliberal government and the Social Democratic government of Schmidt, and what this meant for the future of socialism. As Audier suggests, 'if Foucault assumes a very German-centred point of view, it's because he is questioning the destiny of France and of French socialism in 1979: if the "neoliberal" policy of Barre and Giscard seems to partially imitate the social democratic policy of Schmidt, what does socialism mean today?'[55] This interrogation would divide at the same time both the Left and the Right. As the French economist Christian Stoffaës wrote at the time, 'the debate on the German model is the moment of original divisions within the

53 In Simeon Wade's book on Foucault's Death Valley trip, he recounts a discussion on the subject in which Foucault claims to be aware of Reagan's policy and 'the political change it represents'. Although Foucault had already made several trips to the United States, it was not until 1975, at the invitation of Leo Bersani in Berkeley, that he really discovered California. See Simeon Wade, *Foucault in California*, p. 141.

54 On the details of this relationship during the Giscard presidency, see in particular Valéry Giscard d'Estaing, *Le pouvoir et la vie*, Paris: Compagnie 12, 1988, pp. 124–61.

55 Audier, *Penser le 'néolibéralisme'*, p. 131.

political class: Gaullists and Communists communicate in their grumbling; liberal Giscardians, Rocardian socialists and *cédétistes* [members of the CFDT union] communicate in a barely veiled admiration'.[56] This division would be even stronger in light of the marked lack of enthusiasm among German and UK social democrats for the Common Programme. Giscard would even explain that the day after the 1978 election, the first to rejoice openly at his victory were the social democratic leaders Helmut Schmidt and James Callaghan.[57] From this perspective, Foucault's lectures on biopolitics are deeply concerned with the crisis facing the Union of the Left at that moment, and with the rise of the neoliberal Right behind Giscard, which in many ways broke with the old Gaullist power. As Foucault himself explained in his lectures, we 'pass from a, broadly speaking, Keynesian type of system, which had more or less lingered on in Gaullist policy, to a new art of government, which would be taken up by Giscard'.[58] The French context manifests, then, a neoliberalism surging from different sides and with different actors, transcending the old Left–Right opposition to reshape the whole political framework.

In this context, Foucault – along with some of his contemporaries – saw neoliberalism as an interesting framework within which to rethink the Left as a 'governmentality' rather than a 'simple economic logic'. As Lagasnerie argues, Foucault did not see it as 'something that would function as a political alternative to which a well-defined programme or plan could be attached'.[59] The important point here is that Foucault did not really study neoliberalism as a problem of the 'Left' or the 'Right'. Instead, he was interested in it as a form of governmentality, or what we could call its political ontology, the framework within which it conceived politics and society. As he put it in his lectures:

56 Christian Stoffaës, *La grande menace industrielle*, quoted in Audier, *Penser le 'néolibéralisme'*, p. 215

57 Giscard d'Estaing, *Le pouvoir et la vie*, p. 147.

58 Foucault, *The Birth of Biopolitics*, p. 146.

59 Lagasnerie, *La dernière leçon*, p. 47.

> Liberalism in America is a whole way of being and thinking. It is a type of relation between the governors and the governed much more than a technique of governors with regard to the governed . . . I think this is why American liberalism currently appears not just, or not so much as a political alternative, but let's say as a sort of many-sided, ambiguous, global claim with a foothold in both the right and the left. It is also a sort of utopian focus which is always being revived. It is also a method of thought, a grid of economic and sociological analysis.[60]

The emergent neoliberal governmentality would thus be essential for the philosopher's attempt to find an alternative to 'social-statism' and to open a space for the proliferation of minority practices.

This political context sheds new light on Foucault's reading of neoliberalism. Indeed, since the publication of his lectures in 2004, the majority of authoritative commentators have generally projected onto them their own interpretations of neoliberalism. The enormous contrast between the reception of the published courses and that of the course given at the Collège de France is particularly well illustrated by the first account of it, published in September 1979, in the journal *Autrement*, the emblematic publication of the Second Left. In this piece, written by the journalist Jules Chancel and the management theorist Pierre-Eric Tixier, Foucault's lessons are not at all depicted as a denunciation of neoliberalism. Their article, entitled 'The Desire of Entrepreneurship', argued that with the explosion of alternative economic models in the aftermath of May '68 (such as autonomous and local experimentations within the ecological movement, anti-institutional struggles or self-management alternatives), 'the notion of enterprise' was 'at the centre of this cocktail of ideologies'.[61] In that context, the authors remarked, Giscard's government

60 Foucault, *The Birth of Biopolitics*, pp. 218.

61 Jules Chancel and Pierre-Eric Tixier, 'Le désir d'entreprendre', *Autrement* 20, September 1979, p. 13.

and his neoliberal reforms were surprisingly 'favourable' to the proliferation of small, autonomous 'entrepreneurial' experiments. Using Foucault's lectures on neoliberalism, Chancel and Tixier argued that these 'new entrepreneurs' of the Left could, within the neoliberal framework, 'use the convergences, objective but partial, which exist between their experiences and the governmental perspectives, without falling into the trap, so convenient, of "co-optation"'.[62] In their view, what Foucault helped us to understand was that a subversive use of neoliberalism was possible, that in its 'enterprise-oriented' framework the Left could open spaces for its own anti-'social-statist' politics, to create a 'third sector' of 'creative entrepreneurs' in between the state and the more traditional firms. As Audier observed, 'this first and almost immediate mobilization of Foucault's lectures on neoliberalism . . . is undoubtedly a valuable document because it reveals elements of context that are no longer those of readers of the twenty-first century or even of the nineties, and are generally ignored by them, as if Foucault had written only for them and in their own context'.[63]

The *Autrement* journal intended then to 'rehabilitate' the concept of 'enterprise' within the Left by titling its special issue 'What If Everyone Created His Own Job?' It included articles by Jacques Delors, future president of the European Commission, criticizing the 'invasion of the person by institutions', and by Michel Rocard – Foucault's favourite socialist – arguing that the 'freedom' to be an entrepreneur should be an integral part of the struggle against totalitarianism.[64] Interestingly, this key publication of the French Second Left also included an interview with Bernard Stasi, a former right-wing minister in Giscard's government. Stasi illustrated perfectly what Foucault had sensed about neoliberalism:

62 Ibid., p. 14.

63 Audier, *Penser le 'néolibéralisme'*, p. 19.

64 Michel Rocard, 'Et si big devenait beautiful?', *Autrement* 20, September 1979, p. 155.

the state, whatever its political connotation, necessarily tends to tighten its control, its tutelage, on society. It is necessary, by building all kinds of safeguards, to ensure that society is not crushed by the State, that there is a certain autonomy, spaces of freedom for individuals and natural communities. It is only through the diversification of funding sources that it will be possible to avoid the increase in state control.[65]

Finally, in the same issue, it is worth noting the paper by the sociologists Bernard Rochette and Elie Théofilakis, who argued openly that 'the remedy is simple if a little retro: reinventing the market'.[66] In their view, in the aftermath of '68 and the energy it released, it was obvious that 'the market is no longer only the static equilibrium between a supply and a demand for goods, but the global dynamic process of integration and articulation of all the effervescent elements of a new social order'.[67] Indeed, while the old welfare state affected negatively both economic growth and social justice, the market, if carefully reorganized, could have a 'therapeutic value' in regulating social exchanges. Behind this shift, what was now emerging, on both the Right and the Left, was 'the figure, for a time overshadowed by the planning technocrat, of the entrepreneur'.[68] In this new context, the neoliberal economist, the 'manager' and the 'leftist entrepreneur' could all rejoice together within the spaces freed from statist normativity.[69]

In many ways, this Second Left felt that it sometimes shared more with the Giscardian and neoliberal Right than with the 'social-statism' of its own party. A new field of experimentation was thus opened by this 'new capitalism', creating the conditions

65 Bruno Stasi, 'Réduire le contrôle de l'État', *Autrement* 20, September 1979, p. 161.

66 Bernard Rochette and Elie Théofilakis, 'Avec les "nouveaux économistes", allons tous au marché!', *Autrement* 20, September 1979, p. 175.

67 Ibid.

68 Ibid., p. 176.

69 Ibid.

for new coalitions between past enemies. If this context is important, it is precisely because it gives us a sense of what kind of neoliberalism Foucault was talking about in his lectures, and of the conversation of which they were a part.

Giscard and the 'liberalization' of society

To understand Foucault's intervention, it is crucial to have in mind the presidency of Valéry Giscard d'Estaing between 1974 and 1981. His victory against François Mitterrand in one of the tightest elections in French history (50.81% to 49.19%) was framed under the promise of an 'advanced liberalism' more open to the aspirations of May '68. Giscard's presidency, though often underestimated, marked an important transition in French society. Rather than pushing forward the Gaullist legacy, Giscard inaugurated a more neoliberal Right in French politics. During the first half of his mandate, his 'liberal' programme not only took into account the claims of May '68 on 'societal' issues, but also, by 1978, applied more neoliberal economic doctrines.[70] Two things explain Foucault's interest in this government: first, its domestic policies, which broke with Gaullism and the conservatism of the previous president Georges Pompidou; and second, Giscard's relations with Schmidt's Social Democratic Party in Germany, which proved to be an interesting starting point from which to question the future of the Left in France.

In relation to domestic politics, Giscard was viewed with some interest by a fringe of the 'libertarian' Left. His concept of 'advanced liberalism' aimed to formulate some kind of 'third way between pure liberalism and the statist or bureaucratic interventionism'.[71] In this respect, the first years of his presidency were marked by important reforms that partially met the

70 On the economic policies see Berstein and Sirinelli, *Les années Giscard*.

71 Mathias Bernard, 'Le projet giscardien face aux contraintes du pouvoir', in Berstein and Sirinelli, *Les années Giscard*, p. 15.

aspirations of May '68. As noted by Mathias Bernard, 'the crisis of May '68 transformed [Giscard's] conception of society – insofar as it appeared possible to respond to the anti-authoritarian aspirations of the baby boom generation without jeopardizing an economic organization which, for him, carried the evidence of its effectiveness'.[72] In an attempt to 'modernize' French society and attack 'social prejudices', he also created three new departments: one focusing on the condition of prisoners, one for immigrant workers, and one concerning the condition of women. This led to significant reforms such as the legalization of abortion, the liberalization of contraception, the decriminalization of adultery, the recognition of divorce by mutual consent, the promotion of the integration of immigrant workers, and the improvement of conditions in prisons. Giscard was also the first president to actually go into a prison to visit inmates[73] and to invite immigrant garbage men to the Élysée presidential palace (in 1974).[74] He also reduced the voting age to eighteen.

Giscard's concern for increasing individual freedoms in the aftermath of '68 was accompanied by a more wary relation to state power. He would defend a vision of the state that was neither 'invasive nor arbitrary',[75] including the 'suppression of phone tapping, the refusal of any restrictions of the press even in case of attacks against the president, reaffirmation of the right of asylum',[76] and the end of the censorship of cultural production (especially of movies that had had to be politically evaluated by the censorship commission). In an interview, Foucault even joked about Giscard, saying that he would soon define his project as one of creating 'an

72 Mathias Bernard, *Valéry Giscard D'Estaing. Les ambitions déçues*, Paris: Armand Colin, Paris: 2014, p. 200.

73 Giscard d'Estaing, *Le pouvoir et la vie*, pp. 302–7.

74 Ibid., pp. 308–11. See also Sylvain Laurens, 'Les Maliens à l'Elysée', *Revue Agone* 40, 2008.

75 Bernard, 'Le projet giscardien face aux contraintes du pouvoir', p. 18.

76 Ibid.

anti-repressive society',[77] and that he was annoyed with how the far Left viewed Giscard's achievements. 'When Giscard was elected president', Foucault noted, 'he enacted several original reforms' and 'created a post of under-secretary of state in the Ministry of Justice devoted exclusively to prison problems, and he appointed a woman there'. 'So, straight away', he added, 'the diehard leftists criticized: "Look! It's recuperated by the system!" But I don't think so . . . To succeed is to succeed.'[78]

Finally, Giscard would also defend a new approach to social issues. In an attempt to refuse both the equalization of income, which was seen as integral to totalitarian regimes, and a wild liberalism without any concern for poverty, Giscard would instead work to ensure 'equal opportunity'. As he himself wrote, if he recognized 'a certain level of inequality of resources' as a result of 'the hierarchy of functions' and as the 'inevitable' corollary of economic dynamism, he nevertheless refused to 'recognize the inequality of beings'.[79] Therefore, only the inequality resulting from discrimination, racism or prejudice constituted a problem. As Mathias Bernard argued:

> rejecting the egalitarian utopia, which leads to communism and therefore contradicts the liberal project that was implemented, the President rather gives to the State the dual mission of helping the excluded and correcting the inequality of access to education. The extension of freedom was the challenge of the first year of its mandate; it is now equal opportunities that the government must tackle.[80]

---

77 Foucault, 'Entretien inédit entre Michel Foucault et quatre militants'.

78 Michel Foucault, 'Sexualité et politique', May 1978, in *Dits et Écrits II*, text no. 230, p. 529.

79 Giscard d'Estaing, *Le pouvoir et la vie*, p. 308.

80 Bernard, *Valéry Giscard D'Estaing*, p. 197.

An anti-normative neoliberalism

This emphasis on equality of opportunity explains, in particular, Giscard's pronounced interest in a negative income tax system, as proposed by Milton Friedman. In his view, such a system could address the questions of poverty and exclusion without limiting inequality, and without the 'perverse' effects of egalitarianism on the economy. As Lionel Stoléru – sent by Giscard to the Brookings Institution in Washington to study the system in order to implement it in France – argued, 'doctrines . . . can encourage either a policy to eradicate poverty or a policy seeking to limit the gap between rich and poor.'[81] This involves what he calls 'the border between absolute poverty and relative poverty'. The former simply refers to an arbitrarily determined level (addressed by the negative tax), while the latter relates to broader differences between individuals (addressed by social security and the welfare state). As Stoléru saw it, 'the market economy is able to assimilate actions against absolute poverty' but 'it is unable to digest strong remedies against relative poverty'.[82] In other words, we can struggle against extreme poverty in order to try to create a society with equal opportunity, but we cannot limit inequality itself without hurting the economy.

The replacement of equality with the fight against poverty also involves a transformation of the underlying principle of justice. It is indeed by this fundamental ideological operation that a notion of social justice articulated around equal opportunities is affirmed. If the principle of equality requires a reduction of the income gap, that of equal opportunity only ensures that resources are not then allocated through unfair mechanisms (meaning structures negatively affecting the free competition between individuals). Thus, exclusion, racism and sexism distort the economic game by

81 Lionel Stoléru, *Vaincre la pauvreté dans les pays riches*, Paris: Flammarion, 1974, p. 237.

82 Ibid., p. 287.

promoting some individuals over others. The goal of equal opportunity is therefore not to abolish competition (by establishing genuine equality) but to ensure that it is fair, that we all start from the same starting line. By providing a negative income, it would be possible to overcome discrimination and restore the balance of economic play. The negative income tax system therefore has the advantage of not interfering with the market. Unlike the social security system, it does not limit the market but rather makes everyone part of it. Foucault perceived this aspect of the negative tax very well, noting that:

> it ensures as it were a general security, but at the lowest level, that is to say, the economic mechanisms of the game, the mechanisms of competition and enterprise, will be allowed to function in the rest of society. Above the threshold everyone will have to be an enterprise for himself or for his family. A society formalized on the model of the enterprise, of the competitive enterprise, will be possible above the threshold, and there will be simply a minimum security, that is to say, the nullification of certain risks on the basis of a low-level threshold.[83]

This idea was in tune with the reforms proposed by Giscard on the 'societal' level. Indeed, the negative income tax system, since it guarantees a floor of income, has none of the effects of normalization, discrimination or social control that the old social institutions could have. It was precisely this non-selectivity in the criteria that would particularly appeal to Foucault. In his view, the system was a response to the governmentality and forms of normalization imposed by the old centralized and statist social security institutions. As he notes:

> when it comes to it, the famous distinction that Western governmentality has tried for so long to establish between the good

83 Foucault, *The Birth of Biopolitics*, p. 206.

> and bad poor, between the voluntary and involuntary unemployed, is not important. After all, it does not and should not concern us to know why someone falls below the level of the social game; whether he is a drug addict or voluntarily unemployed is not important. Whatever the reasons, the only problem is whether he is above or below the threshold.[84]

The new system will allow the population that is 'floating' or surplus with respect to the labour market to be assisted 'in a very liberal and much less bureaucratic and disciplinary way than it is by a system focused on full employment which employs mechanisms like those of social security'.[85] Thanks to a mechanism that rejects any distinctions among the 'poor', ultimately 'it is up to people to work if they want or not work if they don't. Above all there is the possibility of not forcing them to work if there is no interest in doing so. They are merely guaranteed the possibility of minimal existence at a given level, and in this way the neoliberal policy can be got to work.'[86] Also in this way, we avoid basically everything Foucault had criticized for years in the course of his work: all those forms of control of the body, of conduct, of sexuality that are so present, yet often hidden, in many socialist policies intended to reduce inequality. That is why, as Stoléru will note, 'what interested Foucault . . . is the passage from a tutelary system to a fiscally neutral system where nothing is asked of anybody, neither of his past nor about his responsibility. There was in it something at the same time socialist and liberal that could make him think.'[87]

The effects of a certain configuration between the state and the dispositives of normalization thus seemed very different in the

84 Ibid., pp. 204–5.

85 Ibid., p. 207.

86 Ibid.

87 Lionel Stoléru, email exchange with Michael C. Behrent, 27 August 2010. We would like to thank Michael C. Behrent for providing us with this document and the necessary details concerning the relationship between Foucault and Stoléru.

new neoliberal France of the 1970s compared to the old Gaullist and statist France. Foucault was particularly struck by this evolution within the realm of sexuality. In a rarely cited interview in 1978 discussed by Audier,[88] Foucault explored the reception of his proposition to de-penalize sexual relations between adults and teenagers. He had offered the proposal to a government commission that France should reduce the legal age of consent to the range of thirteen to fifteen years old as in Scandinavia. In the article, he explained how surprised he was that the reaction of the government (in 1978) was positive and the discussion constructive.

Indeed, in the late 1970s, the idea of sexual relations between adults and teenagers (and, for some, even children) became the object of strong debates within the Parisian intelligentsia. The 'Versailles affair' – in which three men in their mid-forties were given prison sentences after having sexual relations with boys and girls aged between thirteen and fourteen years old – led to several highly publicized petitions to bring the age of consent down to under fifteen. In particular, the gay activist and founder of the FHAR, Guy Hocquenghem, assembled an impressive collection of names under the two letters published in *Le Monde* in January and May 1977, including prestigious authors such as Foucault, Jacques Derrida, Gilles Deleuze, Jean-Paul Sartre, Simone De Beauvoir, Roland Barthes and André Glucksmann, and important writers like Philippe Sollers, Alain Robbe-Grillet and the self-proclaimed paedophile Gabriel Matzneff.[89] While these interventions and the infamous figures defended at the time would generate intense controversies about the Parisian elite's tolerance for the sexual

88 Michel Foucault, 'Michel Foucault, juillet 1978', in J. Le Bitoux, *Entretiens sur la question gay*, Bézier: H&O éditions, 2005, p. 70. Quoted in Audier, *Penser le 'néolibéralisme'*, pp. 374–5. English version, Michel Foucault, 'The gay science', *Critical Inquiry* 37:3, 2011, pp. 385–403. The proposal concerning the age of consent is at p. 402.

89 'A propos d'un proces', *Le Monde*, January 26, 1977, available at lemonde.fr. On Matzneff, see Norimitsu Onishi, 'A Pedophile Writer Is on Trial. So Are the French Elites', *New York Times*, 11–12 February, 2020.

abuse of children, the context nevertheless led the Giscard government to be open to reform.[90]

The main reason Foucault gave for this reaction of the government commission to the proposal was connected quite clearly to the analysis he would give in lectures in the coming year of the decline of the disciplinary or pastoral model of exercising power under neoliberalism – the economic and political cost of repressive governmental measures. He then mobilized the analysis he would make of Gary Becker's theory of crime, noting that 'in the development that we are seeing now, what we are now discovering, is the extraordinary cost of what represents the exercise of repressive power'. He continued: 'Why alienate intellectuals? What is the benefit of a society that would hunt homosexuals? The birth rate? In the age of the contraceptive pill? The fight against syphilis?' In this age of neoliberalism, we understand that 'whenever one commits an act that is exercising power, it costs, and not just economically'.[91] For Foucault, the emergent neoliberalism or Giscardian 'advanced liberalism' thus appeared as a more 'tolerant' and less normative governmentality, perfectly able to respond to the economic and political 'crisis' of the exercise of disciplinary power within the welfare state.

Towards a 'new political culture'

To grasp Foucault's relation to neoliberalism we cannot, therefore, ignore the strong interest that a section of the Left had in the early years of Giscard's presidency in relation to their own quest for an

---

90 See in particular Jean Bérard, 'De la libération des enfants à la violence des pédophiles. La sexualité des mineurs dans les discours politiques des années 1970', *Genre, sexualité & société* 11, 2014; Jean Bérard and Nicolas Sallée, 'Les âges du consentement. Militantisme gai et sexualité des mineurs en France et au Québec (1970–1980)', *Clio. Femmes, Genre, Histoire* 2:42, 2015, pp. 99–124.

91 Foucault, 'Michel Foucault, juillet 1978', p. 71. Foucault, 'The gay science', pp. 402–403.

alternative to the Common Programme. The alternative to Gaullism Giscard seemed to offer opened the door for the Left to make a similar move. This project would be taken up in particular by intellectuals close to the Second Left and the CFDT. Giscard was an important figure for them as he had instituted, within the Right, the turning they hoped to effect within the Left. During a televised debate on the legendary *Apostrophes* set, the editorialist Jean Boissonnat pointed out that 'strange coalitions' were emerging on the political front. A coalition between 'liberals' and '*autogestionnaires*' (advocates of self-management) on the one hand, and, on the other, a front composed of 'nationalists and bureaucrats'. This configuration, which was not superimposed on the 'existing political organizations', amounted in Boissonnat's eyes to a confrontation between 'a left and a right that would be modern' and 'a left and a right that would be archaic'. As Michel Chapuis, Socialist minister under Rocard and an important figure in the Second Left, wrote: 'Facing the new liberal right incarnated by Giscard, it would have been important to give a chance to a new socialist left.'[92]

This French Second Left acquired its name from an influential speech by the Socialist leader (and later prime minister in 1988), Michel Rocard, at the 1977 congress of the Socialist Party, where he made a distinction between two lefts: one 'that was long-dominant, Jacobin, centralized, statist, nationalist and protectionist', and the other, the Second Left, which is 'decentralized' and 'refuses arbitrary domination, that of the bosses as well as of the state'. This Left was to be 'liberating for dependent majorities like women or badly integrated minorities in society: youth, immigrants, and the disabled'.[93] In clear opposition to the programme of the Union of the Left and François Mitterrand, Rocard formulated the idea of a

92 Michel Chapuis, *Si Rocard avait su . . . Témoignage sur la deuxième gauche*, Paris: L'Harmattan, 2007, ebook.

93 Michel Rocard, 'Les deux cultures politiques, discours prononcé aux congrès de Nantes du Parti socialiste en avril 1977', in Michel Rocard, *Parler Vrai*, Paris: Seuil, 1979, p. 80.

strong division between these two 'cultures' within the Left. For him it was clear that, beyond their differences, both Communists and the Mitterrandist majority within the Party had in common a 'strategy of change' 'centred on the conquest of state, activists behaving more like the "soldiers" of an army in the field'.[94]

The most clearly articulated theorization of these 'two cultures' of the Left came in a book by Patrick Viveret (who wrote Rocard's 1977 speech) and Pierre Rosanvallon, published in 1977 under the title *For a New Political Culture*.[95] Viveret and Rosanvallon defended the idea that, since the war, France had been dominated by a political culture in which the state is 'the central element' and 'the motor for the future transition to socialism'.[96] The problem for them was not so much what you could do with the state as the state itself, which was the main tool for social transformation. As they argued, 'the dominant political discourse, from the left or right, puts the difficulty of social transformation, not in its aim, but in the means'.[97] The Second Left was therefore a reaction to a certain conception of social transformation rather than a mere political programme. As Michel Foessel notes, 'the Second Left reacts against two figures of authoritarianism who have lived in peace through the Trente Glorieuses: the national centralism of Gaullism and the supposedly democratic one of the PCF'.[98] Against these two figures of 'statism', the Second Left defended the virtues of 'civil society', human rights and minority rights, and rehabilitated within the Left the idea of entrepreneurship. For them, as Jacques Julliard pointed out in an interview with Michel Rocard, 'socialism is not the suppression of private entrepreneurship, but to the contrary, the possibility for each

94 Michel Rocard, 'Un puissant parti socialiste, intervention à la convention nationale du parti socialiste le 25 novembre 1978', in Rocard, *Parler Vrai*, p. 165.

95 Rosanvallon and Viveret, *Pour une nouvelle culture politique*.

96 Ibid., p. 33.

97 Ibid., p. 11.

98 Michael Foessel, 'De Rocard à Julliard, vie et mort de la deuxième gauche', *Libération*, 25 January 2011.

individual to recover the function of the entrepreneur'.[99] Thus, in the context of their attempt to refuse a 'statist society' and to 'rehabilitate the concept of entrepreneurship', neoliberalism was seen as an interesting intellectual tool with which to invent a new Left, a Left that was no longer opposed to the market. The idea of entrepreneurship will therefore be strongly linked to that of self-management, a model that offered a way to 'fragment sovereignty and politics' into a more modest and decentralized conception of social change. In this vision, as noted by Christofferson, equality was to be reconceptualized 'in terms of autonomy and recognition', in particular of the right to differ.[100]

The intervention of André Gorz was particularly interesting in this respect. An important Marxist thinker of ecology, and an advocate of the end of post-war class politics[101] who was close to the Second Left, Gorz also saw in the rise of French neoliberalism an occasion to rethink the Left. As he put it in a text from 1976, 'it is clear: Giscard comes from the Right. But it does not follow from that, that the liberalization of society is necessarily a right-wing project and that we should abandon it to the Giscardians'.[102] He then stated that 'everywhere in Europe there are now, between neoliberals and neosocialists, exchanges and a partial osmosis'.[103] At their core, these exchanges were not so much about increasing corporate power as they were about struggling against a common enemy: the state. As Gorz argued, 'if Giscard arrives at disengaging the central power and freeing new spaces where we can exercise collective initiative, why not profit from it?' The retreat of the state, provoked by neoliberal policies, would then become a good

99 Michel Rocard, 'Entretien avec Jacques Julliard', in Rocard, *Parler Vrai*, p. 30.

100 Christofferson, *French Intellectuals Against the Left*, p. 218.

101 Especially in André Gorz, *Farewell to the Working Class*, London: Pluto Press, 1982.

102 André Gorz, 'Occupons le terrain', *Le Nouvel Observateur* 116, August 1976, p. 23, quoted in Audier, *Penser le 'néolibéralisme'*, p. 212.

103 Ibid., p. 213.

occasion for an anti-statist Left to 'occupy the field left vacant by power'. He then naturally concluded with a very straightforward question: 'Does the Left want a society where everyone relies on the state for everything: the pollution of our shores, food additives, architecture, abusive layoffs, work accidents, etc.? In that case we will only replace a private carelessness by an administrative carelessness, an employer's arbitrary will with a bureaucratic arbitrary will.' He goes so far as to argue that 'the project of Giscardian society is nothing but a project of deep democratization of the social body itself'.[104] As Audier has pointed out, for Gorz, neoliberalism was obviously not a solution, but 'it could offer significant opportunities for another economic, political and social agenda'.[105] In this sense, neoliberalism could be seen as an interesting tool in its desire to reject a 'statist society' and 'rehabilitate the concept of enterprise'. For a significant section of the Second Left, this necessary evolution was a condition for being able to 'elaborate a plan [that would] break with any economistic, bureaucratic or totalitarian temptation'.[106]

The relations between Foucault and neoliberalism may be understood from a similar perspective. It will then not be very surprising that during the 1970s he would manifest a pronounced interest in this Second Left, with whom he shared the rejection of Mitterandism and of social-statism.[107] Notably, he participated in the 'Vivre à gauche' forum, organized by Rosanvallon and Viveret, whose objective was precisely to bring together all the actors in this emerging new political culture, and saw in these two days of intense discussions the sign of an 'ideological and profound' change.[108] He was also very enthusiastic about the reflections proposed by

104 Ibid.

105 Ibid.

106 Rosanvallon and Viveret, *Pour une nouvelle culture politique*, p. 69.

107 Pierre Rosanvallon, *Notre histoire intellectuelle et politique, 1968–2018*, Paris: Seuil, 2018, p. 102.

108 Foucault, 'Une mobilisation culturelle', September 1977, in *Dits et Écrits II*, text no. 207, p. 330.

Rosanvallon and Viveret in their book. In a letter written to Rosanvallon, Foucault said that he was 'hugely pleased and interested' in the book and that it offered 'a remarkable understanding of our present', 'an accurate diagnosis' that represented 'a breakthrough', 'a true' rather than 'immobilizing' analysis that was really needed.[109] Foucault himself would confirm his support when he declared, in 1983, that 'we have to see that, within the Socialist Party, one of the places where this new left thought was the more active, is around somebody like Michel Rocard.'[110] As Pierre Rosanvallon noted more recently, the idea of a 'progressive alternative' to the 'Common Programme' had 'particularly interested' him.[111] In Foucault's opinion, it was was clear that 'it's not thanks to the PC, thanks to the old SFIO[112] – which did not die before 1972, it took too much time to die – that we have a living left in France.'[113] In 1984, he will even see the failure of the Socialist Party to fulfil the enthusiasm it had provoked in the fact that within the party 'they were afraid of the Rocardians', and that the intellectuals were obviously on the side of Rocard.[114]

In a conversation organized at the University of Chicago in 2012, Gary Becker asked if Foucault was a socialist. In his response, François Ewald made an interesting distinction: 'Socialist, no! On the Left.' Troubled, Becker then asked, 'But well, what does Left mean?'[115] It was precisely this question, regarding the definition of

109 Rosanvallon, *Notre histoire intellectuelle et politique*, p. 100.

110 Michel Foucault, 'Structuralisme et poststructuralisme', spring 1983, in *Dits et Écrits II*, text no. 330, p. 1273.

111 Rosanvallon, *Notre histoire intellectuelle et politique*, p. 100.

112 The SFIO was the historic French Socialist Party created in 1905. The French Communist Party was created out of the SFIO after the congress of Tours in 1920. It would finally disappear with the creation of the Socialist Party in 1969.

113 Michel Foucault, 'Structuralisme et poststructuralisme', p. 1271.

114 'Interview de Michel Foucault', *Actes: cahiers d'action juridique* 45–46, 1984, pp. 3–6, in *Dits et écrits II*, text no. 353, p. 1509.

115 Becker, Ewald and Harcourt, 'Becker on Ewald on Foucault', p. 19.

the Left itself, that was at stake during the fierce political debates in mid-1970s France. What should the Left be? Not only in terms of its programme, but in its very definition? Though the so-called statist Left won at the ballot boxes in 1981, it would not be an exaggeration to say that the Second Left's ideas later had a central importance in the evolution of the Socialist Party.

It is essential to understand that Foucault and many other post-'68 intellectuals took part in the process of thinking about a Left that was not socialist, a Left that would wipe out the legacy of post-war socialism. Describing it as 'crypto-totalitarian', they finally abandoned the socialist project. Since the revolution was no longer desirable, Foucault thought that a new kind of politics should be invented that would open the way for a Left that no longer rejected the market and could therefore create a space free both from the state and from the normativity of the 'social-statist' governmentality (shared by both socialists and Gaullists). Rejecting, as Paul Veyne notes,[116] any 'abstract' or 'general' analysis in his political commitments, Foucault discovered in neoliberalism a fascinating framework for his 'militancy on the margins'[117] and his 'everyday' struggles for the excluded, prisoners, immigrants, or people with mental illness. From this perspective, neoliberalism provided Foucault with interesting insights into how, in accordance with his understanding of social critique, we might 'not be governed too much'. In this sense, as Michaël Foessel argues:

> In defending civil society, the Second Left took for inspiration the libertarian and social thought of '68. From the thought of Michel Foucault to the activism of the CFDT there was an anti-statist consensus. Not 'reform' instead of 'revolution', but

116 Paul Veyne, 'Foucault ne rêvait pas à la révolution', *Le Monde*, 20 March 2018, available at lemonde.fr.

117 Gil Delannoi, *Les années utopiques, 1968–1978*, Paris: La découverte, 1990, p. 61.

> 'micro-resistances' and local experiences against the vertical exercise of power.[118]

This is precisely why the historian Julian Bourg saw in these evolutions a turn toward ethics among the French Left. This turn transformed the main subject of social change, but 'what had been revolutionized was the very notion of revolution itself'.[119]

118 Foessel, 'De Rocard à Julliard'.

119 Julian Bourg, *From Revolution to Ethics: May '68 and Contemporary French Thought*, Montreal: McGill-Queen's University Press, 2007, p. 4.

3

Beyond the Sovereign Subject: Against Interpretation

> I am an experimenter in the sense that I write in order to change myself.
>
> Michel Foucault, 1978[1]

> . . . there is no first or final point of resistance to political power other than in the relationship one has to oneself.
>
> Michel Foucault, 1982[2]

In an interview given to the Italian journalist Duccio Trombadori in 1978, Foucault reconsidered the events to May '68. He argued that, with ten years of hindsight, 'the second half of the sixties' was a 'crucial point in the history of European culture'.[3] Foucault had

1 Michel Foucault, 'Entretien avec Michel Foucault (Conversazione con Michel Foucault)', 1980, in *Dits et écrits II*, text no. 281, p. 861.

2 Michel Foucault, *The Hermeneutics of the Subject: Lectures at the Collège de France 1981–1982*, trans. Graham Burchell, London: Palgrave Macmillan, 2005, p. 252.

3 Foucault, 'Entretien avec Michel Foucault (Conversazione con Michel Foucault)', p. 889; Foucault, *Remarks on Marx*, pp. 108–9.

not, however, grasped the importance of the French events at the time they occurred. In contrast to other thinkers such as Cornelius Castoriadis, Michel de Certeau or Claude Lefort, who had immediately published their interpretation of the events, he remained more or less silent about them, if not deeply critical.

This was perhaps in part because, during the events, he was still teaching at the University of Tunis after he had accepted a three-year contract sponsored by the French government. And his experience of the student movement there – especially in March 1968, during protests against the visit of US vice-president Hubert Humphrey in the context of the Vietnam War – changed him. If before that he had always remained quite cautious about politics, the ruthlessness of the repression in Tunis 'awakened' him politically. He decided to help the movement and the students by hiding them in his apartment, providing them with material for printing manifestos, intervening on behalf of those in prison,[4] and even giving part of his salary to support legal expenses. The extreme violence of the Bourguiba regime, the massive arrests of students and the reports of torture, will then strongly contrast with the French May. Marxism in Tunisia was not just words; it meant incurring an existential threat.

In Tunisia, Foucault thought, Marxism functioned not as a simple theory, but more like a Sorelian myth, allowing students to accept 'formidable risks', putting their own existence and bodies in danger. There, he added, 'everyone was drawn into Marxism with radical violence and intensity and with a staggeringly powerful thrust. For those young people, Marxism did not represent merely a way of analysing reality; it was also a kind of moral force, an existential act that left one stupefied.'[5] Foucault recalled it as a 'formative experience', leading him for the first time to the view that politics, like art and sexuality, could, as James Miller puts it,

4 Miller, *Passion*, p. 171.
5 Foucault, *Remarks on Marx*, pp. 135.

'occasion a kind of limit experience'.[6] One of Foucault's students, Ahmed Othmani, who would later become a human rights and Amnesty International activist, was tortured and sentenced by a special political court to fourteen years in the Burj Al-Roumi jail.[7] Only two weeks after that rigged trial, which saw more than a hundred students locked up, Foucault returned in September 1968 to a Paris that seemed radically less dramatic and rather more mundane.

When he arrived, he viewed with some suspicion what he called the 'generalized hyper-marxization'[8] of the French movement. He even admitted later to having 'hated'[9] the late 1960s microcosm and the band of 'half-fools'[10] he rubbed shoulders with at the University of Vincennes between 1968 and 1970. With his head totally shaved for the first time, Foucault was appointed director of the philosophy department in this brand-new university opened by the then minister of education, Edgar Faure. Created in the immediate aftermath of '68, Vincennes recruited an impressive number of original and leftist thinkers such as Michel Serres, Nicos Poulantzas, Alain Badiou, Étienne Balibar, Jacques Rancière and Gilles Deleuze, and became the first university in France to include a Department of Psychoanalysis.

The university rapidly attracted the leading intellectual figures of the period, such as Noam Chomsky, Roland Barthes and the Italian filmmaker Pier Paolo Pasolini, and drew many of the leftist students out of the Latin Quarter. While the minister had in mind something like a 'French MIT', Vincennes' radical microcosm transformed it quite rapidly into a political battleground for the

---

6 Miller, *Passion*, p. 171.

7 Kathryn Medien, 'Foucault in Tunisia: The Encounter with Intolerable Power', *The Sociological Review*, 68:3, 2020, p. 496.

8 Foucault, 'Entretien avec Michel Foucault (Conversazione con Michel Foucault)', p. 899; Foucault, *Remarks on Marx*, p. 107.

9 Wade, *Foucault in California*, p. 57.

10 Didier Eribon mentions in his biography that Foucault told one of his friends, soon after leaving Vincennes, that he was 'tired of being surrounded by half-fools'. See Eribon, *Michel Foucault* (French version), p. 328.

ultra-left, where a militant of the French Communist Party was seen as part of the Right. On 23 January 1969, only ten days after its opening, the university was occupied by students and some professors, leading to violent clashes with the police. Foucault himself threw some bricks at the police, transforming him into the more militant and activist figure he will later be known as. In June of the same year the government decided to take away the department's qualification to grant degrees, in response to what it saw as 'leftist madness' – specifically in Foucault's department where some professors did not even grade the students. This 'post-'68' ambience was particularly well captured by Lacan's famed seminar hosted at Vincennes in early December 1969 in front of a quite hostile crowd of leftist students. After arguing about his dog Justine, the psychoanalyst guru was interrupted by a young activist who went on stage to undress himself and attempt to elicit from Lacan a Maoist-style self-criticism.[11] 'What you aspire to, as revolutionaries', Lacan responded, before cancelling the seminar, 'is a master. You'll get one.'[12]

Beyond this surreal environment, Foucault was particularly disturbed by the constant debates about revisionism,[13] the interruption of his courses by orthodox Maoists, and the extravagant lectures given in the department such as in Jacques Rancière's course on 'Theory of the Second Step of Marxism–Leninism: Stalinism' or Badiou's teachings on 'The Proletarian Theory of Knowledge'.[14] As he wrote in a letter to his partner Daniel Defert, if for his Tunisian students a reading of Althusser could become an 'immediate imperative', a physical risk, in France it was just a 'pure

11 François Dosse, *La saga des intellectuels français, 1944–1989. II. L'avenir en miettes 1968–1989*, Paris: Gallimard, 2018, pp. 148–9.

12 Jacques Lacan, *Le Séminaire, Livre XVII. L'envers de la psychanalyse 1969–1970*, Paris: Seuil, 1991, p. 239.

13 François Dosse, *Gilles Deleuze. Felix Guattari. Biographie croisée*, Paris: La Découverte, 2009, pp. 408–19.

14 See Charles Soulié, 'Histoire du département de philosophie de Paris VIII. Le destin d'une institution d'avant-garde', *Histoire de l'éducation* 77, 1998, pp. 47–69.

theoretical discourse' sometimes degenerating into monastic liturgy. In fact, Foucault tried to spend as little time as possible at the university, preferring to work at the Bibliothèque Nationale de France, away from the 'permanent revolution' that agitated the campus. Indeed, the excessive themes of some of the courses in the department contrasted strongly with the more classical ones pursued by Foucault[15] and his colleagues such as Châtelet, Serres or, later, Deleuze. All this created a rather unpleasant work environment that he was 'very happy'[16] to leave in December 1970, after being elected to the most prestigious institution in France, the Collège de France.

It was only with the rapid collapse of the many small revolutionary groups, and of Marxism itself as a doctrine, that Foucault's judgement on '68, as much as his intellectual concerns about power and the subject, began to evolve. A new 'horizon of values' was 'emerging' and opening up new questions. If, in the immediate aftermath of the events, it was common to think that 'the Utopian project of the thirties had resumed',[17] Foucault was now convinced that it actually meant the opposite, and that the movement was in fact 'profoundly anti-Marxist'.[18] 'The first consequence of May 1968', he argued, 'was the decline of Marxism as a dogmatic framework, and the emergence of new political, cultural interests concerning personal life.'[19]

Against what we used to think, Foucault claimed, '68 actually meant the end of the 'problematic of the revolution' as it had been conceived since at least 1789. The central function of this

15 Foucault taught that year on the 'Discourse of Sexuality'. See Michel Foucault, *La Sexualité suivi de Le Discours de la Sexualité*, Paris: Gallimard, 2018.

16 Wade, *Foucault in California*, p. 57.

17 Michel Foucault, 'Preface', in Gilles Deleuze and Félix Guattari, *Anti-Oedipus: Capitalism and Schizophrenia*, New York: Viking Press, 1977, pp. xii. 'Préface', *Dits et Écrits II*, text no. 189, p. 133.

18 Michel Foucault, 'Pouvoir et corps', 1975, in *Dits et Écrits I*, text no. 157, 1624.

19 Michel Foucault, 'Une interview de Michel Foucault par Stephen Riggins', in *Dits et Écrits II*, text no. 336, p. 1348; Foucault, *Essential Works*, vol. 1, p. 125.

problematic was to reduce the sphere of politics and the realm of the possible, demanding that 'all other struggles be subordinated to it and remain suspended'.[20] The image of the revolution, in its desire to 'encompass and prioritize a whole range of revolts and contestations in a single effort', had been a deeply 'conservative' and normative project that subjected political struggle to a single meaning. What now became central were all the 'immediate struggles', the proliferation of small battles raising a wide range of problems concerning aspects of 'everyday life'.[21] Even if the 'old flags' were brandished in '68, in fact politics had moved on, into 'new areas' like all these small and minor dispositives of government that shaped our subjectivity. This meant the slow displacement of struggles organized around 'large economic structures and the state apparatus'[22] toward all the diffuse systems of governmentality that seek to conduct our very existence. The question of power then slowly shifted from institutions to how subjects themselves were shaped. This revision of Foucault's judgement with respect to May '68 will coincide in particular with his growing proximity to the anti-totalitarian Left, which represented the most 'libertarian' current of May. Already by the mid-1970s, '68 referred not so much to the largest strike in French history, but to this displacement of the question of the power from institutions toward the dispositives shaping subjects.

Interestingly, Foucault's analysis added to this profound change what he considered another central shift: the end of the 'respect' given to the signifier.[23] This question, however, illustrated an older concern in his work. If he admitted that he 'probably' would not have undertaken the kind of research he did on prisons, power,

20 Michel Foucault, 'La philosophie analytique de la politique', 1978, in *Dits et Écrits II*, text no. 232, p. 547.

21 Michel Foucault, 'Sexualité et politique', May 1978, in *Dits et Écrits II*, text no. 230, p. 529.

22 Michel Foucault, 'Les réponses du philosophe Michel Foucault', November 1975, in *Dits et Écrits I*, text no. 163, p. 1674.

23 Michel Foucault, 'Préface', in *Dits et Écrits II*, text no. 189, p. 133.

sexuality and subjectivity 'without May 68',[24] the question of what he called the 'sovereignty of the signifier' was a longstanding one, even if it would now take on a new political significance. Indeed, what Foucault was referring to here was his radical take on the idea of the author, a notion he had already criticized in *The Order of Things* (1966), the *Archaeology of Knowledge* (1969) and, more explicitly, in his celebrated 1969 lecture, 'What Is an Author?'[25] In this apparently limited sphere occupied by linguistics, discourse analysis and semiotics, Foucault sketched a template that would reappear in his critique of the juridical and political model of power and the moral and philosophical conceptions of the subject. The displacement of the sovereignty of the author in favour of the text as a zone of experimentation became the paradigm for a displacement of the sovereignty of the state for the modes of governmentality and of the sovereignty of the subject for the technologies of the self.

The argument Foucault made in relation to the author was twofold. One part was about the ontology of the text and arose from his archaeological studies. The author was, he wrote, nothing more than 'the ideological figure by which we conjure the proliferation of meaning'.[26] Hence it preserves the unity of the text. The other part was about how his criticism of the concept of the author would give the reader – in other words, the 'subject' – a particular importance in the production and subversion of the text. The dissolution of the author's sovereignty will then allow a new ontology of the text, one of pluralism and difference that will form the basis of a new vision of politics.

Indeed, the political importance of the so-called pluralism inherent in the text as against the figure of the author will be a

24 Foucault, 'Entretien avec Michel Foucault (Conversazione con Michel Foucault)', p. 900; Foucault, *Remarks on Marx*, p. 140.

25 Michel Foucault, 'Qu'est-ce qu'un auteur?', 1969, in *Dits et Écrits I*, text no. 69, pp. 817–49. Michel Foucault, 'What Is an Author?', in *Aesthetics: The Essential Works*, vol. 2, ed. James D. Faubion, London: Allen Lane, 1998, pp. 205–22.

26 Ibid., p. 222.

useful starting point for thinking about the subject and the institutions that bind it to a certain self-interpretation. From this standpoint, there would be a parallel between the institutions of the welfare state – with its penal, medical, psycho-social and therapeutic experts that were the object of the struggles of May – and the text. Such institutions 'subjectify' us into a certain identity, just as 'the author' was the figure by which the text was 'subjected' to a unique meaning. More fundamentally, one could even argue that, starting from the 1970s, Foucault's criticism of the author will constitute an intellectual framework for gradually thinking of the subject as a text: as something that needs to be invented, experienced rather than interpreted. Indeed, what his political trajectory announces in this period is the challenge of two forms of interpretation, each having a common background in the Christianity of the monastic communities.

The first comes from the Christian exegesis of texts; the second, which he discovers a decade later, is a 'hermeneutics of the self' inherited from the techniques of avowal that had constituted the self as an interiority to be constantly verbalized and interpreted. The refocusing of Foucault's entire *History of Sexuality* around a genealogy of modern subjectivity will then place at the heart of his preoccupations the technologies through which we constitute ourselves as ethical subjects. The emergence and study of this hermeneutics of the self – this 'exegesis of the self' 'pinning'[27] us to a certain identity – will henceforth become the central thread of his work and offer a way to think about resistance outside the sovereign and revolutionary model. This interest will explain his later concerns with the Iranian revolution, Zen Buddhism and, for surprisingly similar reasons, neoliberalism. But the original laboratory for this revolt against the sovereignty of the subject and the institutions for the fabrication of subjects would be the interrogation of the function of the author in the text itself.

27 Michel Foucault, 'Questions à Michel Foucault sur la géographie', 1976, in *Dits et Écrits II*, text no. 169, p. 36.

Against the sovereignty of the author

The first part of the argument concerning the ontology of the text was the natural outcome of some of the developments in Foucault's thought by the early 1960s. The main point was that, contrary to what had been thought since at least the French Revolution and the 1793 legislation on the author's right, there was no reason to link the meaning of a text with the author's intention. Since the 'author-form' was 'directly derived from the way in which the Christian tradition has authenticated (or, on the contrary, rejected) texts',[28] it was now necessary to demonstrate that texts had not always worked through this quasi-legal relationship. This was a relationship that allowed the author to 'reign' as a 'sovereign' over the meaning of the text and offered the reader the sole task of 'deciphering' it, in order to establish the 'correct' interpretation. The French semiologist Roland Barthes would see in this evolution the logical consequence of 'rationalism' and of the emerging capitalist ideology. As he wrote, within this discourse, 'the author is defined as the father and owner of his work; literary science thus learns to respect the manuscript and the declared intentions of the author, and the society postulates a legal relation between the author and his *oeuvre*'.[29] The author thus constitutes, in Foucault's terms, 'the regulator of the fictive', playing the role characteristic 'of industrial and bourgeois society', that 'of individualism and private property'.[30] This figure of the author is transformed into some kind of God, and the literary critic into a simple exegete. This tradition was indeed important during the nineteenth century, especially in the work of critics such as Gustave Lanson or Sainte-Beuve, who understood a work of art as the expression of the 'artistic genius' and the 'exceptional' personality of its author.

28 Foucault, 'Qu'est-ce qu'un auteur?', p. 829. Foucault, 'What Is an Author?', p. 214.

29 Roland Barthes, 'De l'œuvre au texte', in *Le bruissement de la langue*, Paris: Seuil, 1984, p. 76.

30 Foucault, 'What Is an Author?', p. 222.

However, by the late 1960s, Foucault will develop an almost completely opposite approach in this area.

The death of the author

When questioned about the fact that he referred to authors like Ricardo, Cuvier or those who wrote the logic of Port-Royal in the *Order of Things*, Foucault argued that what he was referring to was not so much a delimitated thought as the sign of a 'transformation' within discourse itself.[31] For him, the text was always made of 'discursive layers' composed of a 'plurality of concepts and theories'. As he wrote in the *Archaeology of Knowledge*, texts were always 'given' 'in a system of references to other . . . texts' and could only be conceived as a 'network of relations'.[32] To attribute a text to an author was then 'impossible'. In other words, Foucault argued, 'the author does not exist'.[33] The only power the author had, as Barthes argued during the same period, was to 'mix writings', the text being 'a web of quotes, coming from a thousand sources of culture'.[34] Therefore, the author could not be the origin of anything, but just the effect of the 'intertextuality' of discourse itself. This concept, prominently introduced by the literary critic Julia Kristeva in 1966, had been crucial for the literary theorists gravitating around the journal *Tel Quel*,[35] and especially for Barthes himself in his famous 1967 text 'The Death of the Author'. The title was, of course, a reference to Foucault's formula about 'the death of man', and it illustrated the friendship they had shared since 1955. This friendship was nurtured by common concerns and their similar

31 Michel Foucault, 'La situation de Cuvier dans l'histoire de la biologie', in *Dits et Écrits I*, text no. 77, p. 928.

32 Michel Foucault, *L'archéologie du savoir*, Paris: Gallimard, 1969, p. 36.

33 Foucault, 'La situation de Cuvier', p. 929.

34 Roland Barthes, 'La mort de l'auteur', in *Le bruissement de la langue*, pp. 63–9.

35 François Dosse, *Histoire du Structuralisme. Tome II: Le chant du cygne. 1967 à nos jours*, Paris: La Découverte, 1992, p. 73.

interest in the work of Blanchot or Sade, who they thought of as key examples of a literature that had precisely subverted the notion of the author itself.[36]

To give a text an author, Barthes wrote, is to 'to impose on that text a stop clause, to furnish it with a final signification, to close the writing'.[37] In this perspective, the author was one of the great principles of 'rarefaction' of the discourse to which Foucault dedicated his inaugural lecture at the Collège de France in December 1970. 'In the indefinite proliferation that seems to authorize the discourses of fiction', Foucault wrote in the first version of his manuscript, the author's function is precisely to 'establish a law and a limit'.[38] He is then not the 'origin' of an *oeuvre*, he does not 'precede' the text, but is rather, as he had put it earlier, the 'functional principle by which, in our culture, we delimit, exclude, select. In short, the principle by which we hinder free movement, free manipulation, free composition, decomposition, recomposition of fiction.'[39] He makes possible 'a limitation of a cancerous, dangerous proliferation of meanings in a world where we are not only thrifty with its resources and wealth, but with its own discourses and meanings'.[40]

This idea was substantially more radical than older criticisms of the notion like that of Proust in his *Contre Sainte-Beuve*, or even of Mallarmé. Indeed, Proust never really opposed the idea of the author, but carefully argued that we have to differentiate between the person that the writer is in his personal life and what he is as a writer. He thought that looking for meaning in the biography of the author diminished any interest in the text itself. There was, for him, no reason to postulate that they were the same person, that

36 Michel Foucault, 'Interview avec Michel Foucault. Stockholm mars 1968', March 1968, in *Dits et Écrits I*, text no. 54, p. 688.

37 Barthes, 'La mort de l'auteur', p. 68.

38 Michel Foucault, *Œuvres I*, Paris: La Pléiade, 2015, p. 1606.

39 Foucault, 'Qu'est-ce qu'un auteur?', p. 839. Foucault, 'What Is an Author?', p. 221.

40 Ibid.

the 'author' was somehow equivalent to the person. The same can be said for Mallarmé, who was the central topic of the important 1967 double issue of *Aspen* magazine in which Barthes first published his essay on the death of the author, along with contributions by John Cage, Susan Sontag and Robbe-Grillet. However, if Mallarmé did appeal to a certain disappearance of the author – to the 'disappearance of the poet's voice' – this never really implied any claim for the pluralism of the poem or against the fact that there was a meaning to interpret.[41] What Foucault – and Barthes – argued was that if there was no author or unique meaning, then the entire enterprise of interpretation itself was compromised. The discussion became not about how we should interpret the text but about whether there was anything to interpret at all. From the moment we conceived the text as something without an author, Barthes wrote, '"meaning" was no longer an adequate concept',[42] and 'the claim to "decipher" a text becomes completely useless'.[43] We had, according to Foucault, to 'abandon definitively the question of the origin'[44] and accept the inherent plurality of the text.

Experimentation rather than interpretation

By the end of the 1960s, this analysis, accompanied by the works of Derrida or Paul de Man,[45] will be part of a broader reconceptualization of social change wherein the subject will play a growing

41 Molly Nesbit, 'What Was an Author?', *Yale French Studies* 73, 1987, p. 230.

42 Roland Barthes, 'Texte (théorie du)', in *Œuvres Complètes IV*, Paris: Seuil, 2002, p. 449.

43 Barthes, 'La mort de l'auteur', p. 65.

44 Foucault, *L'archéologie du savoir*, p. 57.

45 Indeed, the question of the author was not entirely new since it had been the topic of important publications, notably by the New Criticism school in the late 1940s (especially W.K. Wimsatt and M.C. Beardsley's 1946 text 'The Intentional Fallacy'), but also by the literary critic Paul de Man (especially with his 1967 essay *Criticism and Crisis*) and, finally, by Jacques Derrida, who would publish two important works in 1967, *De la grammatologie* and *L'écriture et la différence*.

role. In a moment of refusal of all kinds of authorities, the abolition of the figure that had governed the text for centuries – the author – opened a space for the reader to become more than just a reader. Indeed, the idea was seductive for May '68 thinkers not only because of its radical take on a certain academic knowledge – was not the teacher a simple spokesperson for the author? – but also for the space it could open up for other readings. In his 1969 lecture to the French Philosophical Society on 'What Is an Author?', Foucault mentions, as examples of texts functioning without author, the 'anonymous text that is read in the street on a wall', which could disrupt the normal 'mode of existence, circulation and functioning'[46] of the discourse in society. This was, of course, a reference to what Barthes called, after the events, the 'wild speech' of May, a 'speech' 'based on invention' whose most iconic representation was precisely the mural inscription, the 'fundamental place of collective writing' that cannot be 'owned or claimed'.[47] The refusal of interpretation meant the constitution of the text as a space of experimentation for the subject.

The old system of literary criticism, through which one 'assigns to a game of confused or even contradictory appearances, a unitary structure, a deep meaning, a "true" explanation', was now coming to an end.[48] Interpretation was slowly being replaced by a new type of practice offering greater freedom to the reader, a practice in which the reader could 'experience the text'. This new relationship opened what Barthes called a 'counter-institutional, counter-parliamentary space'. The student revolt in particular thus constituted the taking, not of the Bastille, but 'of language itself', experienced no longer as an instrument but as an activity. Barthes thought that 'the rustling of language' (*le bruissement de la langue*) was the basis of a new type of utopia. Far from

---

46 Foucault, 'Qu'est-ce qu'un auteur?', p. 838. Foucault, 'What Is an Author?', p. 221.

47 Roland Barthes, 'L'écriture et l'évènement', in *Le bruissement de la langue*, p. 191.

48 Ibid., p. 193.

resembling past utopias – the overthrow of one power by another – this utopia aimed to create 'experiments'.[49] This was a perspective shared by Foucault.

With '68, something crucial was happening. In his 1969 lecture, Foucault argued that the 'precise moment when our society is in a process of change' is the moment where 'the author-function will disappear', allowing texts to 'function again in another mode', one that 'will not be the author anymore', but a mode of 'experimentation'.[50] This is a way of relating to texts that allows us to put them 'in circulation, to make them transit, to disguise them, to deform them, to heat them till incandescence, to glaze them, to multiply them'.[51] The dissolution of the sovereign author thus allowed the emergence of a new ontology of text, inherently pluralist and promoting differentiation.

In a sense, Foucault's emphasis, like that of Barthes before him, was no longer on the text itself or on its meaning, but on the uses subjects can make of it to transform themselves. And that is precisely the role Foucault gave in the following years to the works of Blanchot or Bataille. As he explained in an interview conducted in 1978, what fascinated him about these works was not only that they were 'authorless', but also that 'their problem was not the construction of a system, but a personal experience'.[52] These texts were aimed at changing our relation to ourselves, as dispositives allowing us also to be the authors of our own existence – tools for, as Foucault later wrote, the 'writing of the self'.[53] It will therefore not be surprising that Foucault will conceive his own texts in the

49 Barthes, 'Le bruissement de la langue', in *Le bruissement de la langue*, p. 102.

50 Foucault, 'Qu'est-ce qu'un auteur?', p. 839; Foucault, 'What Is an Author?', p. 222.

51 Michel Foucault, 'La peinture photogénique', in *Dits et Écrits 1, 1954–1975*, text no. 190, p. 1578.

52 Foucault, 'Entretien avec Michel Foucault (Conversazione con Michel Foucault)', p. 862; Foucault, *Remarks on Marx*, p. 30.

53 See, especially, Michel Foucault, 'L'écriture de soi', February 1983, in *Dits et Écrits II*, text no. 329, pp. 1234–49.

same terms, not as a small space appropriated by its creator but, on the contrary, as 'rolling marbles. You capture them, you take them, you throw them again.'[54] When he was asked to write a new preface for the reissue of *History of Madness*, he even went as far as to get rid of the old preface and replace it with a short plea against his own hold on the book. 'I would like that a book', he writes, 'be nothing but the sentences of which it is made', so that it could be 'copied, fragmented, repeated, simulated, split and finally disappeared so that who produced it could never claim the right to be its master, to impose what he wanted to say, or to say what it should be'.[55] The works that mattered to him were, then, those whose function was 'to tear apart the subject from himself, to make sure that he is no longer himself, or that he is brought to his annihilation or dissolution. It is an enterprise of desubjectification.'[56]

This notion of desubjectification is crucial for understanding the profound connection between Foucault's new pluralist ontology of the text and his later conceptualization of an anti-foundationalist subject. Indeed, in the post-1968 decade, his radical shift from *interpretation* to the *experience* the subject has of the text will not remain confined to aesthetics but will provide a more general framework in which to think about power and the way subjects are formed. His rejection of interpretation will become an instrument for understanding how the subject itself is also a 'prisoner' of certain readings of itself, how its inherent plurality is restricted. Indeed, were not all the institutions targeted by May '68 also designed to tie us to a certain understanding of ourselves, to limit the spectre of what we could become? Were they not, like the author, dispositives of 'subjectification'? Was not politics after '68 also an enterprise of 'desubjectification'?

---

54 Foucault, in Roger-Pol Droit, *Michel Foucault, entretiens*, Paris: Odile Jacob, 2004, p. 107.

55 Michel Foucault, 'La monarchie de l'auteur', in Foucault, *Histoire de la folie*, new Foreword to the 1972 edition, p. 10.

56 Foucault, 'Entretien avec Michel Foucault (Conversazione con Michel Foucault)', p. 862; Foucault, *Remarks on Marx*, p. 31.

The rise and fall of the modern subject

By the mid-1970s, this radical critique of Christian exegesis and of the notion of the author it had shaped found an echo in Foucault's work on the relationship between power, truth and subjectivity. Indeed, through his growing interest in avowal, he would focus on the dispositives that, after Antiquity, slowly surround individuals. Against a conception of the individual as a 'primitive atom' facing a 'sovereign power', power was now to be studied in the way it shapes our ethics, or how we constitute ourselves as moral subjects. This 'practical matrix of experience' of oneself then becomes the privileged ground for Foucault's study of the genealogy of the modern subject and the way in which, since the end of Greco-Roman Antiquity, these techniques would slowly trap the subject in a certain definition of itself.

A detour into Foucault's work of this period will explain in particular why, between 1975 and 1983, he reformulated the plan of his *History of Sexuality* so many times and radically altered the direction of his research and lectures. By the time Volumes II and III finally saw the light in 1984, the project had been substantially transformed. The long wait between 1976 and 1984 for these two later volumes indicated not simply a change of content and historical focus but a fundamental shift. In 1976, the key contrast was between our own *scientia sexualis*, which obliges us to render into discourse the truth of sex, and the ancient and oriental *ars erotica*, where truth is drawn from the economy of pleasures itself. By 1984, the key contrast is between modern scientific expertise and the techniques of the self found in Antiquity, techniques that had been institutionalized in the ascetic practices of the Christian pastorate concerned with renouncing the temptations of the flesh and with the verbalization of the inner truth of the subject. As Stuart Elden argues, Foucault shifted 'from a project begun when his focus was the interrelation of power and knowledge to one where truth and subjectivity were to the fore, with new ideas about technologies of the self'.[57]

In the course of this shift, the study of the Christian pastorate would drive Foucault to revise some of the claims made in the first volume of *The History of Sexuality* and in the draft of the second. Foucault's move toward the study of governmentality in his lectures of 1978 and 1979, therefore, should not be read as a definitive rupture with his research on sexuality, but rather as reconfiguring and anticipating his later work on technologies of the self.[58] Indeed, the question of government becomes increasingly important in relation to the self, since the 'government of a polity' can never exist without the 'government of souls'.[59] As Foucault writes in 1978: 'what the history of the pastorate involves, therefore, is the entire history of procedures of human individualization in the West. Let's say also that it involves the history of the subject.'[60] This reformulation highlights the close ties between his genealogy of modern governmentality during his lectures at the Collège de France – which in 1978 included five lectures on the Christian pastorate – and his examination of ancient techniques of the self in the second and third volumes of the *History of Sexuality* and in his lectures from 1980. In other words, 'power relations, governmentality, the government of self and others, and the relationship of self to self' form a series that connects 'the question of politics and the question of ethics'.[61] The question of interpretation – of what Foucault calls 'hermeneutics' – therefore took on a larger dimension, questioning not only how we understand texts, but also how we establish our relationship to ourselves. The self, too, had to be

57 Stuart Elden, 'Review: Michel Foucault, Confessions of the Flesh', *Theory, Culture & Society* blog, 20 March 2018, available at theoryculturesociety.org.

58 Elden, *Foucault's Last Decade*, p. 99.

59 Ibid., p. 96.

60 Michel Foucault, *Security, Territory, Population, Lectures at the Collège de France, 1977-1978*, trans. Graham Burchell, London: Palgrave Macmillan, 2007, p. 184.

61 Foucault, *Hermeneutics of the Subject*, p. 252.

freed from interpretation or, more precisely, from its Christian origin. If, at the end of the 1960s, Foucault sought to free us from the Christian heritage of the hermeneutics of the text, by the early 1980s he would seek to free us from the Christian heritage of the 'hermeneutics of the subject'.

Indeed, Foucault's growing interest in Christianity in the following years explains the significant reorientation of his research. It was through his study of the Council of Trent in the *Abnormals* lectures,[62] and then, in the summer of 1977, his study of the Church Fathers, that Foucault, as Frédéric Gros observes, first focused on 'the moment of emergence of a ritualized obligation, of an injunction of verbalization by the subject of a truth-telling about himself'.[63] For Foucault, these Christian techniques of the self, especially avowal (*aveu*), implied a crucial shift in the way the self was thought of as 'a text or a book that we must decipher, and not something that must be constructed',[64] as it had been in the ancient care of the self. 'It seems to me that an absolutely fundamental aspect of Christianity', Foucault argued in a series of lectures he gave in Louvain in 1981, 'is that it is a religion bearing two sets, two types, two modes of obligation of truth. On the one hand, there is an obligation to believe in a revealed truth or dogma; this is also the truth of the text.' On the other hand, there is 'an obligation of truth that takes the form of the necessary exploration of oneself, of the necessary discovery of a truth within the self, of the fundamental obligation to tell this truth. Truth of the text, truth of the self. Truth of the text, truth of the soul. Hermeneutics of the text, hermeneutics of the self.' There is in Christianity thus 'a fundamental link between . . . reading the text and verbalizing the

62 Especially the lecture of 19 February 1975 on the study of the mutations of confession. See Michel Foucault, *The Abnormals: Lectures at the Collège de France 1974–1975*, trans. Graham Burchell, New York: Picador, 2003, pp. 167–99.

63 Frédéric Gros, 'Avertissement', in Michel Foucault, *Les aveux de la chair*, Paris: Gallimard, 2018, p. iii.

64 Michel Foucault, *L'origine de l'herméneutique de soi*, Paris: Vrin, 2013, pp. 50–1.

self'.[65] The Christian techniques of the self – or at least those that will become and remain dominant – will slowly turn toward deciphering 'the image that God has imprinted in our souls'[66] rather than constituting a subject through physical and spiritual *tests* and exercises. As his commentators note, it is only with Christianity that 'the knowledge of the self, conceived as an exploration and decipherment of the subject, takes ascendancy and the care of the self fades away'.[67]

Foucault's interest in the history of subjectivity would, however, also be a way of questioning our own techniques of subjectification as well as the enormous importance we give, in our societies, to truth when we think about the subject. Why 'has all Western culture turned around this obligation of truth?',[68] asked Foucault. For him, this interrogation constitutes *the* question of the Western subject and requires an understanding of how, historically, this relationship has emerged and taken such a centrality. Studying this story, demonstrating that 'the self is nothing but the historical correlative of technology built in our history', may then help us 'change these technologies'.[69] And it is to this precise task that he devoted his last decade. From this perspective, Foucault's 'turn' toward Antiquity is not the product of a banal academic curiosity. He was interested above all in questioning our contemporary way of constituting ourselves as subjects, in order to redefine critical theory as an attack on the hermeneutics inherited from Christianity. This was a decade that, in the Western world, would profoundly shake this hermeneutics of the self with the emergence of new

65 Michel Foucault, *Wrong-Doing, Truth-Telling: The Function of Avowal in Justice*, trans. Stephen W. Sawer, Chicago: University of Chicago Press, 2014, pp. 165–7.

66 Michel Foucault, *Qu'est-ce que la critique suivi de La culture de soi?* Paris: Vrin, 2015, p. 86.

67 Henri-Paul Fruchaud and Daniele Lorenzini, 'Introduction', in Michel Foucault, *Dire vrai sur soi-même*, Paris: Vrin, 2017, p. 20.

68 Michel Foucault, 'L'éthique du souci de soi comme pratique de la liberté', July–December 1984, in *Dits et Écrits II*, text no. 356, p. 1542.

69 Foucault, *L'origine de l'herméneutique de soi*, p. 90.

forms of revolt in the post-'68 period, from the 'political spirituality' of the Iranian revolution, to the 'gay lifestyle' invented in California, to the rise of a neoliberal governmentality.

The ancient care of the self as 'laboratory'

The genealogy of the modern subject that Foucault worked on the last decade of his life begins in Greco-Roman Antiquity. But this epoch was his privileged field of research precisely because it appeared to manifest 'a way of constituting subjectivity which is radically different from the Christian one'.[70] In that perspective, Antiquity was for Foucault a 'laboratory' in which to better understand our subjectivity and to provide alternatives to the Christian hermeneutics of the self, to 'demonstrate that a concrete alternative did exist'.[71] As Arnold I. Davidson argues, Foucault read Antiquity as a way to make us realize that 'nothing makes the work of invention, to create a new alternative, unimaginable'.[72] If the Christian 'hermeneutics of the self' formed the framework for the modern subject, the ancient 'care of the self' not only helped Foucault to understand the specificity of the turn under Christianity, but also offered him a view of what a more 'autonomous' constitution of the subject could be.

The major difference between these epochs lies in the relation of their two modes of subjectification to power and truth. As Foucault explained in seminars he held in Berkeley in 1983, Christian monastic subjectivity 'is produced within a network of obedience; on the contrary, ancient subjectivity makes room for the autonomous action of the individual (self-mastery)'; 'the most striking

---

70 Laura Cremonesi, Orazio Irrera, Daniele Lorenzini and Martina Tazzioli (eds), *Foucault and the Making of Subjects*, London: Rowan & Littlefield, 2016, p. 8.

71 Arnold I. Davidson, 'La fin de l'herméneutique de soi', in Daniele Lorenzini, Arienne Revel and Arianna Sforzini, eds., *Michel Foucault. Éthique et vérité (1980–1984)*, Paris: Vrin, 2015, p. 73.

72 Ibid.

thing about Greco-Roman culture is the fact that people have what seems to be a real autonomous culture of the self.'[73] This autonomy did not imply a freedom from any relation with power structures, but that the relation to self 'was not at all a matter of obligation based on authority'; it was not something the ancients were 'obliged to do . . . but it was proposed to them as something important, something of great value, and something which could give them the ability to achieve a better life, a more beautiful life, a new type of existence, etc., etc. So you see that it was a matter of personal choice.'[74] As Foucault argued in the second volume of his *History of Sexuality*, in ancient thought ethical principles were not organized as a 'unified' morality, or 'imposed' on subjects, but rather came from 'scattered origins'.[75]

In this specific configuration, the techniques of the self were therefore not integrated 'into religious or political or even educational institutions',[76] but were diffused in the kinds of books or treatises of advice that Foucault studied in Volumes II and III of his *History of Sexuality*. These techniques were then 'exercises on the self through which we try to elaborate ourselves, to transform ourselves and access a certain mode of being'.[77] That is precisely why Foucault did not hesitate to call them 'practices of freedom' through which we can define our sexuality, our relation to power and to truth. In this framework, the 'purpose of Greek philosophical schools was the transformation of the individual', to 'give the individual the ability to live differently, better, happier than others'.[78] Within this care of the self, it is important to understand that the truth of the subject does not lie 'in the depths

73 Foucault, *Qu'est-ce que la critique?*, p. 140.

74 Ibid.

75 Michel Foucault, *Histoire de la sexualité II. L'usage des plaisirs*, Paris: Gallimard, 1984, p. 28.

76 Foucault, *Qu'est-ce que la critique?*, p. 141.

77 Foucault, 'L'éthique du souci de soi', p. 1528.

78 Foucault, *L'origine de l'herméneutique de soi*, p. 41.

of consciousness',[79] as a text to interpret, but acts as a 'force'.[80] Therefore, 'access to this truth is not obtained by an analytic exploration of oneself, but rather by arguments, demonstrations, persuasive examples and rhetorical explanations of a master'; it thereby 'transforms the subject into a nexus, articulating, without discontinuity, the knowledge and the will'.[81] It is a question not of 'discovering' but of 'experiencing' the self. The ancient subject excluded then 'the possibility of a hermeneutics of the self: there was no psychic interiority that could function as a content to be interpreted or avowed'.[82]

The turn to the hermeneutics of the self

Foucault's long detour through Greco-Roman Antiquity thus allowed him to 'clearly highlight the rupture that Christianity represents in the genealogy of the modern (Western) subject'.[83] This marked the precise moment when a fundamental reversal of the relationship with oneself inherited from Antiquity took place. This shift might be understood through the gradual coming to dominance of one of the elements of the two types of confession Foucault finds in early Christianity[84] and outlines in his lectures at Dartmouth from November 1980.[85]

The first type has some continuity with the technologies of the self and involves the practice of *exomologesis*, or 'penitential rites'.[86] This entails technologies of fasting and self-mortification, such as wearing a hair shirt, pouring ashes on one's head or

79 Ibid., p. 17.

80 Ibid., p. 51.

81 Ibid., p. 17.

82 Davidson, 'La fin de l'herméneutique de soi', p. 70.

83 Foucault, *Dire vrai sur soi-même*, p. 14.

84 Michel Foucault, *Histoire de la sexualité IV. Les aveux de la chair*, ed. Frédéric Gros, Paris: Gallimard, 2018, Annexe #2.

85 Michel Foucault, 'About the beginning of the hermeneutics of the self', *Political Theory* 21:2, 1993, pp. 198–227.

86 Ibid., p. 212.

scarring one's own body. The penitent thereby dramatizes the 'willing of his own death as a sinner' and thus enacts a dramatic self-renunciation, a 'self-revelation' that 'is, at the same time, self-destruction'.[87] As Tertullian would have it, the sinner must 'publish himself' through rituals of humiliation to choose the path to purity; for Foucault, *exomologesis* 'was the theatrical representation of the sinner as dead or as dying'.[88] The penitent in early Christian communities, as noted by Jerome, engaged in a kind of ritual renunciation of the flesh itself.

The second type, *exagoreusis*, is found within monastic institutions and involves 'an analytical and continuous verbalization of thoughts' in a 'relation of complete obedience to the will of the spiritual father'.[89] It contains two elements that will come to be increasingly important in Christianity and generalized to all believers in the modern practice of confession and in secular therapeutic and welfare practices: the principle of a lifelong practice of obedience, and the necessity of confession to a spiritual father who listens as the image of God – or later as an expert or therapist. For Foucault this attention to the movement of one's inner thoughts, to their pure or impure origins, and the necessity of the avowal of them to a master, will become fundamental not only in the history of Christianity but in the development of pastoral power in the West. While both types of confession (*exomologesis* and *exagoreusis*) are based on the renunciation of the self, the first will achieve this by a public manifestation of the status of the penitent as a sinner, but only the second will do so by the permanent verbalization of the truth of the sinner. By identifying the very early distinction between these two modes of manifestation of the truth of the sinner, Foucault juxtaposed the renunciation of oneself in one's corporeality to the simultaneous avowal and renunciation of oneself (of the 'flesh') through the verbalization of thought. And he

87 Ibid., pp. 214, 215.
88 Ibid., p. 214.
89 Ibid., pp. 216–19.

makes clear that it is the second form that 'became victorious after centuries and centuries, and it is nowadays dominating'.[90] It is this second type of confession that marks an early move from Greco-Roman technologies of the self to the hermeneutics of the self in Western culture.

In this context, the self must be 'brought to light', 'deciphered', 'interpreted'. This displacement is central to Foucault's view in that it replaces an essentially practical ancient morality, as a 'style of freedom',[91] with a much stricter code of rules, as a 'principle of obedience'. In this sense, rather than being techniques allowing the subject to be transformed, the monastic rules are much more coercive, demanding obedience and the permanent verbalization to the spiritual guide of 'the most imperceptible movements of our self'.[92] It is for this very reason that Foucault perceives in Christianity a 'break in the history of Western subjectivity'[93] and the birth of the modern hermeneutics of the self.

Indeed, Foucault notes that with the monastic communities the 'arts of existence' and 'techniques of the self' inherited from Antiquity would lose 'a certain amount of their importance and autonomy' with their integration 'in the exercise of a pastoral power'.[94] There is, then, a transition from a 'morality that was essentially looking for a personal ethics to morality as obedience to a system of rules',[95] and, beginning in the fifteenth century, to a 'great process of governmentalization of society',[96] encasing ethics in a legal framework made up of constitutions, penal and civil codes, etc. It was at this precise moment that many pastoral and monastic functions were taken up and diffused within political

90 Ibid., p. 222.

91 Michel Foucault, 'Une esthétique de l'existence', July 1984, in *Dits et Écrits II*, text no. 357, p. 1550.

92 Foucault, *L'origine de l'herméneutique de soi*, p. 89.

93 Foucault, *Wrong-Doing, Truth-Telling*, p. 117.

94 Foucault, *Histoire de la sexualité II*, p. 17.

95 Foucault, 'Une esthétique de l'existence', p. 1551.

96 Foucault, *Qu'est-ce que la critique?*, p. 41.

institutions, 'inasmuch as government also begins to want to take responsibility for people's conduct'.[97] This was 'the dream', Foucault argued, 'of a judicial mode of government'.[98]

It is also worth mentioning that Foucault's reading of the Enlightenment is seen precisely as a response to this long decline of the care of the self. He understood the critical attitude of the Enlightenment as the encounter between governmentalization and the assertion of the art of 'not being governed so much'.[99] In the same vein, the 'revolts of conduct' inaugurated by Protestantism that Foucault began to study in *Security, Territory, Population* were also designed in his view as a refusal of both 'the hermeneutics of the text and the hermeneutics of the self'.[100]

However, these techniques and rituals of avowal will not disappear with Protestantism or the Enlightenment but, by the eighteenth century, will continue their diffusion and reproduction through institutions of discipline and authority such as medicine, education, the justice system or psychology, and would come to 'constitute the ground of subjectivity as the role of the positive self, what we would call the permanent anthropologism of Western thought'.[101]

This reorganization of monastic spirituality in what Foucault now called a 'culture of scientific avowal' will gradually constitute 'thought as a field of objective data that must be interpreted'[102] in order to extort the truth from the subject. In Foucault's account, as noted by Davidson, the '*cogitationes* of Cassian, the *cogito* of Descartes, the *ego* of Freud, are specific (and obviously different) configurations of this same space'.[103] Consequently, 'the human

97 Foucault, *Security, Territory, Population*, p. 197.

98 Foucault, *L'origine de l'herméneutique de soi*, p. 112.

99 Foucault, *Qu'est-ce que la critique?*, p. 37.

100 Foucault, *Wrong-Doing, Truth-Telling*, p. 168.

101 Foucault, *L'origine de l'herméneutique de soi*, p. 112.

102 Ibid., p. 89.

103 Arnold. I. Davidson, 'La fin de l'herméneutique de soi', in: Daniele Lorenzini, Ariane Revel and Arianna Sforzini (eds.), *Michel Foucault: éthique et vérité*, Paris: Vrin, 2013, p. 70.

sciences' will 'reintegrate verbalization techniques into a different context' and offer a positive and scientific foundation for man, forming what Foucault called the 'interpretive analysis of the self'.[104] This genealogy, then, explains why truth plays so central a role in our procedures of government, and how a 'regime of truth' was produced that was 'indexed to subjectivity', requiring the individual 'to say not only, "here I am, me who obeys", but in addition "this is what I am, me who obeys . . ." '.[105]

These techniques – such as those of the French psychiatrist Dr Leuret,[106] whose main objective was precisely to obtain from the patient an avowal of his madness – will slowly encompass the entire social body, making us 'prisoners of certain conceptions of ourselves and of our conduct'.[107] Indeed, does not the penal system seek, beyond the punishment of an act, to sketch a *homo criminalis*? Are not social security systems, too, techniques aimed at subjugating individuals to a particular way of life? Even parts of the French and Californian gay movements, organized into revolutionary groups and conceiving what they called 'coming out' as an important political act, were viewed with suspicion by Foucault. Was not this whole strategy, insisting on a form of public avowal, reproducing precisely the kind of subjectification he was trying to avoid? The public affirmation 'I'm a homosexual', he thought, was not only 'the affirmation of a right' but also 'the cage, the trap'. Sexual choices could not, in his view, 'be stabilized' in a category but rather should be 'creators of lifestyles'.[108] Finally, was not Marxism also, with its own heretics, avowals and

---

104 Foucault, *L'origine de l'herméneutique de soi*, p. 65.

105 Michel Foucault, *On the Government of the Living: Lectures at the Collège de France, 1979-1980*, trans. Graham Burchell. London: Palgrave Macmillan, 2014, p. 82.

106 Leuret was a French anatomist and psychiatrist in the mid-nineteenth century. His work on the moral treatment of madness is the opening illustration of the idea of 'truth-telling' and avowal in Foucault's inaugural lecture at Louvain in 1981. See Foucault, *Wrong-Doing and Truth-Telling*, pp. 11–17.

107 Michel Foucault, 'Foucault étudie la raison d'État', 1980, in *Dits et Écrits II*, text no. 280, pp. 256–7.

108 Michel Foucault, 'Entretien avec M. Foucault', in *Dits et Écrits II*, text no. 311, p. 1114.

directors of conscience, interpreting and 'making law' on the Left by pronouncing on the meaning of history? Just as the 'author-form' had aimed at preventing heretical readings of texts, so the institutionalization of the techniques of Christian avowal had 'impoverished' our ethical imagination in terms of the plurality of relationships that we could maintain vis-à-vis ourselves. And, Foucault thought, prior to the 1960s 'nothing has been able to show until now that we could define a strategy external to this.'[109]

The fall of the hermeneutics of the self

It was only by the late 1970s, in the wake of the 'crisis of Occidental thought', May '68 and the emergence of neoliberal governmentality, that this hermeneutics of the self inherited from Christianity appeared to be eroding. For Foucault, it was clear that 'it was no longer acceptable to be governed, in the broad sense of government';[110] all these smaller powers, shaping our relation to ourselves, were now openly 'in crisis, both in the Western world and in the socialist world.'[111] The 1970s therefore constituted, in the eyes of the philosopher, 'a great crisis of reassessment of the problem of the government.'[112]

This shift from exploitation and 'class struggle' to the problem of subjectification will become a recurring theme in Foucault's work. As he himself wrote, if the 'nineteenth century was concerned mainly with the relations between the large economic structures and the state apparatus', it is now 'the problems of small powers and diffuse systems of domination' that have become 'fundamental problems.'[113] While the problem of 'the impoverishment of

109 Foucault, 'L'éthique du souci de soi', p. 1542.

110 Foucault, 'Entretien avec Michel Foucault (Conversazione con Michel Foucault)', p. 891; Foucault, *Remarks on Marx*, p. 144.

111 Foucault, 'Entretien avec Michel Foucault (Conversazione con Michel Foucault)', p. 901; Foucault, *Remarks on Marx*, p. 176.

112 Ibid.

113 Michel Foucault, 'Michel Foucault. Les réponses du philosophe', November 1975, in *Dits et Écrits I*, text no. 163, p. 1674.

those who produce wealth' had not been 'totally solved', it 'no longer arises with the same urgency' and 'finds itself doubled by another problem which is not that of too little wealth, but that of too much power'.[114] From now on, the new forms of resistance had as their essential objective 'the facts of power themselves, much more than what would be something like an economic exploitation, much more than something that would be like an inequality'.[115] Foucault will call this specific pattern of resistance to forms of power 'revolts of conduct'.[116] These are revolts that burst out when what 'institutions offer us is not satisfactory', when 'we seek to organize, to build, to define the relationship to ourselves', and when we try to 'escape a certain model of relation to ourselves', a model proposed to us by 'the political parties or the education system'.[117]

In this perspective, according to Foucault, 'a form of political innovation, political creation and political experimentation' will be pursued 'outside the major political parties and outside their normal or ordinary program'.[118] And while it will not immediately change our institutions or legal systems, it will transform our daily lives, our 'attitudes' and our 'mentality'.[119] It is clear to Foucault that, 'since the sixties, subjectivity, identity, individuality constitute a major political problem', and our priority must be to 'change our subjectivity, our relationship to ourselves'.[120] Henceforth 'all current struggles revolve around the same question: who are we?'[121] As he observed in 1977 at the forum 'Vivre à Gauche', 'innovation does not pass through

114 Foucault, 'La philosophie analytique de la politique', p. 536.

115 Ibid.

116 Foucault, *Security, Territory, Population*, p. 196.

117 Foucault, *Qu'est-ce que la critique?*, p. 140.

118 Michel Foucault, 'Michel Foucault, une interview: sexe, pouvoir et la politique de l'identité', June 1982, in *Dits et Écrits II*, text no. 358, p. 1558.

119 Ibid.

120 Foucault, 'Foucault étudie la raison d'État', p. 857.

121 Michel Foucault, 'Le sujet et le pouvoir', 1982, in *Dits et Écrits II*, text no. 306, p. 1046.

parties, trade unions, bureaucracy and politics anymore. It is an individual, moral concern.'[122] Foucault appears then to draw an interesting historical parallel between the transition from Antiquity to the dominant forms of Christianity and the transition from the old statist France to the rise of neoliberalism after '68. The old morality, which was slowly incorporated into the 'juridical organization' and took the form of a 'juridical structure', is now 'declining and disappearing',[123] opening a path, once again, to the creation of a more autonomous ethic. As he writes:

> in our society today, we remember very well that our ethics, our morality, has been linked to religion during centuries and centuries. It was also linked to civil laws and, in a way, to legal organization, and at a certain point morality took the form, in a way, of a legal structure – think of Kant. You know very well that ethics has been linked to science, that is, to medicine, psychology, even sociology, psychoanalysis, and so on. I think that these three great references of our ethics to religion, law and science are now, if I may say so, worn out. And we know very well that we need ethics, and that we cannot ask religion, law, or science to give us that ethics. We have the example of a Greco-Roman society, where an ethic, and an ethic of great importance, existed without these three references. This ethic is so important that part of our Christian, or so-called Christian, ethics, comes from there. The problem is not at all to return to this Greco-Roman ethic, since part of ours is coming from it. But we know that it is possible to carry out an ethical research, to build a new ethic, to make room for what I should call the ethical imagination, without any reference to religion, law and science.

122 Michel Foucault, 'Une mobilisation culturelle', September 1977, in *Dits et Écrits II*, text no. 207, p. 330.

123 Foucault, *L'origine de l'herméneutique de soi*, p. 112.

> And it is for this reason that, I believe, this analysis of Greco-Roman ethics may be of interest.[124]

We could therefore witness the fact that in French society from the early 1970s, deeply transformed by the emergence of a neoliberal governmentality, 'the idea of morality as obedience to a code of rules is now disappearing, has already disappeared'.[125] Adultery, for example, which was neither legally forbidden nor punished in ancient Greece,[126] but would slowly become with Christianity a matter of law, was finally decriminalized under the Giscard presidency. The 'revolts of conduct' that shaped the 1970s, and the policy of social 'liberalization' adopted by Giscard's government, initiated profound changes that seemed to definitively undermine the Christian hermeneutics of the self and open the path to alternative ways to constitute the self.

'They are not making the revolution', Foucault told the editor of *Le Nouvel Observateur* in 1968 about a student demonstration, 'they are the revolution'.[127] In that sense, 1968 became then not only the starting point for the slow disintegration of the hermeneutics of the self inherited from Christianity but also marked an important shift in how Foucault conceived resistance. This shift toward the subject will also open up new perspectives on how it can play a role in social change. By focusing on the subject, it has been noted, Foucault conceived 'the relation of oneself to oneself as the decisive place of articulation of technologies of power and practices of resistance'.[128]

124 Foucault, *Qu'est-ce que la critique?*, p. 143.

125 Foucault, 'Une esthétique de l'existence', p. 1551.

126 Foucault discusses this example in the introduction to volume 2 of the *History of Sexuality*. See Michel Foucault, *The History of Sexuality, vol. 2: The Use of Pleasure*, trans. Robert Hurley, London: Allen Lane, 1985, p. 17.

127 Eribon, *Michel Foucault* (French version), p. 302.

128 Laura Cremonesi, Arnold I. Davidson, Orazio Irrera, Daniele Lorenzini and Marina Tazzioli, 'Introduction' in Foucault, *L'origine de l'herméneutique de soi*, pp. 12–13.

Against most of the theories that had dominated the post-war period – psychoanalysis and Marxism in particular[129] – he began to define resistance as 'the art of not being governed quite so much.'[130] This is a definition that he will make exactly ten years after the events of May '68 when, in a lecture entitled 'What Is Critique?', he will define the German *Aufklärung* as an 'attitude' of 'resistance' against the 'governmentalization' of society. Interestingly, he gave this important lecture in front of members of the very same French Philosophical Society to whom he gave his speech on the author in 1969. In a fashion, 'What Is an Author?' and 'What Is Critique?' drew together a new way of conceiving the subject, power and resistance to it.

What perhaps distinguishes Foucault from the entire generation of semioticians, deconstructionists and linguists of the 1960s is that he would most clearly and directly apply the lessons learnt in his critiques of the text, of meaning and of the author to the political sphere itself. The linguistic turn would become a political turn. The end of the sovereignty of the author over the text would become the end of the sovereignty of the state, and of those actors such as parties and unions that were focused on state power. And, just as the first critique would allow the text to become a site of plurality and difference in which both the reader and the writer are engaged in self-transformation, so the focus of the political will become that of an experimental domain of self-creation. Foucault's project, being both political and literary or philosophical, thus becomes a 'critical ontology of ourselves' that 'has to be conceived as an attitude, an ethos, a philosophical life in which the critique of what we are is at one and the same time the historical analysis of the limits that are imposed on us and the *ordeal* of their possible

129 When the *Anti-Oedipus* came out Defert remembers a joke Foucault and Deleuze exchanged about their work in March 1972. Jokingly Foucault says to Deleuze 'we must get rid of Freudo-Marxism' and Deleuze responds 'I'll take care of Freud, will you take care of Marx?' In Defert, 'Chronologie', p. 55.

130 Foucault, *Qu'est-ce que la critique?*, p. 37.

transcendence'.[131] The struggle over the text in the 1960s was merely the first or at least the paradigmatic struggle against all those forms of authority, power and knowledge that concerned subjectivity, a struggle which, for Foucault, would prevail today over struggles against domination and economic exploitation. He would conclude that 'the struggle against forms of subjection – against the submission of subjectivity – is becoming more and more important, even though the struggles against forms of domination and exploitation have not disappeared'.[132] One key way to conduct acts of self-transformation, both personal and political, will indeed be the *ordeal*.

131 This is James Miller's translation of the typescript that he says evidently served as the basis of the English translation. Miller, *Passion*, p. 279, p. 445n. See the English version of 'What is Enlightenment?' in *The Foucault Reader*, p. 50.

132 Michel Foucault, 'The Subject and Power', in Hubert L. Dreyfus and Paul Rabinow, *Michel Foucault: Beyond Structuralism and Hermeneutics*, Brighton: Harvester, 1982, p. 213.

4
Ordeals: Personal and Political

> In rising up, the Iranians said to themselves – and this is perhaps the soul of the uprising: 'Of course we have to change this regime and get rid of this man . . . But above all, we have to change ourselves. Our way of being, our relationship with others, with things, with eternity, with God, etc., must be completely changed, and there will only be a true revolution if this radical change in our experience takes place.'
>
> Michel Foucault, 1979[1]

There are two elements in Foucault's writings and lectures that illustrate the radicality of his reconceptualization of the struggles concerning subjectivity and self-transformation. The first is a concern with the different ways in which truth can become manifest, focused particularly on forms he variously viewed as 'experimental', as experiences, tests or, above all, as ordeals, which he held to even in his last writings and lectures on the question of Enlightenment. They would

1 Foucault, 'Iran: The Spirit of a World without a Spirit', in Afary and Anderson, *Foucault and the Iranian Revolution*, p. 255.

be summed up by his notion of the '*épreuve*', a key term barely visible to Anglophone readers, but one that connects his diagnosis of liberal and neoliberal government with his own personal experiences. The second element is found in his journalistic reports and opinion pieces on the contemporary uprising in Iran, which demonstrate that, even in this case, what was at stake was no longer the old political and social conflicts that lead to revolution, but the collective and individual self-transformation of a people through a collective ordeal and the liturgical unfolding of truth. In short, Foucault would search for ways in which truth would become manifest, no longer simply in the rational inquiry of the Enlightenment, but also, and with even greater force, in acts of individual and collective self-transformation.

Veridiction and forms of truth

It is difficult to ascertain the exact date at which Foucault first used the term 'veridiction', which would assume such importance in his final five courses at the Collège de France, and to which he devoted an entire course at the University of Louvain in 1981. Veridiction is a neologism, breaking down into Latinate components as 'veri-diction', literally 'true-speaking', or 'truth-telling'. It is a very simple compound notion.

In his 1979 lectures, *The Birth of Biopolitics*, the term appears when he suggests that, up until the start of the eighteenth century, the market remained a site of 'jurisdiction', that is to say, something coming within the domain of the sovereign's will and law. By the end of that century, however, after the writings of the *économistes*, the market will come to constitute a site of veridiction, that is, of the verification and falsification of governmental practice. 'The market must tell the truth (*dire le vrai*)' and as such 'will command, dictate, and prescribe jurisdictional mechanisms, or the absence of such mechanisms'.[2] Foucault described the market

2 Foucault, *The Birth of Biopolitics*, p. 32.

as becoming a site, a regime, a principle, or a mode of veridiction for liberal forms of government. In liberalism, and particularly in neoliberalism, the mode of veridiction of the market will not involve an investigation into or detailed knowledge of the multifarious exchanges and transactions between economic actors, but will take the form of a test, an *épreuve*, as he says in his course summary of the same lectures. One might say that, for Foucault, the market can act as an ordeal that imposes forms of austerity on government and on the population, that questions whether it is governing too much and in the right way.

The term 'veridiction' appeared in English in 1981 in the translation of a roundtable debate between Foucault and historians dating from 20 May 1978.[3] The date of the roundtable places its first use in the month after Foucault had delivered his first lectures on governmentality, in which the term does not appear, other than in later interventions by the editor and translator.[4] Apparently, it was also used in Foucault's introduction to the 1979 seminar that would accompany the lectures of the next year and which was presumably written some time prior to the advertisements for the seminar and lectures. There, Foucault wrote: 'It is a matter of asking what type of practice governmentality is, inasmuch as it has effects of objectivation and veridiction regarding men themselves by constituting them as subjects.'[5]

We have two pairs, then: 'jurisdiction and veridiction' in the roundtable and the 1979 lectures, and 'objectivation and veridiction' in the introduction to the seminars that accompanied those lectures. This is complicated somewhat in the latter, where the question of the subject is also raised in relation to veridiction. Hence, the concept of veridiction is defined in relation to a series of operations that both specify objects and constitute subjects and

3 Michel Foucault, 'Questions of Method', *Ideology and Consciousness* 8, 1981, pp. 3–14.

4 Foucault, *Security, Territory, Population*, p. 193n.

5 Quoted by Michel Sennelart in 'Course Context', Foucault, *Security, Territory, Population*, p. 387.

that oppose 'truth-telling' to what might be called 'law-speaking', 'jurisdiction' in the broadest and most literal sense of that term.

One avenue for thinking about the new term 'veridiction' would be to focus for a moment on its contrast with, but close relation to, jurisdiction, or its even closer linguistic parallel with *juridiction* in French. Like jurisdiction in English, *juridiction* is an actual term in French, not one of Foucault's conceptual creations. Breaking it in two as *juri-* and *-diction*, we can say that it is derived from the Latin phrase *iuris dictio* ('saying or dictating of law'), *iuris* being the genitive of *ius* (law). So, in Foucault's rendering, truth-speaking confronts and contrasts with law-speaking. However, importantly, the notion of jurisdiction remains dominant in this contrast because it provides the exemplar that justifies the neologism.

But why should Foucault immediately employ a juridical term as the exemplar here, rather than say an ecclesiastical one like 'benediction' or an epistemic one such as 'prediction'? To understand this, we need to return to the way in which he had cast his general project of a history of sexuality a few years earlier, proposing an analytics that would 'free itself completely from a certain representation of power that I would term . . . "juridicio-discursive" '.[6] Elaborating, he stated that this type of power 'is essentially what dictates its law to sex . . . power acts by laying down the rule . . . It speaks, and that is the rule.'[7] In contrast, Foucault will find a form of power in which sex is forced to speak its own truth, or the subject is compelled to speak the truth of sex, through the dispositive of sexuality. Thus, already Foucault identified two axes: a juridical axis of law-speaking and an axis of truth-speaking that might be called veridiction. The central figure of this veridiction in the first volume of his *History of Sexuality* was the confession or the avowal (*aveu*). The confession, a technique that prescribes it as a fundamental duty to render every thought, desire, delectation

6 Michel Foucault, *The History of Sexuality, vol. 1: An Introduction*, trans. Robert Hurley, London: Allen Lane, 1979, p. 82.

7 Ibid., p. 83.

and temptation of the flesh into spoken words, is thus already a form of veridiction. If the *épreuve* or ordeal is a particular *mode* of veridiction, then the *aveu* or avowal is one of its social, political or ethical forms.

The term veridiction is elaborated in Foucault's pseudonymous entry on himself for a *Dictionary of Philosophers* (writing as 'Maurice Florence'). There, he retrospectively described himself as undertaking a 'history of "veridictions", understood as the form according to which discourses capable of being declared true or false are articulated concerning a domain of things'.[8] This project concerned 'games of truth' in which 'the subject is posited as an object of possible knowledge', a description that makes plainer the relation between subject and truth. This had initially taken two forms. The first addressed the formation of the subject in domains of knowledge of the human sciences as a speaking, living and labouring being. The second addressed the form of the subject as an object of knowledge through certain practices such as those of psychiatry, clinical medicine and penality. Now, Foucault described himself as moving on to a third inquiry, where he wished 'to study the constitution of the subject as an object for himself: the procedures by which the subject is led to observe himself, analyse himself, interpret himself, recognize himself as a domain of possible knowledge'.[9] It is clear that this new project still lies within the history of veridiction proposed earlier when he immediately adds: 'In short, this concerns the history of "subjectivity", if what is meant by that term is the way in which the subject experiences himself in a game of truth where he relates to himself.' The date of this text is not given, other than as 'the early eighties', but we have no reason to doubt Stuart Elden's approximate dating of it to around 1980, before the lecture series on *Subjectivity and Truth* in 1981.[10]

8 Foucault, 'Foucault', *Aesthetics*, p. 460.
9 Ibid., p. 461.
10 Elden, *Foucault's Last Decade*, p. 120.

While placing Foucault within the critical tradition of Kant, the dictionary entry moves that tradition away from the search for the universal and formal conditions of a true knowledge of objects towards the interconnected conditions of a certain subjectification and a certain objectification in 'games of truth': 'the rules according to which the subject can say certain things depend on the question of the true and the false'.[11] Veridiction takes historical rather than transcendental forms and should be examined as such. This becomes clearer when we turn to the only lecture series entirely devoted to or organized around the concept of veridiction, the Louvain lectures of 1981.[12] Here, Foucault cut a cross-section of his work of the previous decade to provide a 'political history of veridictions' through three historical segments: Greek 'prelaw', the Christian and medieval linking of certain forms of inquiry with the pastorate, and the avowal in early modern and modern times.

Early on in these lectures, veridiction is distinguished from assertion. Assertion concerns a claim about what is true or false, while veridiction is the act of truth-telling.[13] Thus, assertion refers to an object that is independent of the statement which is measured by logical or factual parameters as true or false, while veridiction concerns the different types of act that can manifest truth. The latter acts take specific social forms such as court testimony, oath-taking, religious acts of prayer, confession, penance and contrition, expressions of faith, and the criminal's avowal of wrong-doing. Many types of veridiction include assertion – or statements answering to the protocols of logic or reporting facts – such as journalistic narrative writing, witness testimony or scientific paper writing, but they are still specific forms in which truth becomes manifest. There are thus many types of veridiction to which correspond different modes of obligation by which the subject is bound to truth. That veridiction was at the heart of

11 Foucault, 'Foucault', *Aesthetics*, p. 460. The relevant footnote is on p. 465.
12 Foucault, *Wrong-Doing and Truth-Telling*.
13 Ibid., pp. 19–20.

Foucault's concerns in these years is indicated by his repeated return to the problem of confession or avowal and his hope of publishing a volume of his *History of Sexuality* on the topic – something that would only come to pass some thirty-five years after his death, and against his stated will.

What is at stake here is that Foucault wished to recover the plurality of the 'possible verbal or non-verbal procedures by which one brings to light what is laid down as true as opposed to false, hidden, inexpressible, unforeseeable, of forgotten', as he says in *The Government of the Living* lecture of 9 January 1980, in the course of defining what he there calls 'alethurgy'.[14] But what is important is not simply an ethnological recognition of the diversity of possible truth procedures, but how this 'alethurgy' is connected to hegemony. Thus, we might seek to understand how the rational inquiry or knowledge of the subject of the Enlightenment came to have hegemonic status and how other kinds of truth persisted or were subjugated in the process. Just as Foucault sought to recover the techniques of the self that had been enclosed in the hermeneutics of the self, he was concerned here with how different forms of truth about the subject had been made subservient to the human sciences which objectify the subject as 'Man' or rely on the subject's confession of truth about themselves. *Aveu* or avowal thus appears as a key concept in both Foucault's history of sexuality and his history of truth.

In his 'first lecture' at Louvain (that is, the one after his 'inaugural' lecture), Foucault referred to the *Iliad* as possibly the first text we have that includes a search for the truth in a judicial process by means of 'something resembling judicial avowal'.[15] In this epic narrative, during the funeral games organized for Patroclus, a dispute arises between Antilochus and Menelaus. Menelaus accuses Antilochus of beating him to second place in the chariot race by irregular means, thereby causing his own crash. And while

14 Foucault, *On the Government of the Living*, p. 8.
15 Foucault, *Wrong-Doing and Truth-Telling*, p. 31.

Homer makes clear in the story that there was a witness, Menelaus dares Antilochus to 'place himself in the ritual position of the oath, standing in front of his horses, holding the whip in his right hand, with the end of the whip touching his horses' foreheads . . . and to swear that he, Antilochus, did not voluntarily thwart Menelaus's chariot through trickery'.[16] At that moment, Antilochus, who had denied any kind of cheating, refuses to take the oath and therefore acknowledges finally the irregularity. For Foucault, this oath is a very specific way to produce the truth in the absence of a judge: truth is achieved not through the testimony of a witness or an inquiry but rather by a 'challenge put forward by one's adversary'[17] to risk his exposure to the wrath of Zeus in whose name the oath is taken.

In his exposition of this episode from the *Iliad*, Foucault returned to a story he had previously addressed in his Rio lectures from 1973. There he concluded that 'the burden of deciding, not who told the truth, but who is right, is entrusted to the struggle, to the challenge, to the risk that everyone will run'.[18] This is also one part of the significance he finds in the story as recounted in Louvain. There is a kind of continuity between the funeral games and the contest and challenge of the oath. The latter is an *agõn*, a confrontation, as might appear in a contest or a game between adversaries.[19] Hence, when Foucault wrote of 'games of truth' – as he did in the dictionary entry – he did not mean playful or childish activities but forms of struggle between opponents.

In the Louvain lectures, however, Foucault emphasized another element in this story: the way Antilochus' actions had disturbed the expected outcome of the race and the result that could have been foreseen according to the charioteers' already known levels of skill and strength. The race should have revealed the order of the

16 Ibid., p. 34.

17 Ibid., p. 37.

18 Michel Foucault, 'La vérité des formes juridiques', June 1974, in *Dits et Écrits I*, text no. 139, p. 1438.

19 Foucault, *Wrong-Doing and Truth-Telling*, pp. 36–7.

true value of the competitors: not only Antilochus and Menelaus but all the others in the race. As a consequence, Foucault describes both the race and the oath in ceremonial terms as 'liturgies of truth' in which, rather than an unpredictable winner emerging from a genuine contest, the race, and the ensuing avowal, consists 'very simply' in 'the liturgical unfolding of a truth already known'.[20] Liturgy is a word derived from the Greek (*leitourgia*) for public services which, in Christian culture, has been restricted to the services conducted by the Church. If one form of veridiction might simply be a confirmation of what is already known, then what we today regard as religious acts or sacraments, such as that of the Eucharist in the Catholic Mass, can be understood as modes of veridiction. As noted above, there are thus multiple modes of veridiction – the inquiry, the test, the examination – that can take many forms: juridical, political, social and religious.

In discussing the episode from the *Iliad*, Foucault drew upon the historical anthropologist, Louis Gernet, and his somewhat dubious notion of a 'prelaw' that exists at a stage prior to the distinction between religion and law. For Foucault, at least in the Greek example, the indeterminacy of the juridical and the religious exists at a stage prior to 'the emergence of an autonomous judicial structure that affirmed its independence, and up to a certain point, its sovereignty'.[21] It is thus historically prior to a judicial procedure in which a judge stands as a third party who decides justice based on witnesses and investigation, leading to an account of the truth of the matter rather than the truth being a stake in a continued 'agonism' – a combat, confrontation or struggle between the parties.

In brief, 'veridiction' – in terms of which Foucault understood his entire project – thus indicates the totality of all the different practices in which truth is manifest in a society, from the juridical-political and the scientific to the ritual and the religious, and the

---

20 Ibid., p. 39.
21 Ibid., p. 49.

way the subject might be assigned a place in relation to those practices or even be fabricated or transformed by them. For Foucault, however, this was neither a matter of a relativistic celebration of the diversity of how truths are manifest, nor of searching for a secret or subjugated practice of truth, but rather of discovering forms of truth that question our given subjectivities and indicate lines of possible self-transformation.

Experimentation and knowledge through the ordeal

This concern for the different forms of the manifestation of truth and their effects on the subject does not commence with the concept of veridiction; rather, we might say, the concept pre-existed its naming in Foucault's thought. As we have seen, Foucault himself returned to an example he had used earlier in his Rio lectures. There we find a conceptual distinction that captures the way in which the vocabulary of the experimentation and the test will become an increasingly important way of describing how we innovate and find new forms of existence and ways of relating to ourselves. If, in the 1960s, the experiment was a way of relating to texts, in the 1970s it became a mode of producing truth that presages a self-transformation.

Foucault observed that, alongside the shift toward the hermeneutics of the self, the Church had instituted, during the Middle Ages, our modern way of relating to truth, which would give shape not only to our judicial system – *l'enquête* (the *inquisitio* or inquiry) – but also ultimately to our rational sciences. In the Rio lectures, Foucault had traced this form of validating truth back to Greek Antiquity through his reading of Sophocles' *Oedipus Rex*. In this play, he observed how the figure of the witness and the search for truth through an inquiry emerged in Greek thought, profoundly transforming the judicial methods and the techniques to produce truth. This would become 'the matrix, the model from which a series of other knowledges – philosophical, rhetorical and empirical – could develop and characterize Greek thought'.[22]

In these same lectures, Foucault identified another procedure of truth: the examination (*l'examen*) that will be central in the production of disciplinary subjects, as discussed in *Discipline and Punish*.[23] But the key innovation in his discussion of Greece is the contrast he drew between inquiry and *l'épreuve* (the test or ordeal), the more typical way through which truth was established in Antiquity.[24] The latter was generally organized around a series of tests, actions and challenges that the subject had to pass through or undertake in order to manifest the truth. In this sense, Menelaus' challenge to Antilochus was not an *inquiry* into the truth of whether he had cheated but an *épreuve* that sought to make clear who was in the position of right.

For Foucault, this very old technique will persist until the twelfth and thirteenth centuries in forms as diverse as verbal tests, in which a certain set of words had to be recited successfully in order to succeed, or physical ordeals and rituals that would submit the individual body to a set of tests.[25] Foucault reminded us, for example, how in France during the Carolingian Empire, a person accused of murder would have to walk on embers and, two days

---

22 Michel Foucault, 'La vérité des formes juridiques', p. 1454; Foucault, 'Truth and Juridical Forms', in *Power: The Essential Works*, vol. 3, ed. James D. Faubion, London: Allen Lane, 2001, p. 34.

23 Foucault, 'Truth and Juridical Forms', p. 5.

24 Foucault first developed this distinction in his 1971–72 lectures, (8 March 1972); see Michel Foucault *Penal Theories and Institutions: Lectures at the Collège de France 1971–1972*, trans. Graham Burchell, London: Palgrave Macmillan, 2019. He also devoted a parenthetical 'little history of truth' to it in his 1973–74 lectures. See Michel Foucault, *Psychiatric Power: Lectures at the Collège de France 1973–74*, trans. Graham Burchell, London: Palgrave Macmillan, 2006, pp. 235–47 (23 January 1974). It is also found in the seminars he held in Brazil during the autumn 1973 entitled 'La verité des forms juridiques' (published in English as 'Truth and Juridical Forms'), and then in a seminar he conducted in Montreal a year later, more explicitly entitled '*l'épreuve et l'enquête*', published as 'La maison des fous', 1975, in *Dits et Écrits I*, p. 1562.

25 Foucault, 'Truth and Juridical Forms', pp. 38–9.

later, if he still had scars on his feet, would be found guilty. Of course, torture and trial by combat would be exemplary forms of the *épreuve* that persisted in Europe until the sixteenth century – and even until the twentieth century, outside the judicial system, in the form of the duel. Truth didn't need to be 'told' or 'found' after a long inquiry involving proofs, witnesses, demonstrations, or examinations of the individual in terms of psychopathology or criminology; justice manifested itself in the ordeal. 'It was a way', Foucault argued, 'of deciding which side God was currently placing the extra chance or strength that ensured the success of one of the two adversaries; this success, if it was acquired regularly, indicated for whose benefit the dispute would be resolved'.[26]

Torture was one exemplary form of the ordeal. 'When the Inquisitors of the Middle Ages tortured someone', Foucault noted, it was not to demonstrate that the convict was guilty, but rather involved 'the judge and the person accused or suspected in a real physical struggle – the rules of which, while not rigged, were of course completely unequal and with no reciprocity – to find out whether or not the suspect would stand up to it'.[27] The acknowledgement of guilt was therefore not a 'proof' of the person's crime, but 'simply the reality of the fact that he had lost in the game, in the confrontation, and could consequently be sentenced. All this could then be inscribed, secondarily as it were, in a system of significations: God, then, has abandoned him, etcetera.' Only with the 'process by which penal justice was brought under State control', Foucault argued, did our societies pass 'from this technique for establishing the truth in the test to the establishment of truth in the certified report, through evidence and demonstration'.[28]

Of course, both these ways of relating to knowledge – 'truth-test-event' and 'truth-demonstration' – should be seen not as ideologies that would obfuscate the way subjects related to truth,

26 Foucault, 'La maison des fous', p. 1562.
27 Foucault, *Psychiatric Power*, p. 240.
28 Ibid.

but as what constituted subjectivities in the first place. In that perspective, our relation to truth and knowledge defines more fundamentally different 'types of subjectivity', different ways of relating and constituting the self. And, while these two opposed types of practices more or less coexisted until the thirteenth century, the '*enquête*' will become the dominant form of production of knowledge with the slow constitution of the sovereign state and the modern arts of government.

Indeed, if the inquiry almost vanished during the Middle Ages, it continued to play a function within the Church in a spiritual and administrative form and would soon become a 'governmental process, an administrative technique, a management method'.[29] In other words, the inquiry became 'a particular way of exercising power'. Conducting souls soon also meant knowing 'their hearts, their acts, their intentions'. The king's prosecutor 'would do the same thing that visiting ecclesiastics did in the parishes, dioceses and communities. He would seek to establish through an *inquisitio*, through an inquiry, whether there had been a crime, what crime it was, and who committed it.'[30] 'What was invented in this reformulation of law', Foucault commented, 'was something that involved not so much the contents of knowledge, as its forms and conditions of possibility. What was invented in law during this period was a particular way of knowing, a condition of possibility of knowledge whose destiny was to be crucial in the Western world.'[31] With the Renaissance, he argued, 'the inquiry developed as a general form of knowledge', as the privileged form for 'authenticating truth', and it would form the matrix in which disciplines such as medicine, botany or zoology would unfold and displace older forms of knowledge relying on the ordeal, such as alchemy.[32] As he argued in a 1974 lecture at the Collège de France:

29 Foucault, 'Truth and Juridical Forms', p. 48.
30 Ibid., p. 47.
31 Ibid., p. 40.
32 Ibid., pp. 50, 52.

> We can say that from the end of the Middle Ages we have seen the entire surface of the Earth, down to the finest grain of things, bodies, and actions, subjected to generalized investigation: a sort of grand inquisitorial parasitism. That is to say, at any time, at any place, and with regard to anything in the world, the question of truth can and must be posed. Truth is everywhere and awaits us everywhere, at any place and at any time. This, very schematically, is the great process that led to this move from a technology of the truth-event to a technology of truth-findings.[33]

We went from the 'truth-ordeal', produced and inscribed in bodies and souls, to the 'truth-finding' conducted with the mediation of scientific instruments. This meant that we were then unable to separate the hermeneutics of the self that became part of our modern form of government from the techniques of the inquiry that shaped our relation to knowledge.

To escape this specific nexus of power, knowledge and subjection Foucault did not, of course, propose a simple return to the ordeal, in the same way he did not envision a simple return to the care of the self. However, as with the care of the self, the ordeal showed that alternative ways of relating to knowledge existed and could create interesting spaces for experimentation, especially at a historical moment where the hermeneutics of the self seemed to be collapsing.

Already, with his distinctions between the inquiry, the examination and the ordeal, Foucault had raised the question of different modes of veridiction. But if the inquiry, originally a juridical form, indicated the direction to the modern natural sciences, and the examination formed the basis of the human sciences and the society of normalization, what did the recovery of the more ancient juridical form of the ordeal presage? Would it, like the techniques of the care of the self, indicate a new manifestation of truth in

33 Foucault, *Psychiatric Power*, p. 246.

UNIVERSITY OF CALIFORNIA, BERKELEY

BERKELEY • DAVIS • IRVINE • LOS ANGELES • RIVERSIDE • SAN DIEGO • SAN FRANCISCO

SANTA BARBARA • SANTA CRUZ

DEPARTMENT OF FRENCH

BERKELEY, CALIFORNIA 94720

14 Ma

Dear Simeon,

Really, I dont know how to thank you for all you have been doing for me last week end. It was a great experience, one of the most important in my life. And I dont mean only the Zabriskie night, but our meeting and the two days we spent together. It is so rare to meet a friend like you with whom it is possible to

Courtesy of ONE Archives, Simeon Wade Papers, USC Libraries.

14 May

Dear Simeon,

Really, I don't know how to thank you for all you have been doing for me last week end. It was a great experience, one of the most important in my life. And I don't mean only the Zabriskie night, but our meeting and the two days we spent together. It is so rare to meet a friend like you with whom it is possible to . . .

Courtesy of ONE Archives, Simeon Wade Papers, USC Libraries.

. . . we found a wonderful boy (not a professional actor, but a young farmer, twenty year old) to play the role of Pierre Rivière. I feel very deeply interested in writing screenplays and I would like to work in this field, next year.

I hope you had a nice summer, in the East, with lot of work and pleasure. I am leaving this night for Brasil, where I'll stay a month; then I'll spend two weeks in New York (1st–15th November)

Love, for you and Michael

Michel F.

My adress in Brasil
c/o LEBRUN
178 PRAÇA ROOSEVELT
SAÕ PAULO

Foucault speaking at a demonstration of the French Democratic Confederation of Labor (CFDT) in support for Polish trade union Solidarność, 13 April 1981. Image Credit: Rue des Archives/Granger.

Foucault arriving at the Teheran airport in September 1978 with the gay activist Thierry Voeltzel to write about the Iranian Revolution for the *Corriere della sera*. Image Credit: Michel Setboun.

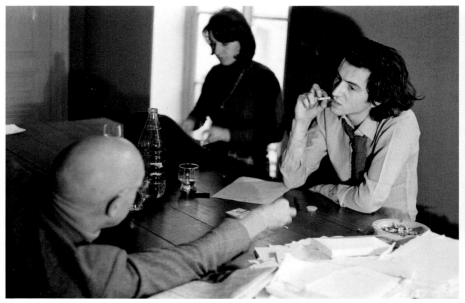

Foucault discussing with Bernard-Henri Levy, at Levy's apartment at Rue Saints-Pères in Paris, for an interview entitled "The End of the Monarchy of Sex" published in *Le Nouvel Observateur* in March 12, 1977. Image Source Credit: Michele Bancilhon via AFP & BELGA.

Foucault and the pianist Michael Stoneman during their trip to the Death Valley in June 1975. Courtesy David Wade.

modes of radical self-transformation that allow us to contest, to challenge or to resist hegemonic forms of truth and subjectivity? This was the problematic that was taking shape from the early 1970s and which, by the end of the decade, would lead Foucault to the conceptual innovation of the idea of 'veridiction'. At the heart of this problematic is the ordeal.

More strikingly, in his last decade, Foucault increasingly thought about his 'limit-experiences' – with LSD, with sadomasochism, or with political spiritualities such as those he witnessed in the Iranian uprising – as ordeals, and thus as alternative ways of producing knowledge and constituting the self. They had convinced him that 'the body, like the soul, was in some sense socially constructed – and therefore, in principle at least, open to being changed'.[34] At that time, and during the next few years, he would also engage in S/M practices in the legendary clubs of the 'leather scene', like the Mineshaft in the meatpacking district of New York and those on Folsom Street in San Francisco. These 'member only' clubs offered jail cells, dungeons and various fantasy environments in which to explore more extreme pleasures. This would be the precise moment when Foucault would call for the 'desexualization of pleasure' to break 'the assimilation of pleasure to sex'.[35] 'Sexuality', he wrote, was only 'an imaginary point', a product of 'power in its grip on bodies and their materiality, their forces, energies, sensations, and pleasures'.[36]

The modern natural sciences observed the human as an object among many, while the human sciences examined the being who laboured, who spoke, and who lived in so many different ways. But they did not exhaust the 'games of truth' that humans had practised and still practise: not only experiments of the imagination in relation to texts, but 'acid tests' with drug taking, near-death

34 Miller, *Passion*, p. 273.

35 Foucault, 'Michel Foucault, une interview: sexe, pouvoir et la politique de l'identité', p. 1557.

36 Quoted in Miller, *Passion*, p. 273.

'experiences', or the comportments and postures of the body and control of the breath in Eastern meditation. All these, and particularly the rituals of torture, the calibrations of pleasure and pain, in S/M practices, allowed Foucault to understand that the human is intrinsically formless, capable of aesthetic and ethical forms of self-creation, of action upon itself, of pitting, folding, assembling its impulses, materialities, forces and energies onto and against themselves with new and unpredictable outcomes. It is only through experiences that resemble the very old mode of veridiction of the *épreuve* that a new conceptualization, understanding and knowledge of souls and bodies, desires and pleasures, can contain the potential of not only self transformation but political transformation.

While it would be purely speculative to draw a direct correlation between the test or 'ordeal' (*l'épreuve*) of intense pleasures and the course of Foucault's thinking, his later work was marked by a much more affirmative attention to subjectivity, to different forms of the manifestation of truth, and to the political possibilities of radical self-creation and self-invention, than had been found in his earlier writings. On his return in June 1975 from his trip to California, Foucault would even write to Simeon Wade that he was completely revising his first volume of the *History of Sexuality*. 'I wrote hundred and hundred (sic) pages', he wrote, 'but they are so bad, that I have to begin again.' An immense amount of documentation and drafts on masturbation, incest, perversion or eugenics was put aside, in order to finally publish the short and abstract volume that would become *The Will to Knowledge*.[37] And while the first edition of this book still announced the initial six-volume plan of his history, it was clear that Foucault had already begun to abandon his original perspective on the topic. 'It was very abruptly, as early as 1975–1976', he said in what would be his last interview, that he 'totally departed' from the style of his

37 Ibid., p. 252; Wade, *Foucault in California*, pp. 28–9.

earlier books and decided to reformulate his entire project as a 'history of the subject'.[38]

In the most controversial of the biographies of Foucault, James Miller would ask whether the 'erotic "ordeal" [could] really enable a human being to grasp creatively, in a "moment of truth", its singular *daimon* – and thus transfigure its historical fate, facilitating "the birth of the new man"'.[39] We think this question should be expanded beyond the limited zone of the erotic, to include the textual, the aesthetic, the political, and even whole ways of life. In this sense, Foucault's lasting legacy may lie in posing a question to previous and more recent eschatologies and philosophies of history. That question would be: beyond the calculability and nullity of the Nietzschean last man produced by the disciplinary mechanisms of modern societies, could we not, through ordeals and experimentations, through forms of asceticism, types of austerity, and even the economic tests of neoliberalism, come to gain more personal autonomy, form new relations of power, undertake new styles of life and perhaps enter into a new 'game' of truth'? After all, did not Foucault himself say that whenever he tried to 'do a theoretical job, it was from elements of [his] own experience: always related to processes that [he] saw unfolding around [him]'?[40]

This is, without a doubt, one of the keys to understanding Foucault's last decade – the use of his own body and soul to open up new possibilities and ways of thinking. Resistance now meant to 'differ' from oneself, to craft the self outside the hermeneutics of the self and the blemishes of modern, scientific inquiry. And that is precisely what the Zen philosophy in Japan, the Taoist Californian communities and even the use of drugs could offer, as ways to test

38 Michel Foucault, 'Le retour de la morale', *Les Nouvelles littéraires* 2937, 1984, pp. 36–41, in *Dits et Écrits II*, text no. 354; see also Elden, *Foucault's Last Decade*, p. 98.

39 Miller, *Passion*, p. 277.

40 Michel Foucault, 'Est-il donc important de penser?' (entretien avec D. Éribon), *Libération* 15, 1981, p. 21, in *Dits et Écrits II*, text no. 296, p. 1000.

the limits of 'Occidental rationality'[41] and create new subjectivities. In the case of Zen, it was during his second trip to Japan in 1978 that Foucault expressed his interest in experiencing Zen Buddhist practices and spent a few days with the Rinzai master Omori Sogen Roshi. The Zen philosophy, Foucault thought, tended to weaken the individual, in contrast to the Christian techniques of the self that sought for 'always more individualization', 'to grasp what is at the bottom of the soul of the individual'. Foucault even remarked that the corporeal component of Zen – in which, through 'body posture in meditation', 'new relationships may exist between mind and body, and new relationships between the body and the outside world' – might help us envision solutions to the 'crisis of the Western concept of revolution'.[42] His insight was not simply to diagnose the existence of a new or renewed 'culture of the self' but to suggest that this culture could displace politics as we had previously known it.

Even AIDS was taken by Foucault, as his companion Daniel Defert has suggested, as a 'limit-experience'. The illness, as Foucault explained to the novelist Hervé Guibert, did not destroy the San Francisco sauna subculture but rather, as he observed during his last trip there in 1983, created 'new solidarities'. 'There have never been so many people in the saunas, and it has become extraordinary', Foucault told Guibert; 'before we never exchanged a word, now we speak'.[43] Alongside all these experimentations with texts and styles of life – the experiences in bath-houses, the acid tests, the ordeals comprising the many significant truth-events that produced alternatives to the old Christian hermeneutics of the self and to the sovereign model of politics it had shaped – there is of course the Iranian revolution. Zig-zagging across the categories of ancient and modern, Occidental and Oriental, it was in Iran that

41 Foucault, 'M. Foucault to zen: zendera taizai-ki', *Dits et Écrits II*, p. 620.

42 Ibid., p. 624.

43 Hervé Guibert, *A l'ami qui ne m'a pas sauvé la vie*, Paris: Gallimard, 1993, p. 30.

Foucault discovered the first case in which the old Western concept of revolution had given way to a collective ordeal, with its liturgies of truth, as a form of collective desire for self-transformation. This was a 'revolution' (he would refuse to even use the term since it reduced what was happening there) driven by a spirituality that, Foucault thought, had 'throughout the centuries given an irreducible strength to everything from the depths of a people that can oppose state power'.[44]

A 'political spirituality' against the sovereign

Foucault's interventions in the ongoing events in Iran in late 1978 and early 1979 occurred just before and contemporaneous with his lectures on neoliberalism at the Collège de France. To mention these interventions is to identify a relatively easy target if one wishes to criticize him, because they perhaps constitute his least successful and most contested public political action. How, many have asked, was it possible that the analyst of micro-powers and resistances could have embraced an understanding of the movement and revolt in Iran as an expression of the undivided collective will of the Iranian people, particularly when others had noted its division into factions, Islamist and secular, nationalist and Marxist, feminist and fundamentalist?[45] How could Foucault not have seen that the dominant trend of the uprising was, as Maxime Rodinson, the noted Middle East scholar, put it on the front page of *Le Monde* in December 1978, closer to an 'archaic fascism' mixing authoritarian police measures with an enforced moral order than to either socially progressive anti-colonialism or Foucault's own transgressive and counter-modern 'political

44 Michel Foucault, 'Tehran: Faith against the Shah', in Afary and Anderson, *Foucault and the Iranian Revolution*, p. 203.

45 This is one of the key points that emerges in Afary and Anderson's *Foucault and the Iranian Revolution*. See for example, pp. 123–4.

spirituality'?[46] How could he have dismissed the objections of an Iranian woman and taken so long to acknowledge, in spite of the many protests from feminists, what he would later only grudgingly call the regime's 'subjugation of women'?[47] And why would he remain silent on the persecution of religious and ethnic minorities and gay people?

To be sure, his writings on Iran should not be judged as if they were fully formed social and political analyses but as a series of 'journalistic reports' for the Italian daily newspaper, *Corriere della sera*. Nevertheless, if Foucault's early illusions about the Iranian revolution were an exaggerated and one-sided form of views shared by many others at the time, the most important concern for us is how these writings are consistent with his more general habits of thought, not only in the late 1970s but also throughout his career.

At first glance, Foucault's Iran reports would seem to share very little with his concerns in the lectures on neoliberalism. If neoliberalism is to be understood as a 'renovation of liberalism'[48] and thus as heir to one of the main currents that constitute the European Enlightenment, what he discovered in his two visits to Iran was the insufficiency of Western political perspectives when confronted with the events there. Indeed, the major critical study of his relation to these events, Janet Afary and Kevin Anderson's *Foucault and the Iranian Revolution*, views Foucault's position as sustained by a kind of romantic Orientalism and an enthusiasm for Islamist pre- or anti-modern 'political spirituality' that would leave him insensitive to the authoritarian, hierarchical and violently repressive nature of

46 Maxime Rodinson, 'Islam Resurgent?', in Afary and Anderson, *Foucault and the Iranian Revolution*, p. 233.

47 See Atoussa H., 'An Iranian Woman Writes', and Michel Foucault, 'Foucault's Response to Atoussa H.', in Afary and Anderson, *Foucault and the Iranian Revolution*, pp. 209–10 and p. 210.

48 The name of the centre to be established after the Walter Lippmann Colloquium, held just before the Second World War, was to be *Centre International d'Études pour la Rénovation du Libéralisme*. See Foucault, *The Birth of Biopolitics*, p. 152n.

the movement and subsequent regime charismatically led by the Ayatollah Ruhollah Khomeini, in particular its treatment of women, dissenters, ethnic and religious minorities, and gay people.[49]

At the time, Foucault came under intense criticism for his 'blindness' from feminists, Marxists and scholars of Iran and Islam, as documented by Afary and Anderson. As they show, these criticisms were followed by Foucault's silence on Iran after he finally expressed some concern about the trials taking place under the new regime in April 1979, in an open letter to the Iranian prime minister, Mehdi Bazargan.[50] In response to Afary and Anderson's work, major commentators on Foucault and religion concede what Jeremy Carrette calls his 'aberrations in political judgment'[51] and James Bernauer his 'misjudgements about the likely future course of the revolution'.[52] The debate that followed Afary and Anderson's book thus did not concern whether Foucault erred in his predictions, such as that 'Islamic government' would not be under the control of a religious hierarchy, that liberties would be respected and the rights of minorities protected, and that there would be no inequality between men and women under a Shi'ite 'separate but equal' doctrine.[53] Rather, the debate concerned what even the *Foucault Studies* journal would call the source of his 'critical failure'.[54] Was it indeed something integral to his own intellectual

49 See Afary and Anderson, *Foucault and the Iranian Revolution*, p. 162: 'In February and March 1979 alone, there were sixteen executions for crimes related to sexual violations.'

50 Michel Foucault, 'Open Letter to Prime Minister Mehdi Bazargan', in Afary and Anderson, *Foucault and the Iranian Revolution*, p. 263.

51 Jeremy Carrette, 'Review of *Foucault and the Iranian Revolution: Gender and the Seductions of Islamism*, by Janet Afary and Kevin B. Anderson', *Journal of the American Academy of Religion* 74:2, 2006, p. 531.

52 James Bernauer, 'An uncritical Foucault? Foucault and the Iranian Revolution', *Philosophy and Social Criticism* 32:6, 2006, p. 781.

53 Michel Foucault, 'What are the Iranians Dreaming About?', in Afary and Anderson, *Foucault and the Iranian Revolution*, pp. 205–6.

54 Richard Lynch, 'Review of *Foucault and the Iranian Revolution: Gender and the Seductions of Islamism*, by Janet Afary and Kevin B. Anderson', *Foucault Studies* 4, 2007, p. 176.

and analytical frameworks that led Foucault astray, or was his critical failure merely a contingent feature of his journalistic attempt to grasp the complicated, unfolding chain of events in Iran in the autumn of 1978 and the spring of 1979?

Our concern then is not so much with the reason for his blindness toward the oppressive potential of the emerging regime, but rather with how he observed the events in Iran. In this respect, there are a certain number of themes we can draw attention to that resonate with the broader ones we explore in this book and provide new insights into them.

The first concerns the question of revolution. Foucault was very reluctant to use the term to describe what was happening in Iran. In his first synthesis of his journalism for the French public in *Le Nouvel Observateur* in October 1978, he claimed that in response to the question 'what do you want?' he had not heard the word 'revolution' once in his entire stay in Iran. Rather, 'four out of five times', he said, someone would answer, 'an Islamic government'.[55] In an interview published in March the following year, he claimed that when Western intellectuals identify a revolution they refer to two dynamics: one of 'the class struggle and social confrontation'; the other of a 'vanguard, class, party, or political ideology'.[56] Citing François Furet's reinterpretation of the French Revolution that denied its contemporary political salience, he argued that while the class struggle may have been present in Iran, it did not appear in an immediate or transparent way, and that rather than political ideology he found a 'religion of combat and sacrifice'.[57]

This view can be elucidated in relation to Foucault's multiple references to Marx's epigram that religion is the 'opium of the people'. The first appears in a dialogue in Tehran with a prominent

55 Foucault, 'What Are the Iranians Dreaming About?', p. 205.

56 Michel Foucault, 'Iran: The Spirit of a World without a Spirit', in Afary and Anderson, *Foucault and the Iranian Revolution*, p. 251.

57 Ibid., p. 252.

Iranian intellectual in which Foucault says he has heard three or four people in Iran say that Marx was wrong with this phrase and, having read several books on Shi'ism, he had indeed discovered the 'historically undeniable' role of this religion in 'a political awakening, in maintaining political consciousness, in inciting and fomenting political awareness'.[58] In his third report from Iran, in October, he repeats the same point, saying that Marx's epigram is the phrase that makes Iranians sneer the most.[59] Finally, in an interview later in Paris, he repeats the critique of the phrase, and adds that Marx's preceding sentence is closer to the Iranian case: 'Let us say, then, that Islam, in that year of 1978, was not the opium of the people but precisely because it was the spirit of a world without a spirit.'[60]

The key point here is that the typical analysis of revolution, inherited from the French Revolution via Marx, would distinguish between the conjunctural effects of actors and ideologies and the underlying social and material contradictions. This, for Foucault, led to an underestimation and reduction of the role of Shi'ism in the Iran case. Oddly, however, this perspective was not that of either the Western intellectual or of the journalist's attempt to write a 'history of the present', but of the man Foucault called 'the saint', the Ayatollah Khomeini himself, who was in Paris at the end of his exile at the time. As Afary and Anderson note, in his October denunciation of both Marxism and Iranian students abroad, Khomeini proclaimed:

> They say Islam is opium! That religion as a whole is opium! . . . [When in fact] the prophet of Islam, and other Muslims, fought the wealthy. Now the [leftist opposition] has injected the thought [in people's minds] that it is the rich who introduced

58 Michel Foucault, 'Dialogue between Michel Foucault and Baqir Parham', in Afary and Anderson, *Foucault and the Iranian Revolution*, p. 186.

59 Michel Foucault, 'Tehran: Faith against the Shah', in Afary and Anderson, *Foucault and the Iranian Revolution*, p. 186.

60 Foucault, 'Iran: The Spirit of a World without a Spirit', p. 255.

> religion! All these machinations are so they could separate you from one another and from the Quran.[61]

In the Tehran dialogue, Foucault concluded that Marx's statement was only correct for a particular kind of Christianity that 'was the product of political choices and joint tactics by states, or the government bureaucracies, and the church organization during the nineteenth century'.[62] In fact, he was so taken by the use of cassettes and loudspeakers to broadcast the mullahs' sermons and calls to arms in the streets that he compared them to European examples of religious revolts of conduct: 'These voices, as terrible as must have been that of Savonarola in Florence, the voices of the Anabaptists in Munster, or those of the Presbyterians at the time of Cromwell, resounded through the whole village, the whole neighbourhood.'[63] He returned to the Anabaptists more than once. During the German Peasants' War of the sixteenth century, Anabaptism, like Shi'ism in Iran, 'was a movement that rejected the power of the state, government bureaucracy, social and religious hierarchies, everything'.[64] Religion, far from sending the masses into a drugged sleep, could galvanize them into a potent force against the existing order of things.

In sum, the case of Iran undermined the whole modern European concept of revolution. In his last statement on the matter, which was also a defence of the positions he had taken, Foucault announced that the Iranian revolt had marked a break with the political paradigms of revolution dominant since 1789:

> Then came the age of 'revolution'. For two centuries, it hung over (*surplombe*) history, organized our perception of time, and polarized hopes. The age of revolution has constituted a gigantic

61 Khomeini, in Afary and Anderson, *Foucault and the Iranian Revolution*, p. 76.

62 Foucault, 'Dialogue', p. 187.

63 Foucault, 'Tehran: Faith against the Shah', p. 201.

64 Foucault, 'Dialogue', p. 187.

> effort to acclimate uprisings within a rational and controllable history. 'Revolution' gave these uprisings a legitimacy, sorted out their good and bad forms, and defined their laws of development. For uprisings, it established preliminary conditions, objectives, and ways of bringing them to an end. Even the profession of revolutionary was defined. By thus repatriating revolt into the discourse of revolution, it was said, the uprising would appear in all its truth and continue to its true conclusion. This was a marvelous promise. Some will say that the uprising thus found itself colonized by *realpolitik*. Others will say that the dimension of a rational history was opened to it. I prefer the question that Horkheimer used to ask, a naïve question, and a little feverish: 'But is it really so desirable, this revolution?'[65]

Foucault, in effect, claimed that the Iranian revolution was really the end of the revolution as it had been known since 1789. He castigated Marxist and liberal intellectuals for seeking to apply the paradigm of European revolution to Iran. By emphasizing the different factions involved in the struggle, by calling for compromises between political groups, or by waiting for the real, material forces to unveil themselves, they denied what he called the 'irreducibility' of the struggle of the Iranian people.[66] The paradigm of revolution reduced the singularity of religiously inspired sacrifice, and of political demonstrations as religious ceremony and liturgy, to the worn out categories of class struggle and ideology.

The second major theme of his reading of the Iranian case is thus condensed in the notion of 'political spirituality'. In October 1978, he would exclaim: 'For the people who inhabit this land, what is the point of searching, even at the cost of their own lives, for this thing whose possibility we have forgotten since the

65 Michel Foucault, 'Is It Useless to Revolt?', in Afary and Anderson, *Foucault and the Iranian Revolution*, p. 264.

66 On Foucault's use of the term, 'irreducible' in relation to Iran, see Afary and Anderson, *Foucault and the Iranian Revolution*, passim, especially pp. 84–5.

Renaissance and the great crisis of Christianity, a *political spirituality*. I can already hear the French laughing, but I know that they are wrong.'[67] Foucault here conceives of political spirituality as an entry of the spiritual into politics. Like the Christian dissidents at the end of the Middle Ages, Shi'ism provides a liturgy for a community that could interpolate its members into an oppositional 'absolutely collective will' irreducible to whatever social forces may be operative. As such, it 'has been the vocabulary, the ceremonial, the timeless drama into which one could fit the historical drama of a people that pitted its very existence against that of its sovereign.'[68]

In Foucault's understanding, there were no divisions and splits in the collective will of the Iranian people. When confronted by his interviewers with the example of Mao in China, he replied that Iran was completely unlike the case of the Cultural Revolution and that what 'gives it such beauty, and at the same time such gravity, is that there is only one confrontation: between the entire people and the state power threatening them with its weapons and police . . . on the one side, the entire will of the people, on the other the machine guns.'[69] As Afary and Anderson point out, while his critique of vulgar Marxism may have been correct, it 'was curious how Foucault characterized Iranian Shi'ism as a "timeless", unified, historico-cultural discourse system, one that completely overrode those "contradictions" with which, he acknowledged in passing, Iranian society was "shot through"'.[70]

Foucault's analysis of Iran evades the complexities of power relations he had diagnosed in modern European society and grasps the events through the lens of a kind of populism in which the unified will of the people rises up against the regime and its elites. The force of this unity is the political spirituality of the Iranian

67 Foucault, 'What Are Iranians Dreaming About?', p. 209 (original emphasis).
68 Foucault, 'Iran: The Spirit of a World without a Spirit', p. 252.
69 Ibid., pp. 253–4.
70 Afary and Anderson, *Foucault and the Iranian Revolution*, p. 123.

people and its point of articulation is the charismatic figure of Khomeini:

> The situation in Iran can be understood as a great joust under traditional emblems, those of the king and the saint, the armed ruler and the destitute exile, the despot faced with the man who stands up bare-handed and is acclaimed by a people. This image has its own power, but it also speaks to a reality to which millions of dead have just subscribed.[71]

The word 'joust' reminds us of the ritual combat between knights in the Middle Ages, and returns us to Foucault's alternative history of truth focused on the *épreuve*. But perhaps even more extraordinary is this image of an acclamatory movement unified through mortal sacrifice by a saintly leader fighting a sovereign. This analysis seems to be the inverse of everything Foucault had written about the complex relations of power that traverse the social body of modern societies. It is closer to the notions of democracy found in the writings of Carl Schmitt,[72] and the political imaginary is closer to the populist movements found in Europe and elsewhere today. Indeed, if one were to look for a vocabulary to talk about the apparently non-rational, anti-elitist rise of populism in Europe and the United States in the early twenty-first century, it would be the one Foucault uses in his discussion of Iran.

In one area, Foucault's analysis of Shi'ism reprises important elements of his thinking at that time. It is remarkably close to his analysis of the forms of 'counter-conduct' to the Christian pastorate he found in late medieval and early modern times in his lectures earlier the same year (in 1978). There he identified forms of asceticism, with their mastery of self and the world, as being in direct

71 Foucault, 'What Are Iranians Dreaming About?', p. 204.

72 See Mitchell Dean, 'Three Forms of Democratic Acclamation', *Telos* 179, 2017, pp. 9–32. The relationship between charismatic leadership and acclamations in democracy is explored by Max Weber, *Economy and Society*, Berkeley: University of California Press, 2013, pp. 1121–30.

opposition to the principles of pastoral obedience.[73] So too the principle of equality between members of a religious community confronted the pastor's privileged power or authority.[74] Further, in his analysis of Christian communities, he lists mysticism, Scripture and eschatological beliefs as bases of opposition.

Foucault's diagnosis of the political force of Shi'ism had all these features. He seemed to accept the Shi'ite prejudice that opposed the egalitarian justice of the founding imams of Shi'ism to the corruption of early Sunni caliphs. He regarded the clerics not as equivalent to the clergy of institutional Christianity, with their strict division from the laity, but as direct relays of the will of the people, 'like so many photographic plates on which the anger and aspirations of the community are marked'.[75] Like the Christian counter-movements, Shi'ism would celebrate the asceticism found in 'the exemplary sacrifices of the imams',[76] around whom was formed a cohesive community with an indivisible collective will, now in opposition to the regime of the Shah, his army and his Western allies. The Scripture of the Quran would provide a symbolic language for its counter-conducts. Moreover, with respect to eschatology, Foucault notes the Shi'ite expectation of the return of the Twelfth Iman (Mahdi), who will institute the reign of the true order of Islam on earth, quoting the moderate Ayatollah Shariamadari's claim that 'we are waiting for the Mahdi, but each day we fight for a good government'.[77] The relation to death and sacrifice is never far from his mind, as when he considers 'rituals of martyrdom' such as the 'wedding' ceremonies that commemorate the youths killed in the struggle.[78] In sum, Foucault's analysis of Shi'ism was an almost point by point transposition of his analysis of Christian counter-conducts as responses to the 'great governmentalization' of society.

73 Foucault, *Security, Territory, Population*, pp. 206–7.
74 Ibid., pp. 208–10.
75 Foucault, 'Tehran: Faith against the Shah', p. 202.
76 Ibid., p. 201.
77 Ibid.
78 Ibid., p. 200.

The means by which this political spirituality would achieve the goal of Islamic government would be self-transformation, which is the third key theme here. Foucault conceived the Iranian revolution not in terms of political and social transformation but primarily as a change of subjectivity, and with that a change of everyday life. For the Iranians, 'religion was like the promise and the guarantee of finding something that would radically change their subjectivity'.[79] In the words Foucault attributed to them: 'But above all we have to change ourselves. Our way of being, our relationship with others, with things, with eternity, with God, etc., must be completely changed, and there will only be a true revolution if this radical change in experience takes place.'[80]

This radical self-transformation had two registers for Foucault. First, there was the formation of the unified and indivisible 'collective will', in which the desire for change entailed a willingness for sacrifice even to the point to death. Second, there was the promise of new forms of ordinary and everyday existence, with new relations and a new community. All this was to be accomplished without the techniques of discipline required of an armed class struggle. Rather, the people opposed the armed regime with their 'bare hands',[81] and achieved their everyday goal of self-transformation in 'a kind of tragic liturgy of suffering and death, unleashing, through ritualized demonstrations of defiance, the latent counter-power of a people, both to topple a regime – and to transfigure itself spiritually'.[82] Rather than a political revolution in the post-French Revolution sense, what was happening in Iran was akin to an individual and collective limit-experience, a liturgy of self-sacrifice, and above all an ordeal or *épreuve*, in which every

79 Foucault, 'Iran: The Spirit of a World without a Spirit', p. 255.

80 Ibid.

81 Michel Foucault, 'A Revolt with Bare Hands', in Afary and Anderson, *Foucault and the Iranian Revolution*, p. 211, and Foucault, 'The Mythical Leader of the Iranian Revolt', in ibid., p. 222.

82 Miller, *Passion*, p. 307.

participant, by making their confrontation with the Shah a matter of life or death, was transformed by it.

While a chastened Foucault would remain silent on Iran from mid-1979, he returned to his view of what was at stake in a revolution in his lectures some four years later. In 1983, he found in Kant's references to the French Revolution in his *Conflict of the Faculties* an analysis of the signs of whether humankind is constantly progressing:

> Kant says, it is not the Revolution itself which is significant . . . not the revolutionary drama itself . . . What is significant is the way the Revolution exists as spectacle, the way in which it is greeted everywhere by spectators who are not participants, but observers, witnesses, and those who, for better or worse, let themselves be caught up in it . . . What is important . . . is that all around the Revolution there is, he says, 'sympathy of aspiration which borders on enthusiasm'.[83]

What was important for Foucault, then, was not the reality of the Revolution, the bloody mess that it was, the material forces and antagonisms of which it was composed, but the wish fulfilment of its spectators bordering on enthusiasm. This was not only an analysis of Kant's view. It was also, at least in part, a description of Foucault's own enthusiasm for the Iranian case. In other words, just as the displacement of the sovereignty of the author enabled both reader and writer to create themselves through the text, it is no longer the revolutionary actors – their motives, interests and reasons – that matter in the Revolution, but the way the Revolution acts as an occasion for spectators and participants alike to transform themselves. This would seem to be the central lesson of Foucault's reading of the Iranian revolution.

83 Michel Foucault, *Government of Self and Others: Lectures at the Collège de France 1982–1983*, trans. Graham Burchell, London: Palgrave Macmillan, 2010, pp. 17–18.

The Revolution had thus become, for Foucault, not so much an act of social and political transformation of an oppressed people or class as an act of individual and collective self-transformation for spectators such as himself, to be sure, but also for its participants. Its 'truth' was revealed not in the cold calculus of social forces, their compromises, alignments and confrontations, but in the collective ordeal, with its sacrifices and possibility of death, that each member of a spiritually unified people was willing to undertake. In his reporting on the case, he belittled all attempts to foreground the analysis of the different factions involved in the uprising and dismissed all appeals for compromise or a political solution. Despite some qualifications of his earlier enthusiasm in his final word on the matter, written as an act of self-justification in May 1979, Foucault never retracted his fundamental understanding of what had happened:

> Concerning the enigma of the uprising, for those who sought in Iran not the 'deep reasons' for the movement, but the manner in which it was lived; for those who tried to understand what was going on in the heads of these men and women when they risked their lives, one thing was striking. They inscribed, on the borders of heaven and earth, in a dream-history that was as religious as it was political, all their hunger, their humiliation, their hatred of the regime and their will to bring it down. They confronted the Pahlavis in a game where each one staked his life and his death, a game that was also about sacrifices and millennial promises. Thus came the celebrated demonstrations, which played such an important role. These demonstrations could, at the same time, respond concretely to the threat of the army (to the point of paralysing it), unfold according to the rhythm of religious ceremonies, and finally refer to a timeless drama in which power is always accursed. This drama caused a surprising superimposition to appear in the middle of the twentieth century: a movement strong enough to bring down a seemingly well-armed regime, all the while remaining in touch with the

> old dreams that were once familiar to the West, when it too wanted to inscribe the figures of spirituality on the ground of politics.[84]

Through a sacrificial ordeal involving the risk of death, during the liturgies of public demonstrations that would acclaim their living saint, and under the inspiration of a millennial eschatology, Iranians were seeking, collectively in their political struggle and as individuals in their everyday lives, a self-transformation. The problem of subjectivity and of the autonomous self-creation and recreation of the subject in opposition to different forms of power was never far from Foucault's concern at this time.

What he found remarkable was a political spirituality acting as a counter-conduct that entailed a radical self-transformation through ascesis, mortification rituals, public penitence, millenarian beliefs, and other ordeals. He thus admired the political deployment of the *épreuve* in Shi'ite Iran as he had in the Christian 'revolts of conduct' of the Middle Ages and early modern period. He also found the same elements in Iran that he had found in the practices of *exomologesis* in early Christianity. What he objected to in Western Christianity was its avowal of an inner truth and of the formation of a subjectivity through an investigation of the truth of its identity. As we have seen, this project would be inherited by the engineers of the modern soul in the contexts of scientific inquiry and expertise and the structures of the welfare state. It is indeed this question of subjectivity that brings us to Foucault's final lesson from the Iran experience, in relation to its treatment of what in the West had come to be called 'sexuality'. After his experiences in Tunisia in 1968, and upon his arrival in Iran ten years later, Foucault appeared to believe that there would be a greater acceptance of homosexual acts and relations within Islam, including in Shi'ism.[85] In *The Use of Pleasure*, he would note with appreciation

84 Foucault, 'Is It Useless to Revolt?', pp. 264–5.

85 Afary and Anderson, *Foucault and the Iranian Revolution*, pp. 140–3.

the reservation of the term 'true love' for the 'love of boys' in ancient Greek aristocratic culture. Such relationships, fraught with difficulties concerning the boy's future status as a citizen, gave rise to an 'aesthetics of existence' regulated not by a moral code but by 'forms of austerity'.[86] Similarly, Shi'ism (including in Khomeini's own advice manual) acknowledges the existence of sexual acts between males, including penetration, but links them to purification and penitential rituals rather than confessions or avowals or moral or legal proscription.[87] In both cases, there is an 'economy of acts' rather than the question of identity and the existence of self-imposed ethical forms to deal with pleasures. What Foucault objected to – and this is perhaps the final and most important reason why he was attracted to the potential of the Iranian uprising – was how modern Western culture, with its roots in the confessional culture of Christianity, sought the truth of desire in its avowal of what lies in the depths of subjectivity.

Whether in the subjugated genealogy of Christian revolts against the hermeneutics of the self, in the meaning of the Iranian revolution, or in the ancient ethics of the self, what Foucault sought was neither liberation from sexual repression nor the contestation of unequal power in erotic relations, nor even especially the acknowledgement of homosexual identity, but an 'exit' or 'way out' from the power relations that dominate by 'subjectification', an ethics grounded in avowal and in the modern Western figure of the subject that is constantly asked to speak its own truth. In classical Antiquity and in Islam he found an older and more discrete economy of acts and pleasures that was the preserve of the adult and often aristocratic male, an economy that prescribed the conditions under which such males could access the bodies of younger males (and, to a lesser extent, women), not through a moral code but through forms of austerity or techniques of the self, ones that would restrict women to a separate domain of the household. It

86 Foucault, *The Use of Pleasure*, p. 253.
87 Afary and Anderson, *Foucault and the Iranian Revolution*, pp. 159–60.

might be remarked that Foucault placed this economy of pleasures in the domain of ethics, but virtually ignored its relation to the economy of powers he had insisted on elsewhere. If there is an example in more recent times of this self-governed economy of pleasures it is Bill Clinton's 'don't ask, don't tell' principle for military personnel, in contrast to the public form of individual avowal termed 'coming out' encouraged by the gay movement of Foucault's own time.

Curiously, Foucault would also seek that same exit from power relations, and from the public, expert and personal elicitation of subjectivities, in the 'environmental' interventions of neoliberalism that, he contended, could regulate individuals through the shaping of choice without the fabrication of subjectivities.

5
The Revolution Beheaded

> My role – but it's a too pompous term – is to show people that they are much freer than they think.
>
> Michel Foucault, 1982[1]

In a 1977 discussion with the founder of the anti-psychiatry movement, David Cooper, Foucault argued controversially against the characterization of rape as a sexual crime. In his view, there was a serious problem with making rape a 'specific' kind of aggression by including the sexual motive and thus including the question of sexuality within the law. Why should rape be considered in a different way than being stabbed or punched in the face? Foucault was indeed very suspicious of the will of the feminist movement to give 'a judicial specificity to the physical attack that involves sex', to give 'sexuality itself' a 'predominant function' 'in the body'.[2] This

1 Michel Foucault, 'Vérité, pouvoir et soi,' October 1982, in *Dits et Écrits II*, text no. 362, p. 1597.

2 Michel Foucault, 'Enfermement, psychiatrie, prison,' October 1977, in *Dits et Écrits II*, text no. 209, p. 354.

conception would only contribute to the larger movement within French law that, since the nineteenth century, sought to 'protect', 'surround' and 'invest' sexuality 'with a legislation that won't be the same for the rest of the body'.[3]

Indeed, before the early nineteenth century, Foucault showed, the French penal code did not mention any 'sexual offences'. It was not until the mid-nineteenth century that the law was progressively informed by the new psychiatric categories of 'necrophilia', 'pederasty', 'homosexuality', 'exhibitionism' or 'kleptomania'. These categories will slowly constitute a 'psychiatric and criminological continuum along which it is possible to interrogate in medical terms any and all degrees on the penal scale'.[4] This development will shape legislation until the late 1960s, when, depending on the sexual orientation of the subject, punishment will vary. Foucault was therefore afraid that the penalization of rape would only reinforce this logic that tends to introduce into the legal system new forms of knowledge of the self from psychiatry, psychology, anthropology, and so forth.[5] He was afraid that the introduction of the sexual motive into the characterization of the crime would contribute to the kind of shifts that the 'anthropological school' operated: 'from the crime to the criminal, from the act committed to the danger that is potentially inherent in the individual, and from a modulated punishment of the guilty party to the absolute protection of others'.[6]

The key to this development is the growing role of the avowal as a technology within the penal system, which would displace the question of truth from the crime onto the veridiction of the criminal subject himself. In this new framework, the judge says to the prosecuted: 'do not just tell me what you did without telling me, at the same time and through that, who you are'.[7] This is

3 Ibid., p. 353.
4 Foucault, *Wrong-Doing, Truth-Telling*, p. 220.
5 Foucault, *L'origine de l'herméneutique de soi*, p. 114.
6 Foucault, *Wrong-Doing, Truth-Telling*, p. 223.
7 Ibid., p. 215.

precisely what, in the eyes of Foucault, will 'derail the entire system', the reason why 'we were also trying to have emerge a subjectivity that maintained a significant relationship to his crime'.[8]

Indeed, 'beyond the avowal, a confession is required, an examination of conscience, an explanation of the self, a highlight of what we are'.[9] This way of shaping the self of the criminal is precisely what Foucault had been trying to criticize in his late work: the will not only to judge the crime, but also to 'constitute a certain kind of self, as through the penal system, the criminal has to understand himself as a criminal'.[10] Therefore, what was at stake for Foucault was the historical 'trend' of the judicial system, the will to 'adapt the modalities of the punishment to the nature of the criminal'.[11] It is now a question of punishing, not the act, but the deep motivations and instincts of a *criminal subject*. As he argued in the lectures delivered at Dartmouth College in 1980:

> there is perhaps a sexual motivation to something like a murder or a robbery or whatever. But we have a penal code that condemns these kinds of actions because they are a murder or a robbery, whether the motivation is sexual or not. And I noticed that, at least in the French judicial practice, the fact that the lawyers, the judges, the prosecutor find a sexual motivation always has completely uncontrollable consequences.[12]

'The fact that sexual differentiation, sexual preference, sexual activity, can be a matter of legislation', he insisted, is 'something that cannot be tolerated'.[13]

---

8 Ibid., pp. 211–12.

9 Michel Foucault, 'L'évolution de la notion d' "individu dangereux" dans la psychiatrie légale du XIXe siècle', 1978, in *Dits et Écrits II*, text no. 220, p. 444.

10 Foucault, *Qu'est-ce que la critique?*, pp. 114–15.

11 Foucault, 'L'évolution de la notion d' "individu dangereux" ', p. 452.

12 Foucault, *L'origine de l'herméneutique de soi*, p. 115.

13 Ibid., p. 114.

Foucault thus placed the question of rape within the more general project of removing any notion of sexuality from the law. His point in this debate is therefore not that we should not condemn rape as such – obviously we should – but that we should avoid the dynamic within law that shapes subjects (the mad, perverts, criminals) and instead try to conceive a legal system that does not rest on forms of knowledge of the human sciences, that does not tend to produce effects in terms of the way we understand ourselves, and that is, therefore, less normative. If Foucault would moderate his position to the audience at Dartmouth – eventually acknowledging that we cannot avoid including the sexual motive in the case of rape[14] – this controversy nevertheless illustrates the centrality that the subject and techniques of subjectification will have in his work during the last decade of his life.

Foucault redefined the question of resistance as a refusal of the dispositives of subjectification at the heart of his analysis. This new framework thus defines both the reconceptualization of the subject as a battlefield, and that of politics as the promotion of new forms of subjectivity. The focus of the critique is now localized at the level of the 'relations that are woven between subject, power and truth'.[15] The analytical and political ground of the 'final Foucault' was no longer the history of knowledge and of the *episteme*, nor the great fresco of the disciplining of undesirable bodies, but the subject itself.

In this regard, it is essential to keep in mind the importance neoliberalism had (both as an emerging governmentality in France during the 1970s and as a theory) in Foucault's slow formulation of a theory of social change and resistance. Indeed, neoliberalism

14 Asked about the issue at Dartmouth, he would qualify his 1977 position in these terms: 'What I wanted to say is that there is a problem: I think the law has nothing to do with sex but I believe, on the other hand, that rape must be condemned and that sexuality cannot be separated from rape. This is a problem: how to solve it?' Ibid., p. 115.

15 Foucault, *Qu'est-ce que la critique?*, p. 23.

seemed to him to be a 'non-moral' and 'non-juridical'[16] form of governmentality capable of breaking with the structures inherited from Christianity and opening the space for new forms of subjectivity. Foucault's intellectual evolution during his last decade thus has a stronger relation to the rise of neoliberalism than is generally acknowledged.

The self as a battlefield

In the years immediately after his 'acid test' in Death Valley, Foucault not only refocused his *History of Sexuality* on the subject but also turned toward his redefinition of the subject as a privileged place for politics. He tried to show to what extent power was not only a constraint on the subject, but also had a productive dimension. As he stated in his 1976 course, we

> do not have to conceive the individual as a sort of elementary nucleus, a primitive atom, a multiple and silent material to which power would apply, against which power would hit, which would subject individuals or break them. In fact, what makes the body, gestures, speeches, and desires that are identified and constituted as individuals, this is precisely one of the first effects of power.[17]

Nonetheless, this 'production' of the subject still seems to function independently of the subject itself. Foucault realized that he had been 'insisting too much . . . on the techniques of domination',[18] and he was beginning to feel that power could not be understood as a 'pure violence or strict constraint'.[19] As François Ewald puts it,

16 Becker, Ewald and Harcourt, 'Becker on Ewald on Foucault', p. 5.

17 Michel Foucault, *Il faut défendre la société*, Paris: Hautes Études/Gallimard Seuil, 1997, p. 27.

18 Foucault, *L'origine de l'herméneutique de soi*, p. 39.

19 Ibid.

it still seemed that the subject 'is decided by power relations';[20] in other words, it was left 'without agency to respond to that power'[21] and was therefore unable to differentiate itself from the liberal subject or the one discovered in Marxist political economy, in which it is reduced to an object. Indeed, as Foucault argued in *The Birth of Biopolitics*, in economic analysis from Adam Smith to Keynes, the worker is not an agent, but rather a function of the whole economic system. Within that intellectual framework, shared by Ricardo and Marx, the worker is always 'passive' and only finds work 'thanks to a certain rate of investment'.[22]

This reading is inspired in particular by Gary Becker's analysis of human capital which, unlike that of Marx, deals with work as a 'human behavior' and with 'the internal rationality of this human behavior'.[23] In other words, the Beckerian analysis of work takes the worker's point of view instead of viewing work simply as a disembodied variable that intervenes in production. In Foucault's eyes, Becker and the other American neoliberals had ensured 'for the first time . . . that the worker is not present in the economic analysis as an object – the object of supply and demand in the form of labor power – but an *active* economic subject'.[24] However, while by the mid-1970s Foucault had invested a lot of energy in dismissing a Marxist understanding of the struggles of his time, his subject was still produced by power relations in the same way as the worker was produced by a political economy.

A decisive turn began in 1978 with Foucault's study of pastoral power and governmentality in *Security, Territory, Population*. This was followed by his careful study of neoliberalism the next year,[25] when he was 'increasingly focused on paying attention to the

20 Becker, Ewald and Harcourt, 'Becker on Ewald on Foucault', p. 7.

21 Dilts, 'From "entrepreneur of the self" to "care of the self"', p. 141.

22 Foucault, *The Birth of Biopolitics*, p. 220.

23 Ibid., p. 223.

24 Ibid.

25 See, in particular, Mitchell Dean, *Critical and Effective Histories: Foucault's Methods and Historical Sociology*, London: Routledge, 1994, pp. 174–93.

relationships to oneself, to the techniques through which these relationships have been shaped'.[26] In a way, this opened the path to thinking of the subject as a possible space for transformation. Power was now not to be seen as essentially repressive or disciplinary, but as a subtle 'mixture . . . of technologies of constraint and technologies of the self'.[27] This duality at the heart of power itself would lead to a more attentive exploration in the 1978 and 1979 lectures of the topics of Christian pastorate and neoliberalism, as Foucault migrated 'from a study of practices of objectification (discipline and biopolitics) to a study of practices of self-initiated subjectification (ethics)'.[28] Thus two faces of a same coin emerge: 'the action of power upon individuals in order to shape their subjectivity (the dimension of the conduct and government of the others)', and, concomitantly, 'the action of individuals upon themselves in order to contrast such a power (the dimension of the conduct and government of oneself)'.[29]

This perspective offers Foucault the possibility of conceiving an autonomy for the subject without falling back into the framework of humanism, thus allowing him to seriously study the problem of freedom and resistance to power.[30] This perspective is then amplified with his view of American neoliberalism as a new approach to the economic subject. *Homo œconomicus* is now 'an entrepreneur of the self'.[31] Whether approached as a producer or a consumer, the economic subject is active and must be considered as its own capital, from which it sources both income and satisfaction. Even consumption must be seen as an activity, and the individuals who consume thus produce their own satisfaction.

This is why Ewald argued that 'Foucault's turn to practices of the self [was] at least partially prompted by the work of the American

26 Foucault, *Qu'est-ce que la critique?*, p. 85.

27 Foucault, *L'origine de l'herméneutique de soi*, p. 39.

28 Ben Golder, *Foucault and the Politics of Rights*, Stanford: Stanford University Press, 2015, p. 51.

29 Cremonesi et al. (eds), *Foucault and the Making of Subjects*, p. 7.

30 Dean, *Critical and Effective Histories*, p. 175.

31 Foucault, *The Birth of Biopolitics*, pp. 226, 230.

neo-liberals'. If this link seems at first counterintuitive, Ewald claimed that to a certain extent the shift from 'macroeconomics to microeconomics' and 'from wealth to human behavior' managed by Becker was 'parallel to the change that Foucault operated within philosophy with regard to the study of power'.[32] In his view, Foucault found in neoliberalism an interesting solution to the question of the place the subject itself had within the field of power. This is what would lead Ewald to argue – as we have noted – that Foucault would find in the human capital approach something like 'a step between his earlier theory of power and the later Foucault lectures about subjectivity'.[33] This gave Foucault access to a subtler understanding of the subject within power relations, granting it a degree of freedom (and possible resistance) that was previously lacking from his work.

As Ewald mentioned during his discussion with Becker, how the neoliberal economists had conceived human agents was 'very close' to 'what Foucault searched for with his theory of the subject and of subjectivity'.[34] Indeed, for Ewald, it was obvious that Foucault was fascinated by how, in the work of Becker and Schultz, 'the agent, in the economy, is always deciding, making decisions', especially because this could give him a solution to the problem with his own 'theory of power', where it was 'difficult to think how the subject decides'.[35] In that perspective, the specific challenges that neoliberal authors had to deal with – dissolving the classical opposition between labour and capital and constituting an acting subject – are surprisingly close to Foucault's own intellectual concerns. Indeed, to quote Andrew Dilts, the neoliberal *homo oeconomicus* 'is a subject that is constituted primarily through practices, and in that sense, precisely the kind of subject that Foucault is interested in explicating'.[36] Neoliberal theory 'opens

32 Becker, Ewald and Harcourt, 'Becker on Ewald on Foucault', p. 6.

33 Ibid., p. 7.

34 Ibid.

35 Ibid.

36 Dilts, 'From "entrepreneur of the self" to "care of the self"', p. 132.

the grounds of subjectivity, re-directs [Foucault's] attention beyond the ways in which we are made subjects by force relations and allows him to think about the role that subjects play in their own formation'.[37]

Foucault's turn to the subject is then closely associated with the neoliberal analysis that allowed economics, in the same way, to 'move over the side of the subject'.[38] If neoliberalism succeeded in looking at work from the point of view of the worker, Foucault had now to succeed in understanding the relations of power from the perspective of the subject. This shift partly explains the long delay between *The Will to Knowledge*, published in 1976, and the second and third volumes of the *History of Sexuality* published in 1984 (and also the fourth volume, not published until 2018). In the meantime, it was not only the entire plan of the project that was modified but the very direction of Foucault's research and teachings. He explained this reorientation in the second volume of *The History of Sexuality*: his work was now oriented to understanding how 'individuals recognize themselves as subjects of "sexuality"'.[39] In his view, this perspective was essential because traditional history often assumes sexuality as an invariant – changing only through the mutations of power mechanisms – putting out of sight the story of the desiring subject as such and therefore leaving the subject without any kind of agency. As he argued in an interview, 'instead of studying sexuality on the borders of knowledge and power, I have tried to investigate how the experience of sexuality and desire was constituted for the subject himself'.[40]

The Foucauldian subject is now therefore an 'active' agent, constituting itself through a set of practices that can neither be reduced to nor explained completely by its environment. Foucault began then to think about power in a new way: within any form of

37 Ibid.

38 Foucault, *The Birth of Biopolitics*, p. 252.

39 Foucault, *The Use of Pleasure*, p. 4.

40 Foucault, 'Une esthétique de l'existence', p. 1549.

conduct and governmentality, there is always 'the immanent possibility of a counter-conduct'; 'power and resistance' are always 'interlocked'.[41] Ben Golder explains that the aim for Foucault is to 'excavate the hidden margin of freedom immanent to all contingent human arrangements, and what it thereby demonstrates is the sustaining possibility of their being otherwise than they are now, so as to show, as Foucault puts it, that people are "much freer than they feel" '.[42] Resistance is always a 'struggle from within'.

This original articulation between forms of knowledge, power relations and subjectification techniques will therefore give an essential freedom to the individual. The subject is now not just the single product of oppression but constitutes itself in a productive, positive relationship to the procedures of governmentality. As emphasized by Frédéric Gros, now 'forms of subjectivity, or specific knowledge, can act as a resistance to certain governmentality procedures'.[43] Self-invention becomes a potential space of freedom and autonomy that individuals can mobilize against the forms of subjectivity that are heteronomously fabricated for them. This approach therefore introduces an essential dimension into Foucault's reflection on power. By focusing on the subject, he now sees the relation of self as the fundamental element of resistance faced with technologies of power and government. If for Foucault there is no outside of power, there is nevertheless freedom at the heart of power relations. As he clarifies: in the 'relations of power, there is inevitably a possibility of resistance, because if there was no possibility of resistance – violent resistance, of running away, of cunning strategies that reverse the situation – there would be no power relations'. Indeed, in his opinion, 'there can be no power relations except insofar as the subjects are free'.[44] And even if there

41 Golder, *Foucault and the Politics of Rights*, p. 57.

42 Ibid., p. 58.

43 Frédéric Gros, *Michel Foucault*, Paris: Presses Universitaires de France, 1996, ebook.

44 Foucault, 'L'éthique du souci de soi', p. 1539. See also Dean, *Critical and Effective Histories*, pp. 177–8.

is 'nowhere we are free of any power relations', 'we can always change the situation', 'there are always possibilities of changing the situation'.[45] Thus, 'resistance is a component of this strategic relation that constitutes power', it 'always relies upon the situation against which it struggles'.[46]

Resistance as 'desubjectification'

It was within this new intellectual framework that Foucault slowly re-thought the resistance of his time as a struggle against everything that assigns us to a certain relationship with ourselves, against all that impoverishes our ethical imagination. In this sense, the most important legacy of May '68 was not anti-statism – the communists too wanted to abolish the state – but the criticism of the power relations and knowledge on which Foucault believed the state relies. The aim was to disarticulate the 'bundle of relationships that ties . . . power, truth and the subject' together and which had as its essential function 'the desubjectification of what one might call the politics of truth'.[47] As he argued, the struggles of his time were no longer 'attacks on a particular institution of power, or group, or class, or elite, but rather a particular technique, a form of power'.[48]

This form of power, relying precisely on what Foucault had called 'truth-inquiry', the *enquête*, influences everyday life as it 'classifies individuals into categories and defines their own individuality, attaches them to their identity, imposes on them a law of truth which they must recognize and which others must recognize in them. It is a form of power that transforms individuals into

45 Foucault, 'Michel Foucault, une interview: sexe, pouvoir et la politique de l'identité', p. 1559.

46 Ibid., p. 1560.

47 Foucault, *Qu'est-ce que la critique?*, p. 39.

48 Michel Foucault, 'Le sujet et le pouvoir', 1982, in *Dits et Écrits II*, text no. 306, p. 1046.

subjects.'[49] It is not a power that represses or exploits, but rather one that 'subjectifies'. Therefore, the problem of institutions is not the 'class interests' they are supposed to serve, but the way in which they assign us a certain identity.

Such revolts obviously opposed a certain kind of state power, but not as it was conceived by many organizations on the Left during the period. Foucault did not believe in seizing state power. The question was more about the state as 'a matrix of individualization or a new form of pastoral power' rather than an institution that must be controlled or abolished. For Foucault, 'the problem we are facing today, which is at once political, ethical, social and philosophical, is not to try to free the individual from the state and its institutions, but to free it from the State and the type of individualization associated with it'.[50] In the same way that we should not be seeking to 'liberate' our sexuality, it is not a question of getting rid of the state (or taking control of it), but of refusing the forms of normalization it imposes on our lives and the way it shapes our relation to truth and therefore to ourselves: 'the problem, then, is not to emancipate, it is not to "liberate" the self, but to consider how it would be possible to develop new types, new kinds of relations to ourselves'.[51] Foucault's anti-statism was therefore not a refusal of the state as such, but of all those techniques, devices and technologies that are designed to shape our relationship with ourselves.

This new perspective symbolized the radical displacement of the question of power outside the figure of the sovereign. We had, in Foucault's words, to 'cut off the head of the king' and localize power not only 'within the state apparatus' but also 'aside', 'above', 'under it', at a level 'much smaller, of our everyday life'.[52] As he argued, '68 revealed that the problem with the 'old left' was that it

49 Ibid.
50 Foucault, 'Le sujet et le pouvoir', p. 1051.
51 Foucault, *Qu'est-ce que la critique?*, p. 98.
52 Foucault, 'Pouvoir et corps', p. 1626.

always seemed think within the framework of the 'sovereign', that is, 'in juridical terms',[53] no matter how 'revolutionary' it thought itself to be. This old notion of 'revolution', Foucault thought, can leave quite unaltered the 'relations of power that [have] allowed the state to function'.[54] Power had to be thought in relation to the constitution of the subject, and not just in opposition to it, as if the subject could be something already existing outside of it, something that had to be found, deciphered or liberated. Therefore, power had to be challenged by the creation of new forms of living, in the same way that the power of the author over the text was challenged by the production of new readings of and experiments with the text. It was now necessary to experience one's subjectivity outside the hermeneutics of the self.

The main task of the struggles of the 1970s and '80s was therefore to 'promote new forms of subjectivity by refusing the kind of individuality that has been imposed on us for several centuries'.[55] Foucault's understanding of power and liberty therefore put the 'invention of the self' at the centre of his politics, profoundly changing the logic of resistance. He thus sought to reformulate the Enlightenment project, as we seen, in terms of the desubjectification of the politics of truth. The art of unravelling the links between power, subject and truth defined, in his eyes, a critical philosophical tradition 'that seeks the conditions and indefinite possibilities of a transformation of the subject, of our own transformation',[56] 'of a permanent creation of ourselves in our autonomy'.[57] It is no longer a question of seeking the limits of our knowledge but of constituting a more autonomous relation to oneself than that of modern forms of subjectification. As Judith Revel has pointed out,

---

53 Michel Foucault, '"La fonction politique de l'intellectuel". Entretien avec Michel Foucault', 1977, in *Dits et Écrits II*, text no. 192, p. 146.

54 Ibid., p. 151.

55 Foucault, 'Le sujet et le pouvoir', p. 1050.

56 Foucault, *L'origine de l'herméneutique de soi*, p. 37n.

57 Michel Foucault, 'Qu'est-ce que les Lumières?', 1984, in *Dits et Écrits II*, text no. 339, p. 1392.

Foucault's critique 'consisted of displacing the place of thought and politics', just like the Greek Cynics who made a public scandal of their own existence; a scandal whose main characteristic was that it 'substituted life for words, or more exactly, absorbed words into something wider which is precisely the experimentation of lifestyles'.[58]

Proliferation against power

May '68 thus opened the way for 'a new kind of revolution', a type of revolution that could disentangle the self from all the dispositives of 'assujettissement' and normalization, and thereby improve our capacities of self-transformation. This idea shaped a very different kind of revolution, one disrupting the state from within. Indeed, when conceived outside the old sovereign model, the state appears as an apparatus that constantly relies on a set of pre-existing micro-powers functioning in sexual relations, schools, family structures, knowledge, and scientific techniques. 'In general', Foucault argued during an interview he gave in Japan,

> we favor state power. Many people think that other forms of power derive from it. Now I think that, without going so far as to say that state power derives from other forms of power, it is at least based on them, and it is they which allow state power to exist. How can we say that all the power relations that exist between the two sexes, between adults and children, in the family, in the offices, between the sick and the healthy, between the normal and the abnormal, derive from state power? If we want to change state power, we must change the various relationships of power that operate in society. Otherwise, society

58 Judith Revel, 'N'oubliez pas d'inventer votre vie', *La Revue Internationale des Livres et des Idées*, 5 June 2010.

> does not change. For example, in the USSR, the ruling class changed but the old power relations remained. What is important are these power relations which function independently of the individuals who have state power.[59]

As he argued, 'the state, with its great judicial, military and other apparatuses, represents only the guarantee, the armature of a whole network of powers which passes through other channels, different from these principal ways'.[60] But what '68 demonstrated was that it would be an illusion to think that the state actually 'controlled all these plans'. Subverting these relations from within, by promoting new forms of self and existence, could then work as a mode of conceiving change far more radical than that of the party-form of the early twentieth century, which Foucault characterized as the 'most sterilizing political invention since the 19th century'.[61]

This was a transformation whose aim would be – as Gilles Deleuze wrote along the same lines – to make proliferate and stimulate 'all kinds of mutant machines' that would 'lead wars, combine themselves, and draw a plane of consistency that undermines the plane of organization of the world and states', and which is able to produce 'huge displacements' 'below the state'.[62] In the same way that '68 taught us to 'distort' texts, images and videos, as in the movies of Guy Debord, transforming society was now also about 'undermining', 'softening' and 'subverting' the norms that shape us rather than 'overthrowing' the state as such. This 'molecular' revolution, as Deleuze and Guattari called it, would then

59 Michel Foucault, 'La société disciplinaire en crise', *Asahi Jaanaru* 19, 1978, in *Dits et Écrits II*, text no. 231, p. 533.

60 Michel Foucault, 'Les réponses du philosophe Michel Foucault', November 1975, in *Dits et Écrits I*, text no. 163, p. 1680.

61 Michel Foucault, 'Interview de Michel Foucault', June 1984, in *Dits et Écrits II*, text no. 353, p. 1509.

62 Gilles Deleuze and Claire Parnet, *Dialogues*, Paris: Flammarion, 2008, pp. 175–6.

fundamentally displace the space for politics from the figure of the sovereign to the subjects themselves.

The self was now the crucial place where we could produce not only new forms of reading, experiences and knowledge but also new ways of living the world. This is what Foucault called 'activism as a testimony of life' and in which he sees the conditions of a 'revolutionary life'.[63] And this is why, by the early 1980s, he was speaking of 'creating cultural forms', of 'inventing', for example, 'new gay lifestyles'. The 'gay culture' that seemed to fascinate him was crucial to the extent that it 'invents terms of relations, ways of life, value types, forms of exchange between individuals that are truly new, that are not stackable nor homogeneous to the general cultural forms'.[64] Only through 'the creation of new forms of life, relationships, friendships, in society, art, culture, new forms that will be established through our sexual, ethical and political choices', will it be possible to 'affirm ourselves not only as an identity, but as a creative force'.[65] This new knowledge, produced through original practices and ordeals, and these new forms of relationship, although specific to a certain group, can, however, be diffused into the social body and change it from within.

Thus, in Foucault's eyes, 'gay culture will not be simply a homosexual choice for homosexuals. This will create relationships that are, to a certain extent, transposable to heterosexuals.' It can help move sexual pleasure from 'the normative field of sexuality and its categories, thereby making pleasure the point of crystallization of a new culture'. By inventing new forms of relationships, non-homosexuals can also 'can enrich their lives by modifying their own relationships'.[66] These new forms of existence could then

63 Michel Foucault, *Le courage de la vérité*, Paris: Seuil/EHESS/Gallimard, 2009, p. 170.

64 Michel Foucault, 'Le triomphe social du plaisir sexuel: une conversation avec Michel Foucault', October 1982, in *Dits et Écrits II*, text no. 313, p. 1130.

65 Foucault, 'Michel Foucault, une interview: sexe, pouvoir et la politique de l'identité', p. 1555.

66 Ibid., p. 1130.

irrigate the whole society, ushering in a deep transformation in the way each person sees their relation to themselves and to others. Tiny transformations could, then, somehow have aggregate effects that will in the end provoke profound shifts in society. The same goes for S/M practices, which Foucault saw as creating 'new possibilities of pleasure, which we had not imagined before'. Even drugs could become sources of new and 'very intense pleasure'.[67]

Revolution now meant to invent ourselves as works of art. But a very particular kind of work of art, a work of art without an author, a work that could proliferate and constantly differ from itself. Change here has no intentional direction – as with a party-based politics – but is produced through immanent and decentralized practices. Foucault partially developed this idea through his study of the ancient care of the self as an attempt 'to bring out alternatives to the yoke of the hermeneutics of the self'.[68] This historical research is then a way, as Arnold Davidson claimed, 'to show us that a concrete alternative existed and, therefore, that nothing makes unimaginable the work of invention that will create a new alternative, by undoing our own subjectification'.[69] In a 1977 interview with Bernard-Henri Lévy, Foucault clearly linked his research to a broader political vision aimed at rethinking our relation to ourselves: 'it is a question, I do not say to rediscover, but indeed to manufacture other forms of pleasures, relations, coexistences, links, loves, intensities'.[70] In such a configuration, it is clear that antiquity becomes his laboratory in which to think about alternative forms of subject-formation.

A 'new ethic' would then promote the extension of 'the surface of possible dissidence',[71] a transformation whose aim would be to

67 Ibid., p. 1556.

68 Davidson, 'La fin de l'herméneutique de soi', p. 73.

69 Ibid.

70 Foucault, 'Non au sexe roi', p. 261; Foucault, 'End of the Monarchy of Sex', p. 218.

71 Michel Foucault, 'Préface', in M. Debard and J-L. Hennig, *Les juges kaki*, Paris: Moreau, 1977, in *Dits et Écrits II*, text no. 191, p. 140.

make subjectivities proliferate. In a sense, with '68, neither the text nor the subject had to be 'interpreted' or discovered, but rather constituted through an 'aesthetics of the existence' that would disrupt power relations. Power did not have to be taken and the subject did not have to be freed from repression but rather constituted through 'practices of freedom'. We had to get rid of, Foucault argued, 'the fundamental hypothesis of the hermeneutics of the self, which is that we must find in ourselves a profound truth that is hidden and must be deciphered as a book, an obscure book, a prophetic book, a divine book'.[72] And, for this task, ethics – understood as the relation to the self – became the crucial political task following 1968. The subject, rather than institutions, became the privileged field in which to think about politics.

This framework was essential to Foucault precisely because his understanding of politics as a form of resistance to normalization and subjectification implied a commitment to *difference* in our relationship to ourselves. Indeed, Foucault did not plea for identity, but rather for a certain form of pluralism in society and within ourselves. As he wrote, 'the relationships we have to have with ourselves are not ones of identity, rather, they must be relationships of differentiation, of creation, of innovation. To be the same is really boring.'[73] We don't need to 'discover' our 'true identity' (a form of essentialism Foucault always repudiated), but to 'refuse what we are'[74] in a certain configuration of power and knowledge in order to open up spaces for our freedom to be 'other'. In this regard, the struggles of the 1970s are fundamentally for a right to differ from oneself.

72 Foucault, *L'origine de l'herméneutique de soi*, p. 133.

73 Foucault, 'Michel Foucault, une interview: sexe, pouvoir et la politique de l'identité', p. 1558.

74 Foucault, 'Le sujet et le pouvoir', p. 1051.

Neoliberalism: a framework for pluralism

This new conception of resistance as self-invention through a critique of the state and its *assujettissement* techniques resonates with the unfolding of neoliberal governmentality, which Foucault considered to be less normative, more open to plurality and to the creation of new spaces for experimentation. The forms of power Foucault denounced are distinguished from the 'economic forms of exploitation' in that they operate on our relation to ourselves. The struggles are thus aimed at a pastoral type of power 'of religious origin', operative 'in the West since the Middle Ages', and that 'claims to conduct and direct men throughout their lives', taking charge 'of the existence of men in their detail and in their unfolding from birth until death'.[75] But, with the deployment of neoliberalism in French society, it is precisely this type of power that is challenged. It is fundamental here to understand neoliberalism as a withdrawal not from the state, but from its subjugation techniques, from the jurisdiction of morality; hence the profound connection between the deployment of neoliberalism as a form of governmentality and Foucault's defence of the invention of new subjectivities. Indeed, far from being an obstacle to such forms of resistance, neoliberalism seems to offer a less restrictive framework for the development of a more autonomous ethic.

A technology of the environment

Foucault saw neoliberalism as a form of governmentality more tolerant of minority practices. In Geoffroy de Lagasnerie's view, he

> advances that the central concept of the neoliberal approach is not that of freedom, but that of plurality . . . In other words, neoliberalism must be conceived as a meditation on multiplicity, a reflection on society which places the theme of plurality in

75 Michel Foucault, 'La philosophie analytique de la politique', p. 548.

> its centre. The specificity of this paradigm is to force us to ask what it means to live in a society made up of individuals or groups who experiment with different ways of life.[76]

In an indirect critique of the Situationists and Guy Debord, Foucault defined neoliberalism not as a society of consumption nor as a force of uniformization through discipline, but rather as a 'game of differentiations'.[77] As he claimed in his 1979 lectures, neoliberalism, as it was conceived by the Ordoliberals, 'and which has now become the program of most governments in capitalist countries, absolutely does not seek the constitution' of 'standardizing market society', but, 'on the contrary, obtaining a society that is not orientated towards the commodity and the uniformity of the commodity, but towards the multiplicity and differentiation of enterprises'.[78] It is not a society of consumers, but an 'enterprise society'. Similarly, he was careful to distinguish neoliberalism from a disciplinary society. It 'is not at all the ideal or project of an exhaustively disciplinary society in which the legal network hemming in individuals is taken over and extended internally by, let's say, normative mechanisms'.[79]

According to Foucault, American neoliberalism envisages a form of regulation that is not that of a sovereign power exercised through law or a disciplinary society with its norms, nor even that of the general standardization of a biopolitics of population. In other words, it does not involve the forms of regulation studied by Foucault prior to his 1978–79 lectures. It is not a society in which 'a mechanism of general normalization and the exclusion of those who cannot be normalized is needed', but, to the contrary, a society

76 Lagasnerie, *La dernière leçon*, p. 65.
77 Foucault, *The Birth of Biopolitics*, p. 142.
78 Ibid., p. 149.
79 Ibid., p. 259.

> in which there is an optimization of systems of difference, in which the field is left open to fluctuating processes, in which minority individuals and practices are tolerated, in which action is brought to bear on the rules of the game rather than on the players, and finally in which there is an environmental type of intervention instead of the internal subjugation of individuals.[80]

In Foucault's view, neoliberalism does not tell us how to live, how to behave; 'it is a rule of the economic game and not a purposeful economic-social control'.[81] As a 'technology of the environment', it leads to 'a massive withdrawal with regard to the normative-disciplinary system'[82] of liberal governmentality. It is not 'a standardizing, identificatory, hierarchical individualization, but an environmentalism open to unknowns and transversal phenomena'.[83] It would, however, be mistaken to suggest that Foucault has no reservations about the neoliberal project of manipulating choice through environmental interventions of the behavioural type.[84] Yet these would seem simply to be the costs – in his language, the 'dangers' – of a form of regulation that he finds has certain benefits, or 'potentials'. Chief among these potentials is that regulation no longer entails the internal 'subjectification' (*assujettissement*) of the individual. We need to attend to the French phrase translated into English as 'the internal subjugation of individuals'. *Assujettissement* has a dual meaning in Foucault's thought: it is not only subjection in the sense of 'submission to' or 'subjugation', but also entails the fabrication or production of subjectivity. This dual meaning is underlined by his use of the adjective 'internal' to emphasize not the external forms of subjugation (as the equivalent of domination) but the internal forms of subjugation as subjectification, as the fabrication of subjectivity

80 Ibid., pp. 259–60.
81 Ibid., p. 173.
82 Ibid., p. 260n.
83 Ibid., p. 261n.
84 Ibid., p. 271.

through relations of power and knowledge. Thus, Foucault here distinguished the neoliberal programme from those forms of regulation and power that subjugate individuals through the production of subjectivity, that is, through tying individuals to the 'truth' of their identity as, for example, an 'occasional criminal', a 'recidivist', a 'dangerous individual', etc. For Foucault, neoliberalism does not subjectify in this sense. Rather, it opens up a space for tolerating minority individuals and practices and optimizing systems of differences. For a thinker who had analysed in such depth a 'society of normalization', the discovery of a form of regulation that does not normalize through the fabrication of subjectivity is, as Foucault himself might have said, a colossal conclusion.

It would thus be a mistake to think, as argued by Pierre Dardot and Christian Laval,[85] that Foucault offered us an account of neoliberal practices of subjectification or of neoliberal subjectivity. Rather, what he claimed is that neoliberalism offers us a way out of subjectification, an exit from the double-bind that ties the production of who we are to our domination, the making of subjectivity to subjugation. What it offers us, in short, is a way out of the Christian hermeneutics of the self.

An anti-normative governmentality

The key aspect of this shift lies then precisely in how neoliberalism relates to the subject. On this matter, Foucault takes as his exemplar Becker's 1968 analysis of crime.[86] Becker's definition of crime will occasion, in Foucault's view, a fundamental reversal of the modern judicial system. In the modern perspective, the act was the important aspect of the crime, a crime being an act punished by the law. This definition was already a non-substantialist and

85 Pierre Dardot and Christian Laval, *The New Way of the World: On Neoliberal Society*, London: Verso, 2013.

86 Gary S. Becker, 'Crime and Punishment: An Economic Approach', *Journal of Political Economy* 76:2, 1968, pp. 169–217.

economic understanding of the crime (only the law defines it, and the one who is punished is already a *homo oeconomicus*), but the emphasis on the act will rapidly become a problem.

Indeed, the fact that the law is 'indexed to the acts which breach the law'[87] necessarily requires it to know what kind of act the crime is precisely. How to characterize it? And who is punished? In this perspective, as Foucault argued, 'the actual application of the law . . . can only be directed at an individual.'[88] This dynamic within the system leads to a 'series of slippages', making us pass from '*homo oeconomicus* to *homo legalis*, to *homo penalis*, and finally to *homo criminalis*.'[89] The utilitarian perspective has not been able to stop the 'inflation of forms and bodies of knowledge' and the slow 'psychological, sociological, and anthropological problematization of the person on whom the law is applied.'[90] The idea of the criminal is born: someone who, by his innate structure or his environment, by deviating from a norm, by his belonging to a population or a class, by his social deviation or his psychopathology, now embodies a certain identity.

> we arrived in a sense at the end of the ambiguity. *Homo legalis*, *homo penalis* is now taken up within an anthropology of crime which replaces, of course, the rigorous and very economic mechanics of the law: there is an inflation of forms and bodies of knowledge, of discourse, a multiplication of authorities and decision-making elements, and the parasitic invasion of the sentence in the name of the law by individualizing measures in the name of the norm.[91]

This is precisely the dynamic that was at stake when Foucault discussed the question of rape: the dynamic that characterizes

87 Foucault, *The Birth of Biopolitics*, p. 249.
88 Ibid., pp. 249–50.
89 Ibid., p. 250.
90 Ibid.
91 Ibid., p. 250.

certain acts (as ones of sexuality) and then finishes by characterizing certain individuals (as rapists). Starting from a specific act, one risks shaping more general subjectivities that are supposed to characterize the person in their entirety. Neoliberalism, while also part of an economic analysis of crime, offers a stimulating alternative in that it focuses attention on the subject's point of view rather than the act. According to Foucault, the strength of such an approach to crime and punishment is precisely that it works without translating economic theory into an institutional and legal form. Indeed, as Foucault notes, Becker will notoriously define crime not as an 'action condemned by the law', but rather as 'any action that makes the individual run the risk of being condemned to a penalty'.[92] The central difference here is that we are no longer observing from the point of view of the act itself, but from the 'point of view of the person who commits the crime, or who will commit the crime, while keeping the same content of the definition'.[93] In this definition, we are placed on the side of the subject and thus evade the determinations of subjectivity found in disciplines such as psychopathology or criminal anthropology. In neoliberalism, Foucault adds, we ask: 'what is the crime for him, that is to say, for the subject of an action, for the subject of a form of conduct or behavior? Well, it is whatever it is that puts him at risk of punishment.'[94]

The effect of this shift toward the subject is quite radical in the eyes of Foucault. Indeed, as he argued, by defining the crime simply as something that exposes an individual to punishment by the law there is now 'no difference between an infraction of the highway code and a premeditated murder'.[95] Therefore, and this is central, 'the criminal is not distinguished in any way by or interrogated on the basis of moral or anthropological traits. The

92 Ibid., p. 251.
93 Ibid., p. 252.
94 Ibid.
95 Ibid., p. 253

criminal is nothing other than absolutely anyone whomsoever. The criminal, any person, is treated only as anyone whomsoever who invests in an action, expects a profit from it, and who accepts the risk of a loss.'[96] As Becker argued in his influential essay, 'persons become "criminals", therefore, not because their basic motivation differs from that of other persons, but because their benefits and costs differ'.[97] Under that framework, as noted by Becker himself, a 'theory of criminal behavior can dispense with special theories of anomie, psychological inadequacies, or inheritance of special traits and simply extend the economist's usual analysis of choice'.[98]

Therefore, Foucault argued, even if Becker's theories 'move over to the side of individual subject', this 'does not involve throwing psychological knowledge or an anthropological content into the analysis'.[99] This point is essential because Foucault did not read this *homo oeconomicus* as a naturalization of the maximization of its interest. For him, the fact that we consider the subject 'only as *homo oeconomicus*' does not mean 'that the whole subject is considered as *homo oeconomicus* . . . considering the subject as *homo oeconomicus* does not imply an anthropological identification of any behavior whatsoever with economic behavior'.[100] The point is rather that the 'grid of intelligibility' that we use to explain behavior is economic but assumes very little about the subject itself. This means that 'the surface of contact between the individual and the power exercised on him, and so the principle of the regulation of power over the individual, will be only this kind of grid of *homo oeconomicus*. *Homo oeconomicus* is the interface of government and the individual. But this does not mean that every individual, every subject is an economic man.'[101]

96 Ibid.
97 Becker, 'Crime and Punishment', p. 176.
98 Ibid., p. 170.
99 Foucault, *The Birth of Biopolitics*, p. 252.
100 Ibid.
101 Ibid., pp. 252–3.

Foucault's interpretation was perfectly consistent with what Becker wrote in a 1962 article entitled 'Irrational Behavior and Economic Theory'.[102] The American economist argued that his theory does not require that the subject be rational. Indeed economic 'theory is much more compatible with irrational behaviour than had been previously suspected'.[103] The problem comes from an environment that pushes people in some directions rather than others. The objective of a neoliberal governmentality would not be to force agents to make certain decisions, but simply to create an economic environment in which an 'optimal' number of agents will be encouraged to make the expected economic choices. It is also interesting to note that in May 2012, when Becker is confronted with the lectures in which Foucault discussed his work, he will formulate his ideas in the same terms:

> What the theory of human capital says is that people – it's part of the theory of human development – people can develop themselves in various ways. They are not simply programmed to go down, in a particular way . . . Of course, how they want to develop themselves will be a function of the environment they're in, the governmental and other environments, what other people are doing. So they can develop themselves.[104]

The analysis that associates crime with a rational act from the point of view of the subject cannot therefore lead to the eradication of criminal acts. On the contrary, cost/benefit analysis aims to define the 'optimal' level of crime. Since it is no longer the act of an individual that has to be addressed, but simply the wrong incentives to such action, the only aim of economics is to optimize the environment in order to effectively reduce the incentive for crime.

102 Gary S. Becker, 'Irrational behavior and Economic Theory', *Journal of Political Economy* 70:1, 1962, pp. 1–13.

103 Ibid., p. 2.

104 Becker, Ewald and Harcourt, 'Becker on Ewald on Foucault', p. 18.

Thus, in the case of shoplifting for example, the challenge for the store is to reduce theft without spending more than the losses avoided. The store defines the amount of surveillance that reduces petty theft without making it disappear completely (which would probably cost too much). The question therefore lies in the 'optimal' value of stolen goods that the owner is willing to 'tolerate', given the exorbitant cost of a reduction beyond this percentage. This idea will be extended to many other fields by the Chicago School of economics. For example, George Stigler, who won the Nobel Prize in 1982, will elaborate models to calculate the 'optimal percentage of car accidents', while Milton Friedman, with his negative income tax, will define an 'optimal' number of people who may stay unemployed. It was this framework, which might be called the neoliberal *desubjectification* of the criminal and other social categories, that led Foucault to draw broader conclusions about the forms of power he studied in his last decade: sovereignty, discipline and biopolitics. Since power is omnipresent, Foucault's thinking did not aspire to free the individual from power, but to increase their autonomy vis-à-vis its functioning.

The negative income tax as desubjectification

From this perspective, the idea of the negative income tax was of great interest to Foucault. This proposal elaborated by Friedman in the early 1940s, which consists in guaranteeing an absolute floor of income, will seduce important figures on the Left attracted by its strong anti-normative potential, and will later become a popular proposal under various guises such as universal basic income. In contrast to a complex social security system, the negative income tax guarantees a certain level of income for everyone, regardless of their situation or behaviour. There is no conditionality or deservingness attached to it.

Of course, Friedman's approach like Becker's never made any reference to 'special theories of anomie, psychological inadequacies, or inheritance of special traits', but explained poverty and unemployment as a pure product of the welfare state and minimum wage legislation. Poverty and unemployment, in this prism, were therefore no longer the result of a personal or social pathology but rather of a rational decision in the context of the welfare state's removal of the incentive to work, or, on the employer's side, a rational decision to abjure hiring new employees because of excessively high labour costs. Attitudes toward work should not therefore be relevant when it comes to receiving the negative tax from the system; the problem was not the players but, according to Friedman, 'to adjust the rules of the game'.[105] The normative aspects of welfare were missing the point: 'it would be far better to give the indigent money and let them spend it according to their values'.[106]

Friedman's tax was designed as way to transform the structure of *incentives*, not as a method to 're-educate' the poor in any form of workfare. His approach represented a remarkable turn away from 'full employment' objectives and made it unnecessary to worry about those unable to find a job. Such citizens, he claimed, could just remain without work and live at a minimal level of existence. As Foucault noted in his 1979 comment on this proposal, the new system would allow for assistance to the 'floating' or surplus population with respect to the labour market 'in a very liberal and much less bureaucratic and disciplinary way than it is by a system focused on full employment which employs mechanisms like those of social security'.[107] The central feature of Friedman's proposal was that it made individuals 'responsible for their lives without imposing a defined anthropological model' on them,[108] and, more importantly, as Foucault added, without involving 'an

105 Milton Friedman, 'The Distribution of Income and the Welfare Activities of Government', Lecture, Wabash College, 20 June 1956, p. 7.

106 Milton Friedman, 'The Case for the Negative Income Tax: A View from the Right', *Proceedings of the National Symposium on Guaranteed Income*, 9 December 1966, p. 114.

107 Foucault, *The Birth of Biopolitics*, p. 207.

108 Pestaña, *Foucault, la gauche et la politique*, p. 122.

anthropology of work.'[109] The rules are indeed imposed on players, shaping the 'environment', but the players 'remain free in their game.'[110]

An 'intelligent use' of neoliberalism

As we have seen, Foucault found in American neoliberalism a stimulating alternative to the pastoral power that shapes our subjectivity. Neoliberalism offers a type of governmentality that is particularly attractive because of its 'non-moral' and 'non-juridical' framework that breaks with the pastoral and avowal structures inherited from Christianity and opens the space for new forms of more autonomous subjectivity. For Foucault, the crucial point about this new governmentality was that it no longer indexed the subject to a specific regime of truth, but created a framework that will allow certain forms of pluralism and autonomy in the subject's relation to itself. As Ewald notes, Foucault's challenge is to find a form of governmentality that will 'be free from morality and from the law'. Neoliberalism's birth in Giscard's France of the mid-1970s is, then, a specific moment that opens a space in which to question the long history of the self in the Western world. The specific place mid-1970s France had in Foucault's genealogy of the subject, alongside the inspiration offered by California, can then be understood within his more general analysis of neoliberalism as a form of governmentality. Here, Gary Becker was, for Foucault, 'a moment in the very long story of truth-telling', a moment of 'a truth-telling free from a moral and juridical framework',[111] freed from the inquiry (*enquête*).

---

109 Foucault, *The Birth of Biopolitics*, p. 252.

110 Ibid., p. 174.

111 Ewald, in Becker, Ewald and Harcourt, 'Becker on Ewald on Foucault', p. 5.

Of course, none of this represents an alternative to power since, for Foucault, power is omnipresent. It is not a question of trying to free oneself from *all* types of power, but of finding an alternative solution to *particular types* of power and regulation. The important thing in the case of neoliberalism is that, unlike in disciplinary forms of power, it is not formed by 'decisions which someone takes for others' but by 'a set of rules which determine the way each must play a game whose outcome is not known by anyone'.[112] As noted by José Luis Moreno Pestaña, Foucault believed that 'neoliberalism does not project its models on the individual: they have no performative effect and do not project any form of normality; they are only part of a framework of comprehensibility for understanding the behavior of the subject'.[113] 'Behind what may seem at first sight to be the most frightening commercial cynicism', philosopher Isabelle Garo adds, 'lies a real critical power, which Foucault does not miss: criticism of any essentialization of feelings and behaviours, from the maternal nature to the Eternal feminine, critical of any eternity of norms at the same time. No other approach to human behaviour offers such an a-moralistic, Nietzschean, or de-anthropologizing perspective of genuine explosive power.'[114] In the eyes of Foucault, neoliberalism proceeds to an 'anthropological erasure (*gommage anthropologique*)' in its understanding of human actions.[115]

As Audier points out, it was quite clear to Foucault that neoliberalism was a new form of governmentality that, while in many ways no better than others, nonetheless 'offered margins of freedom, especially for minority practices – drugs, sex, refusal to work, etc'. Therefore, 'this apparent ambiguity of Foucault's relation to neoliberalism offers a landmark in the way he tried to reinvent subjectivity, sexuality and even welfare by crossing and surpassing

112 Foucault, *The Birth of Biopolitics*, p. 173.
113 Pestaña, *Foucault, la gauche et la politique*, p. 122.
114 Garo, *Foucault, Deleuze, Althusser & Marx*, p. 175.
115 Foucault, *The Birth of Biopolitics*, p. 259; *Naissance de la biopolitique*, p. 264.

neoliberalism, in short by metabolizing it, but certainly not by rejecting it as an opponent from which there would be nothing to learn and integrate'. In short, Audier concludes, an 'intelligent use' of neoliberalism was both possible and perhaps necessary.[116]

May '68 and the end of the Revolution with a capital 'R' marked the death, in Foucault's words, of two kinds of sovereignty: first, the old model of textual interpretation; second, a conception of social transformation centred on the state. In both cases Foucault marked this death by making the subject's experimentation with new ways of constituting the self the centre of his attention. The displacement of the question of meaning to the subject's experience is deeply connected to the displacement of the question of seizing power in favour of inventing new forms of culture and lifestyles.[117] The experimentations the subject could undertake with a text or with new forms of existence were to become the starting point for what Julian Bourg calls the 'ethical turn' that would, in less than a decade, profoundly transform the notion of revolution itself in French thought.[118] The question of the model of society is then replaced by the question of how we should live in society. In other words, Foucault offered us 'an art', a 'lifestyle, a way of thinking and living', rather than a political strategy. This 'molecular' revolution would then fundamentally displace the space of politics from the figure of the sovereign to the subjects themselves. In other words, ethics had now become Foucault's main framework for the understanding of politics.

This complete redefinition of politics in terms of subjectivity must, however, be seen as a starting point for the production of a neoliberal Left more committed to equal opportunity and the

116 Audier, 'Quand Foucault découvre le néolibéralisme'.

117 On this see especially Walter Benn Michaels, *The Shape of the Signifier*, Princeton: Princeton University Press, 2004.

118 Bourg, *From Revolution to Ethics: May '68 and Contemporary French Thought*, p. 4.

respect of difference than to abolishing the exploitation of humans by other humans. 'Don't forget to invent your life', Foucault concluded in the early 1980s. Doesn't this sound familiar to Gary Becker's injunction that we should not forget to be entrepreneurs of ourselves? This turn would have ambivalent political outcomes in the years following Foucault's death in June 1984. Indeed, by explicitly elevating the 'relation to the self' to the 'first and ultimate' point of 'resistance to political power',[119] Foucault somehow paradoxically reduced the scope of critical theory despite his claim to be its heir. His reshaping of 'critique' as the promotion of the experimentation of new lifestyles often sidelined politics conducted through parties, trade unions, strikes or even governmental action. If the May '68 slogan 'everything is political' made it possible to interrogate a broad array of power relations that had previously been invisible, it also went along with a retreat from collective action. As the big macroeconomic variables became increasingly inaccessible, a retreat into the relationship with the self, or the transformation of language, made a virtue of necessity, one in which a 'happening' in a chic art gallery could be branded as a subversion of social order.

Ironically, this very focus on the 'micropolitics' of everyday life put out of reach the very economic institutions that shaped the framework under which the actuality of 'everyday' life would be lived. Faced with the accelerating neoliberal revolution this new concept of social transformation appeared unable to face the challenge of exploitation – a notion that Foucault himself thought had become irrelevant – which was now taking on a global dimension. Indeed, Claude Lefort has argued that, rather than expanding the political, Foucault's theory 'pulverized the social' by its 'elusion' of the role and the importance of institutions like 'the state' or

119 Michel Foucault, *L'herméneutique du sujet*, Paris: Gallimard/Seuil, 2001, p. 241. Foucault will, however, nuance this view a few years later in 'L'éthique du souci de soi', pp. 1547–8. There, the relation of oneself to oneself is fundamental to the exercise of and resistance to power understood as 'governmentality' but not necessarily to power as 'domination'.

'classes'.[120] However, with his assumption that capitalism and power rested on a wide array of micro-powers operating at the level of sexual relations, schooling, family structures, expertise, science, and so on, Foucault implicitly thought that we could subvert the social order by acting at this microlevel, that is, in 'daily life'. Through the styling of one's existence and the creation of spaces of experimentation it was, he thought, possible to transform the whole social edifice from within. The idea was that capitalism, by its very nature, is connected to certain forms of social and cultural organization: that to reproduce itself, it needs, for example, a patriarchal family structure. But history has instead shown that, while capitalism *can* mobilize such structures, it is also quite capable of accommodating, even promoting, other ways of life or family structures, turning them into excellent markets to be conquered. In fact, the decentralized 'molecular revolution' model appeared to be rather inefficient when applied to the field of economic relations. Even more disturbingly, the idea that change had to be thought in terms of the aggregation of individual decisions had a rather surprising resonance with the rising paradigm of the sovereign consumer. As the aggregation of capital reached a level unprecedented in human history, going beyond even Marx's expectations, the molecular revolution appeared more as the sign of a historical defeat than as a new concept of revolution. *Who we are?* became the key question for a generation of theorists, replacing the traditional socialist question *what do we own?*

120 Claude Lefort, 'Maintenant', in *Le temps présent*, Paris: Belin, 2007, p. 285.

6

Foucault's Normativity

> It is clear, even if one admits that Marx will disappear for now, that he will reappear one day.
>
> Michel Foucault, 1983[1]

The general question of the normativity of Foucault's work was raised long ago by thinkers such as Nancy Fraser and Jürgen Habermas.[2] They were right to raise such concerns, particularly given the largely decontextualized reception of Foucault internationally during the 1980s. Today, however, it is possible to say that Foucault's legacy is neither that of a 'young conservative', practising a total rejection of modernity, nor particularly 'normatively confused'. As we have argued, his positions were bound up with

1 Michel Foucault, 'Critical Theory/Intellectual History', in *Politics, Philosophy, Culture: Interviews and Other Writings 1977–1984*, ed. Lawrence D. Kritzman, New York: Routledge, 1988, p. 45.

2 Nancy Fraser, *Unruly Practices: Power, Discourse and Gender in Contemporary Social Theory*, Minneapolis: University of Minnesota Press, 1989; Jürgen Habermas, *The New Conservativism: Cultural Criticism and the Historians' Debate*, Cambridge: Polity Press, 1989.

those of a new and emergent centre-left that would come to link a certain kind of transformational politics with experiments in neoliberal technologies of government. Foucault was very clear about where he stood in relation to totalitarianism, communist and Marxist politics, and the modes of subjectification inherited by the experts of the welfare state from the mainstream of what he conceived of as Western Christian culture.

If we were to add to this debate it would be to say that Foucault engaged with different types of normativity. His 'genealogies' resisted taking explicit stances on the material they analysed, but exemplified or performed their normativity by showing how what is given or taken for granted need not be the case, and using diverse examples as resources to conceive of new and different possibilities. We might call this a kind of exemplary normativity.[3] But this did not stop Foucault from also taking direct political stances and making specific recommendations on law and policy, or on where we should stand in relation to specific events, political ideologies or organizational forms. This chapter returns to a number of the characteristic stances and attitudes that constituted the 'style of thought' Foucault embraced in his final decade, and from which emerged the political and social orientations of his intellectual legacy. We start with his writings and interviews concerning legislation on sexuality and morality because they attest both to exemplary normativity and to direct normative political and policy stances.

Sexuality and morality

In his memoir, Edmund White, who was a close friend of Foucault, recalls an incident after the latter had just given a talk at New York

3 Compare David Owen, 'Genealogy as Exemplary Critique: Reflections on Foucault and the Imagination of the Political', *Economy and Society* 24:4, 1995, pp. 489–506.

University in the early 1980s. The lecture was on late pagan and early Christian sexual ethics. When pressed as to the relation of this analysis to the present, White recalls, Foucault stormed out of the room in a rage. But White does not neglect to explain why this question mattered to members of the gay community: 'if we were hanging on every word surely we did so because we wanted to know exactly where our culture had gone wrong. We wanted to return to the golden, nuanced liberality of paganism. Foucault knew this – privately, as it were – but for methodological reasons, if nothing else, he wanted to limit his claims to contemporary relevance.'[4]

It is true that Foucault himself regularly denied that any explicit normative conclusions could be drawn from his history of sexuality. When asked at Berkeley in 1983 whether classical Greece constituted a Golden Age he replied: 'I think there is no exemplary value in a period which is not our period . . . it is not anything to get back to.'[5] However, he immediately added: 'But we do have an example of an ethical experience which implied a very strong connection between pleasure and desire.' The seminar White refers to might have been the one Foucault conducted with Richard Sennett at the Institute of Humanities, in which he presented material from the not yet published *Les aveux de la chair*, and which led to the article, 'Sexuality and Solitude', first published in the *London Review of Books*. Here Foucault posed a direct equivalence between Christianity as a dogma, with its hermeneutics of the text, in which there is 'the obligation to hold certain books as a permanent source of truth', and Christianity as a 'confession', with its hermeneutics of the subject. In this article, Foucault makes it plain that it is Christianity as a 'confession' that bequeaths to the modern subject 'the duty to explore who he is, what is happening

4 See Michael Behrent, 'Review, Michel Foucault, *Histoire de la sexualité, vol. 4, Les Aveux de la chair*', *H-France Review* 20:23, 2020, p. 10. See Edmund White, *My Lives: A Memoir*, New York: Harper Perennial, 2007, p. 196.

5 Michel Foucault, 'On the Genealogy of Ethics: An Overview of Work in Progress', in *The Foucault Reader*, p. 347.

within himself, the faults he may have committed, the temptations to which he is exposed'.[6] It is from Christianity that this subject inherited the obligation 'to tell these things to other people, and thus to bear witness against himself'.

In this article, the key thing about the hermeneutics of the self is that it is constituted by a dual operation. On the one hand, we must tell the truth about ourselves; on the other, we must renounce ourselves. 'That is what we would call the spiral of truth formulation and reality renouncement which is at the heart of the Christian techniques of the self'.[7] And central to this renunciation of the self in Christianity is the notion of the 'flesh'. While that notion was discussed in the first volume of the *History of Sexuality*, its centrality is underscored by it constituting the main topic of the fourth volume. The 'flesh' is the locus of temptations and impure thoughts and so constitutes the foundation of sinfulness and wickedness and humankind's revolt against God. As Foucault put it in summary form, the flesh becomes the 'ethical substance' for Christians, in contrast to the pleasures, or *aphrodisia*, of the Greeks, and sexuality for we moderns.[8]

In 'Sexuality and Solitude', as in *Les aveux de la chair*, Foucault illustrated this transition from the Greeks' concern with the use of pleasures in relations to others (boys, women, slaves) to the Christian preoccupation with the flesh. He did this through a reading of Augustine's ruminations on the action of the sexual organs. While Augustine admitted that sexual relations occurred in Paradise before the Fall, every part of Adam's body 'was perfectly obedient to the soul and the will'.[9] With the Fall, when Adam wanted to escape God's will and gain his own, he lost control of himself and particularly over his sexual organs. When Adam covered his genitals, it was not because he was ashamed of them

6 Michel Foucault, 'Sexuality and Solitude', in *Ethics, Subjectivity and Truth*, p. 178.

7 Ibid.

8 Foucault, 'On the Genealogy of Ethics', p. 353.

9 Foucault, 'Sexuality and Solitude', p. 181; *Les aveux de la chair*, p. 175.

but because of 'the fact his sexual organs were moving by themselves without his consent'.

The difference between Greek and Christian sexual ethics then can be summarized quite simply: 'Sex in erection is the image of man revolted against God.'[10] Using Artemidorus as his foil, Foucault argued that, while both the Greeks and the Christians are dominated by the theme and form of male or 'phallic sexuality', for the latter 'the main question is not . . . the problem of penetration – it is the problem of erection. As a result, it is not the problem of a relationship to other people but the problem of the relationship of oneself to oneself, or, more precisely the relationship between one's will and involuntary assertions.'[11]

In the fourth volume of his history, Foucault argued that sex is to man what man is to God – a 'rebel'. 'Man's man, erected before him and against him.'[12] Linking this vision of sexuality to psychoanalysis, Foucault noted that Augustine called the principle of the autonomous movements of sexual organs *libido*. The erection of the penis is thus at the heart of the Christian ethic of the flesh, of a conception of an ethical substance to be worked on that rebels against the subject's will. It thus leads us to a 'spiritual struggle' that consists not, as with Plato, in turning upwards toward eternity but 'in turning our eyes continuously downward or inward in order to decipher, among the movements of the soul, which ones come from the libido.'[13]

It is difficult to read the final section of *The Use of Pleasure* on 'True Love', or the love of boys, without viewing it as an exploration of a playful and careful use of pleasure without subjectification, however delayed and restricted the consummation of a relationship between the man and the boy might be in courtship rituals subject to different 'forms of austerity'.[14] It would seem,

10 Foucault, 'Sexuality and Solitude', p. 181.
11 Ibid., p. 182.
12 Foucault, *Les aveux de la chair*, p. 336.
13 Foucault, 'Sexuality and Solitude', p. 182.
14 Foucault, *The Use of Pleasure*, p. 249.

indeed, that pleasure was intensified due to the cautious way advances could be made, the restrictions on what could be done including in the giving of gifts, and the risk of disapprobation for the 'passive' boy who would one day assume the role of the 'active' free citizen. In these ethics, Foucault must have noticed something similar to the 'economy of acts and pleasures' between males he experienced in Islamic societies in Tunisia and later in Iran. And even if he would say, of the Greek ethos of virility and the obsession with penetration, that 'all that is quite disgusting',[15] there was still something to learn from a practice and ethos so clearly different from the psychosocial discourses on homosexuality he criticized, or the gay liberation project of 'coming out', of which he was suspicious lest it become a renewed public confession of one's inner truth.

Nonetheless, this practice of the love of boys was productive of something quite different from the Christian sinful individual. 'In broad terms, what is important to grasp here is not why the Greeks had a fondness for boys but why they had a "pederasty"; that is, why they elaborated a courtship practice, a moral reflection and – as we shall see – a philosophical asceticism, around that fondness.'[16] This 'aesthetics of existence'[17] would seem far superior to the onanistic ethics of the subject bequeathed by Christianity in which the subject is controlled by a desire it must renounce. The hermeneutics of the self is ultimately constituted by a this-worldly asceticism that finds sexual and bodily pleasures repugnant and dangerous and constitutes the truth of the subject through the experience of abhorrence. Now, as Foucault concluded, 'the main question of sexual ethics has

15 Foucault, 'On the Genealogy of Ethics', p. 346. Curiously, Foucault does not seem to offer any evidence of an 'obsession with penetration' in the four volumes of the history of sexuality, apart from the analysis of sexual dreams by Artemidorus in his second century CE text, *The Interpretation of Dreams*. See Michel Foucault, *The History of Sexuality, vol. 3: The Care of the Self*, trans. Robert Hurley, London: Allen Lane, 1986, pp. 29–34.

16 Foucault, *The Use of Pleasure*, p. 214.

17 Ibid., p. 253.

moved from relations to people, and from the penetration model to the relation to oneself and to the erection problem'.[18] However neutral a posture Foucault might have liked to maintain in relation to his historical material, he could not refrain from remarking that for the Greeks this 'masturbation problem' was largely ignored or neglected, 'a thing for slaves and for satyrs, but not for free citizens'. We leave aside the implications of his use of this phallocentric example here, but note that Foucault devoted scant attention to ancient writings on lesbianism and, for some commentators, never managed to integrate his account of the general subordination of women and the ethics of the 'true love' of boys in Greek society in a coherent and systematic way.[19]

What Foucault took from the Greeks was not so much a specific pagan ethics or even a model of contemporary conduct but the possibility of ethics as leading to an 'aesthetics of existence', or what he called elsewhere a 'way of life'. As he put it in an interview with the magazine, *Gai Pied*:

> A way of life can be shared among individuals of different age, status, and social activity. It can yield intense relations not resembling those that are institutionalized. It seems to me that a way of life can yield a culture and an ethics. To be 'gay', I think, is not to identify with the psychological traits and the visible masks of the homosexual but to try to define and develop a way of life.[20]

For Foucault, this way of life runs counter to certain discourses associated with the liberation movements of the 1960s which, in many ways, represent the peak of the hermeneutics of the self as an overcoming of repression and a verbalizing of the truth about the

18 Foucault, 'Sexuality and Solitude', p. 183.

19 Afary and Anderson, *Foucault and the Iranian Revolution*, p. 145.

20 Michel Foucault, 'Friendship as a Way of Life', in *Ethics, Subjectivity and Truth*, p. 138.

self. In contrast, here it is not a question of liberating the self, but of creating a 'new mode of life' that, at least, uses the ancient 'aesthetics of existence' as a point of reference, an exemplar rather than a model.[21] This is much more than a question of individual rights; it is about how many kinds of relations can exist outside of conventional marriage, relations that 'should be able to find their codes not in institutions but in possible support'.[22] It was precisely the possibility of the emergence of these new experimental ways of life and the retraction of the juridical regulation of relations that Foucault found in the anti-repressive measures concerning sexual morality enacted by the 'advanced liberalism' of Giscard's France.

Foucault's explicit position on matters of sexual morality was thus twofold. On the one hand, he supported 'the overall movement tending to liberalism', such as became possible under the Commission on Penal Law, even if he feared a 'disturbing movement' in the opposite direction.[23] In this sense, his positions were consistent, reflecting what might be called a radical libertarian stance. We have mentioned already his views on expunging sexuality from the law on rape and on paedophilia. After a discussion about a child's ability to express their feelings about sexual relations, he would also insist that 'an age barrier laid down by law does not have much sense'.[24] In general, Foucault sought to remove 'sexuality' from juridical and penal codes, and to seek punishment for only the coercive and violent aspects of it.

On the other hand, sexuality has become a 'mode of life'. As for the reader or writer of a text, or the participant or spectator in a revolution, sexuality is about creation, invention and experimentation. As he said in an interview with *The Advocate* in 1982: 'We

---

21 Michel Foucault, 'Social Triumph of the Sexual Will', in *Ethics, Subjectivity and Truth*, p. 158.

22 Ibid.

23 Michel Foucault, 'Sexual Morality and the Law', in *Politics, Philosophy, Culture: Interviews and Other Writings 1977–1984*, ed. Lawrence D. Kritzman, New York: Routledge, 1988, p. 272.

24 Ibid., p. 284.

have to understand that with our desires, through our desires, go new forms of relationships, new forms of love, new forms of creation. Sex is not a fatality: it's a possibility for creative life.'[25] This twofold relation to sexual morality that takes a position against juridical regulation, and removes sexuality from the field of scientific knowledge in order for it to become a form of self-creation, would seem intimately connected to what Foucault claimed to have found in ancient sexual ethics.

While many of Foucault's specific proposals were clearly of the time, and he might not have supported them today, it would seem that it is precisely this constellation of values that is clearly reflected in his analysis of sexuality in ancient times. As Afary and Anderson have pointed out, it is strange that a thinker so focused on technologies of power with minute articulations on the body would fail to analyse the class, ethnic and gender subtexts of male–male sexual relations in Greece that appear in the work of other scholars, including that of Kenneth J. Dover's *Greek Homosexuality*, an important influence on Foucault.[26] Nor, they continue, did he appreciate the inequality between the two male partners in same-sex relations in the ancient world, or the degree to which such relationships were subject to detailed juridical structures and involved complex economic dimensions between an aristocratic man (*erastes*), with the time and resources to pursue and cultivate a relationship, and his object of affection (the *paidika*). Moreover, the *paidika* had to be careful not to be reproached by his friends of his own age, or, worse, to accept gifts that might lead him to be accused of 'prostitution'. Indeed, the boy's father, if wealthy enough, would often employ slaves 'to watch the boy like a hawk'.[27] As Afary and Anderson conclude: 'How is it that Foucault never critiqued or questioned the

25 Michel Foucault, 'Sex, Power and the Politics of Identity', in *Ethics, Subjectivity and Truth: The Essential Works*, vol. 1, ed. Paul Rabinow, New York: The New Press, 1997 p. 163.

26 Afary and Anderson, *Foucault and the Iranian Revolution*, pp. 146–51.

27 Ibid., p. 148.

difference in power in these relations and instead celebrated the point of view of the erastes?'[28]

While Foucault's intellectual and political positions remain to some degree idiosyncratic, it is not entirely incorrect to propose that he sought to encourage a shift from what he held to be a now out-of-date class politics, focused on the juridical order of state, to one of radical self-creation within what we can broadly call 'identity politics', focused on everyday life issues of sexuality, friendship, family relations, and so on. But there is a double problem with regard to his formulations of this shift, which not only sidelined class politics but also disabled what has come to be called identity politics. First, there was the evident downplaying of the significance of struggles around class, exploitation and inequality conducted in relation to and against the juridical order of the state. But, second, many of the key achievements of the post-'70s movements of sexual liberation have been within this juridical order: banning discrimination according to gender or sexuality; making mutual consent between partners the basis of legitimate sexual relations; decriminalizing homosexual acts; and the public recognition of same-sex relations in marriage equality. By limiting sexual ethics to the domain of the ordeal and of experimentation outside of law and institutions, Foucault condemned these movements to a sterile cultural and lifestyle politics that risked silencing the subordinate group and ignoring the hypocrisy and double standards of the dominant one that he had observed in ancient male-to-male sexual relations. Whether with respect to class exploitation, or in relation to his own favoured domain of personal relations, Foucault's framework would appear to have compromised his capacity to address questions of inequality.

28 Ibid., p. 155.

The revolution

Let us follow the trajectory of Foucault's thinking about revolution – for there is one more step in its evolution. We have seen that he announced the end of the European concept of revolution that commenced with the French Revolution. He sought to displace the conceptual structure of the revolution/state couple with his analyses of power, as Ewald observed.[29] More normatively, he wrote in the context of the anti-totalitarian current in French thought that located the problem with Marxism and socialism not in any particularly historical instance, such as Stalinism, but in the desire for revolution itself. This desire was, for Foucault, ultimately conservative, as it acclimated and codified uprisings and resistances. The end of the revolution had implications for Foucault's own disposition toward the emergent neoliberal centre-left formation of the Second Left and his rejection of political formations such as the Union of the Left.

In his diagnoses of contemporary events, he came to understand both May '68 and the Iranian uprising in 1978 in terms of the end of the revolution. Both were, ultimately, struggles around subjectivity, and had their first and final bases in resistance as a relation of self to self: the former in the experimentations with and movements of everyday life; the latter in the renewal of the ordeals, sacrifices and liturgies of a political spirituality now lost in the West.

With the benefit of these reflections, it is of little surprise that, in what turned out to be his final lectures, Foucault returned to and in a sense completed his thinking about the revolution. Here, in a discussion of the descendants of ancient Cynicism, he turned to the question of militancy and the revolutionary life in modern Europe. He began by noting and quickly passing over two organizational versions of that life: the secret society and the established

29 François Ewald, 'Foucault and the Contemporary Scene', *Philosophy and Social Criticism* 25:3, 1999, 81–91.

political party or institution, established respectively in the first and final decades of the nineteenth century. What he was most interested in was 'the style of existence specific to revolutionary militancy',[30] which he tries to link to Cynic notions of the 'other life' and of the scandalous life. 'The resurgence of leftism as a permanent tendency', he argued, 'has always taken place not by basing itself on the organizational dimension, but on the dimensions of militantism comprising secret sociality or style of life, and sometimes in the paradox of a secret sociality which manifests itself and makes itself visible in scandalous forms of life.'[31]

He also observed that this scandalous life became inverted in France, particularly since the 1920s and in the French Communist Party. The 'scandal of the revolutionary life' was now inverted in the conformism of the institutional structures of the PCF, with its model of 'accepted values, customary behaviour, and traditional schemas of conduct, as opposed to bourgeois decadence or leftist madness'.[32] What is important about these comments is not the chagrin directed at the Communist Party but the fact that what intrigued Foucault about revolutionary politics was not its organization or goals but its existence as a way of life. So, a kind of circle is indeed completed here. Not only do movements concerning the transformations of subjectivity in everyday life render the old concept of revolution obsolete and totalitarian, but revolutionary movements themselves should be judged according to the very lifestyles they adopt, and whether they choose to be scandalous or conformist, decadent or morally upright. Whether it was the student militant groups in Tunisia or the French ultra-Maoist group 'Gauche Prolétarienne', what Foucault enjoyed in these revolutionary groups was always more the way they engaged their whole existence and body in the struggle rather than their politics

30 Michel Foucault, *The Courage of Truth: Lectures at the Collège de France 1983–1984*, trans. Graham Burchell, London: Palgrave Macmillan, 2011, p. 184.

31 Ibid., p. 185.

32 Ibid., p. 186.

per se. It was how, as James Miller astutely observed, they transformed politics into a 'limit-experience'.

Neither were the lessons of the ordeal forgotten here. If militancy is a 'bearing witness to the true life by one's life itself',[33] then it too can become sacrificial, even of one's own life. Nihilism, anarchism and terrorism become 'a practice of life taken to the point of dying for truth . . . of making the truth burst out to the point of losing one's life or causing the blood of others to flow'.[34] Not only is the revolution at an end but it can be seen for what it always was, a lifestyle and the choice of a lifestyle. Faced with the alternative between a normativity based on the attempt to combat fundamental inequality through revolutionary organization, or one that celebrated a scandalous lifestyle and the enthusiasm of the spectator, Foucault invariably displayed a preference for the latter consistent with his own anti-institutional politics of everyday life.

Inequality and neoliberal governmentality

Still, it remains strange that Foucault had so little to say, even in his discussions of economics, about inequality. On one of the few occasions he addressed the issue, it was to elucidate the Ordoliberals' rejection of social policy as a 'counterpoint' to the way in which the economy generates inequality.[35] He attributed a quotation, which his editors are unable to verify, to the Ordoliberal economist, Wilhelm Röpke: 'Inequality is the same for all.'[36] For the Ordoliberals, this enigmatic formula means that the inequality the economic game creates 'is a kind of general regulator of society that everyone has to accept and abide by'. For them, the point of social policy is not equalization but 'merely ensuring a vital

33 Ibid., p. 184.
34 Ibid., p. 185.
35 Foucault, *The Birth of Biopolitics*, pp. 142–3.
36 Ibid., p. 143.

minimum'. The problem of social policy is not equality but poverty. As the French civil servant and *polytechnicien* Lionel Stoléru put it, the problem is not the *causes* of poverty but its *effects*, or, in Foucault's formulation, not *relative* but *absolute* poverty, even if one recognizes that the latter is defined in relation to a particular society.[37] It was here, as we have seen, that Foucault became fascinated by the aims of a negative tax system that could secure, in Milton Friedman's words, 'a floor below which no man's income . . . could fall',[38] and make possible an environmental regulation outside the sovereign, biopolitical and disciplinary dispositives.

In these remarks, Foucault's diagnosis of his present gives a remarkable centrality to neoliberalism's aims in social policy and to its problematization of the welfare state. Perhaps the main reason he would say so little about inequality is that he associated redistribution with the disciplinary and pastoral regime of subjectification (*assujettissement*) he found in the welfare state and with the politics of communist and conventional socialist parties. Today, however, we are no longer seeking to replace this regime of *assujettissement*, which would dominate through the construction of subjectivities, with the more open spaces of self-governing. Nor is our central concern how the fight against inequality creates dependency in a system of social rights. Rather we are witnessing a problematization of the so-called 'welfare reform' initiated by a neoliberal governmentality more generally, and the consequent abandonment to 'precarity' of greater sections of the population. Furthermore, it is not the mainstream Left that is raising these issues but, at least in France, a movement that has much in common with a form of resistance to power that Foucault would have clearly recognized.

There is no doubt that questions of inequality, redistribution and social justice have been raised with a vengeance by the *gilets*

37 Ibid., pp. 204–6.

38 Friedman, Quoted in Austin C. Wehrwein, 'Economist Says Negative Tax Should Replace All Poverty Aid', *New York Times*, 16 December 1965.

jaunes in France from late 2018. In many ways, they remind us of Foucault's plebeian resistances: they are without apparent leaders, of a heterogeneous social composition, and politically polyvalent; an unruly and in some degree violent assemblage emerging first around a single issue (fuel prices and taxes) and connected as a network, this time made possible by the realm of the virtual. Their polyvalence opened up the possibility that different forces and authorities, for all kinds of political reasons, would recode their actions as ignoring climate change or as examples of contemporary xenophobia. Yet, as more than one commentator notes, the key to their agenda is 'social justice and democratic renewal', while their 'discourse . . . displaces the social question from the traditional focus on poverty to a more explosive discussion of inequality'.[39]

Their protests thus stand at the limit of a liberal or neoliberal governmentality, and the French government's response has accordingly been an odd mixture. On the one hand, there is the kind of hyper-governmentality of Emmanuel Macron's 'great national debate', a kind of excess of consultation, of meetings, assemblies and online platforms, which nevertheless failed to mention the key issue of a solidarity tax on wealth but included the populist consideration of quotas on immigration.[40] This is in response to an irreversible crisis of liberal governmentality. As Étienne Balibar put it quickly, paraphrasing Lenin: 'the crisis is irreversible when those from above can no longer govern as before, and those from below no longer want to be governed as before.'[41]

On the other hand, we discover all the faces of sovereignty. There is the theological face: in line with Macron's 'Jupiterian' approach to governing, there are no intermediate associations,

39 Didier Fassin and Anne-Claire Defossez, 'An Improbable Movement? Macron's France and the Rise of the Gilets Jaunes', *New Left Review* 115, 2019, p. 84.

40 Jeremy Harding, 'Among the *Gilets Jaunes*', *London Review of Books*, 21 March 2019, p. 8.

41 Étienne Balibar, 'Les gilets jaunes: le sens du face à face', Mediapart, 13 December 2018.

trade unions or even political parties, but only the unmediated relation of the transcendent sovereign and the people, something similar to what Foucault observed in the relation between Khomeini and the Iranians.[42] This revival of a sovereigntist relation appears in the depositions lodged at town halls known as 'cahiers de doléances', reviving the testimonies of the three estates initiated by Louis XVI in 1789. But there is also the emergency face: the use of force without restraint against protestors as if their actions amounted to a civil war. Every tear-gas projectile and rubber bullet, and every injury caused by them, to the eyes, hands, faces and bodies of the protesters, attests to the failure of the imposition of a neoliberal governmentality.

But, descending from the Jupiterian heights and from the political perplexity of the *gilets jaunes*, we can find something like an intelligible trade-union politics in France during the strikes of Christmas and New Year 2019–20. Here, far from the end of conventional politics envisaged by Foucault, we witnessed a classic confrontation pitching the trade unions against Macron's attempt to transform the French pension system. The General Confederation of Workers (CGT) would even invoke the ideals of the French Revolution when opposing the neoliberal slogan 'you make out [*sic*] for yourself': 'With us, it's all about solidarity: liberty, equality, fraternity.'[43] The general secretary of the CGT, Philippe Martinez, made clear what was at stake on French television: 'It's a choice of society that's at the heart of this reform.' Meanwhile, it is noteworthy that the CFDT, Foucault's favoured trade-union interlocutors, continued to work on a compromise with the government, suggesting, perhaps, that the search for a left governmentality is still alive. Interestingly, the same opposition between the CGT and the CFDT characterized the 2016 reform to

42 Harding, 'Among the *Gilets Jaunes*', p. 3; Fassin and Defossez, 'An Improbable Movement?', p. 82.

43 Adam Nossiter, 'At the Heart of France's Long Strikes, a Fight Between the Haves and the Have-nots', *New York Times*, 9 January 2020.

revise France's Labour Code to make it easier for companies to lay off workers. As the government faced the most significant social unrest of the Hollande presidency, the prime minister, Manuel Valls, was forced to pass the bill without a vote in the parliament. During the conflict, François Ewald would condemn the CGT's 'immobilism' and the French 'nostalgia for the revolutionary gesture'. To Ewald, it was clear that the strikes against the reform were 'condemned to failure' because 'we can't stop history'. The CFDT on the other hand, in being willing to negotiate with the government, had understood, Ewald added, the 'inevitability' of this legislative 'modernization'.[44] It is difficult to pretend that these positions were anything but consequences of the project Foucault initiated four decades earlier.

Given this kind of evidence, however, an end of politics, and a banishment of the revolution from the horizon of the politics, has clearly not occurred in France itself. And politics, in the mundane form of the conflict between classes, between classes and the state, and the factional rivalry of different political actors, simply continues, no matter the number of intellectual pronouncements of its death or how many times it has been theoretically displaced. Our point is not to offer a definitive diagnosis of events still ongoing at the time of writing but to suggest that these events reveal the poverty of key themes in the Foucauldian legacy. Its claims about an end of politics, the displacement of the discourse of sovereignty by neoliberal techniques of government, and the relation to self as the most significant contemporary form of resistance, are not only out of touch with the concerns of today but have perhaps contributed to our intellectual predicament and the political mess that those societies once called 'liberal democracies' find themselves in.

Consequently, if Foucault remains enormously influential at the theoretical end of the humanities and social sciences, perhaps his influence is changing in form. We might have finished with David

44 François Ewald, 'La loi travail et les mythes français', *Les Échos*, 6 June 2016, p. 12.

Halperin's (ironic or not) 'Saint Foucault'[45] who could do no wrong, who mysteriously appeared as the American 'grad-school' icon on the correct side of every political debate, and who represented, as Sartre put it regarding Marxism, the 'unsurpassable horizon' of a certain critical and radical thought. We are moving to a much more detailed understanding of how Foucault acted in and responded to the world in which he lived, and of the strengths and the downsides of his experimental ethos. For a multitude of important thinkers, he has become the starting point, not the endpoint, for getting to grips with the problems of our present. Foucault's engagement with forms of economic liberalism, and his triple affirmation, however qualified, of the ideals, policies and positions associated with different aspects of neoliberalism, were important moments in his work and marked a fundamental shift in its trajectory. This does not mean that Foucault was a card-carrying member of the 'Neoliberal Thought Collective', that he uncritically endorsed neoliberalism, or that the entirety or essence of his work is tainted by it. Nor does it mean that the use of his work necessarily carries the assumptions of neoliberalism with it. We must, however, grasp his relationship with neoliberalism in its own context and interrogate the repercussions of it for our present.

This interrogation can take as a starting point three elements that circumscribe Foucault's relationship to neoliberalism and its relevance to our present: the programmatic claims of neoliberalism; the diagnosis it offers of society and its consequent policy prescriptions; and its concrete political manifestations. First, as we have seen in relation to the question of subjectivity, Foucault found certain features in the ideal or programmatic form of the neoliberalism of the Chicago School attractive, in particular that it envisages a kind of regulation outside sovereign, disciplinary and biopolitical forms, and that it regulates without the fabrication of subjectivities while optimizing differences and tolerating minority

45 David Halperin, *Saint Foucault: Towards a Gay Hagiography*, New York: Oxford University Press, 1995.

groups and practices. Strangely, he would find in the Islamic Orient and in ancient Greece a similar point of attraction: forms of sexual conduct between males subject to forms of ritualized austerity, but not connected to the production of subjectivities.

Second, Foucault showed a certain acceptance of the neoliberal diagnosis of the current problems of the welfare state as creating dependency, as unresponsive or not 'active', and as expensive, while also perceiving the benefits for the autonomy of the subject that would follow from a negative tax system. Finally, with regard to concrete political alignments, he displayed an affinity with the Second Left – those factions of French social democracy that opposed the 'social-statism' of the old political formations – and displayed a willingness to adopt neoliberal ideas and solutions. As we have stressed throughout, Foucault was caught in the paradox that his anti-formal politics actually found a place relatively easily in the conventional political spectrum.

It may of course be objected to these observations that the term 'neoliberalism' is today so nebulous and overused that applying it to Foucault can only be interpreted as a form of denunciation. While this may often be the case, we have nevertheless tried to situate the 'neoliberalism' on which Foucault drew in the most precise way possible. To observe the different aspects of this relationship, however, is not to imply that his thought was entirely corrupted by neoliberalism. It is simply a matter of indicating a much more serious and fundamental engagement with a contemporary form of economic liberalism than is usually allowed in the Foucauldian commentary. Nonetheless, we must insist that Foucault's political commitments meant that his reading of neoliberalism went far beyond a strictly 'value neutral' or 'historical' interest.[46]

But if Foucault was not a member of the neoliberal thought collective, what was his role in the dissemination of a certain

---

46 As one could infer from the reading of Stuart Elden. See his *Foucault's Last Decade*, p. 103.

normative ensemble that connected a left politics with neoliberal technologies of government? Let us turn to his final visits to the land he so loved and that embodied in its very lifestyles so many of his political aspirations.

The California Foucault

Foucault's time at the University of California, Berkeley, in the 1980s allows us to complete something of another circle, given that we began our investigations with his 'acid test' in California some eight years earlier. Andrew Zimmermann has argued that the Berkeley visits gave rise to a 'California Foucault', 'a moment when he experimented with liberal alternatives to the left theories of the first decades of his career'.[47] While there is indeed something in this view, it perhaps underestimates the extent to which Foucault made possible the re-entry into an all-too-receptive American context of the very specific politics – that of the French Second Left – that had already oriented itself to both American neoliberalism and a 'lifestyle politics'. The California Foucault had a specific canon in relation to his earlier work, one that announced the relative displacement of struggles over economic exploitation by those over subjectivity,[48] and would propose a programme for a genealogy of the 'government of the social' in both liberal-capitalist and authoritarian-statist regimes. The encounter at Berkeley would leave an important mark on the reception of Foucault's thinking not only in the United States but throughout the Anglophone

47 Andrew Zimmerman, 'Foucault in Berkeley and Magnitogorsk: Totalitarianism and the Limits of Liberal Critique', *Contemporary European History* 23:2, 2014, p. 225.

48 Especially, Foucault, 'The Subject and Power', which had been published in 1982 in Dreyfus and Rabinow, *Michel Foucault*, pp. 208–26. See *History of the Present* 1, 1985, p. 14, for a 'Methodological Bibliography' that also includes several pieces by Foucault and Jacques Donzelot from the English journal, *Ideology and Consciousness*, including the 1979 translation of the lecture, 'On Governmentality'.

world. In this context, Foucault's normativity was not so much a matter of him taking a particular value position as of him acting as a point of exchange that fostered a certain outlook, a mode of perception, comprehension and synthesis, or, perhaps more precisely, a 'style of thought'.[49]

The California Foucault can then be viewed as a key moment in the interchange – via the charismatic thinker – between a theoretically driven academic progressivism in California and a particular French intellectual-political formation. Neoliberalism would be imported into American progressive thought not directly but through the French political and intellectual dispositives of self-management and post-structuralism. A key record of Foucault's time at Berkeley, particularly in 1983, and of this intellectual-political reception of him, is found in the Berkeley newsletter, *History of the Present*, whose four issues appeared in the years immediately following Foucault's death (1985–88). A brief look over their contents is highly instructive.

In the first issue, there is a report on a project of a Berkeley-based working group centred around Foucault in the fall of 1983. The group would 'investigate the 1920s and the rationalities of government that make possible the Welfare State, fascisms and Stalinism'.[50] Foucault favoured this as a 'contemporary topic' – it is noteworthy that it is reported in the present tense – that 'would establish lasting connections between Berkeley and Paris'.[51] The legacy of French anti-totalitarianism is clear in the framing of the topic. It casts suspicion on the emergence of the welfare state in the United States and elsewhere, while naming the key enemies identified by anti-totalitarianism (Soviet socialism) and

---

49 On the idea of 'thought styles' and their relation to 'thought collectives', see Dieter Plehwe, 'Neoliberal Thought Collectives: Integrating Social Science and Intellectual History', in Damien Cahill, Melinda Cooper, Martijn Konings and David Primrose (eds), *The SAGE Handbook of Neoliberalism*, London: Sage, 2018, pp. 85–97.

50 'Foucault in Berkeley', *History of the Present* 1, 1985, p. 6.

51 Ibid., p. 15.

affirming the social and political superiority of liberal democratic regimes.

In the same issue, a long article apparently intended for this project takes on a pro-American inflection in its conclusions. 'The government of working and social life in the USA and the USSR' converged somewhat in 'the government of the social' during the twentieth century. Despite this convergence, the article concludes that 'Soviet regimes have been all along readier to use repression.'[52] By contrast, US repression was 'constrained by constitutional guarantees and the question of public morality'. The US would 'rely on a less violent and ponderous and more refined and subtle exercise of power', appealing to consumerism and inter-generational advancement, and thus use a 'greater "economy" of power and force than the Soviet Union'.[53] With no doubt greater intellectual precision and historical analysis, this position certainly shares elements of the critique of the welfare state and state intervention advanced in Hayek's *Road to Serfdom*, alerting us to the dangers of welfarist interventions in the capitalist economy. Yet, the apparent advantages of the United States could only be affirmed from the airy atmosphere of a prestigious campus, in that they ignore the history of its imperialism, foreign wars and occupations, the treatment of African Americans after the end of slavery, the repression of working-class organizations, and much else besides.

The second issue of the newsletter includes an interview on social security that Foucault had given to the head of the CFDT, Robert Bono, originally called 'A finite system faces an infinite demand'. Among other things, it rehearses neoliberal tropes by notoriously calling for a complete restructuring of the French welfare system to prevent dependency, and denies that health could be a right (while rhapsodizing over an imagined institute exercising

52 Keith Gandal and Stephen Kotkin, 'Governing Work and Social Life in the USA and the USSR', *History of the Present* 1, 1985, p. 13.

53 Ibid.

the right to a joyful, drug-assisted suicide).[54] Underlining the point of transmission and exchange that Berkeley was, there is an interview with Bono himself conducted by Paul Rabinow and Keith Gandal. He speaks of the new kind of relations that a mass organization such as the CFDT could have with intellectuals or *libertaires* like Foucault, Bourdieu, Touraine and Rosanvallon, 'for whom freedom and human rights are inseparable from the fight for life itself'.[55] This and other pieces situate Foucault's politics squarely in relation to the mobilization against the Polish military takeover, social security reform and the work of Médecins sans Frontières, thus connecting at a practical political level anti-totalitarianism, the critique of the welfare state and the emergent human rights politics.[56]

There is also an attempt in this issue to draw a key contrast between Foucault's relation to the Second Left and the relation of intellectuals to the Communist Party, exemplified by Jean-Paul Sartre. While the conceptual point of the contrast, expressed in terms of 'teamwork', 'functionality' and 'autonomy', is often difficult to see, its affirmation of a centrist and anti-communist position within the French political spectrum was very clear, as was its stress on the 'problems of dependence that arise from social security'.[57] Indeed, Foucault's own study of the 'historical production of individual experiences' such as 'mental illness, crime, sexuality and dependency' is invoked to make plain the way his genealogies identify the targets of this new form of politics, which will valorize the experiences of mental patients, welfare recipients and prisoners, over the knowledge of experts and conventional social reformers.

54 Michel Foucault and Robert Bono, 'The Risks of Security', *History of the Present* 2, 1986, pp. 4–5, 11–14.

55 Robert Bono, 'Intellectuals and Labor Unions', *History of the Present* 2, 1986, p. 3.

56 Keith Gandal, 'Intellectual Work as a Political Tool', *History of the Present* 2, 1986, p. 7.

57 Ibid., p. 6.

Finally, we note that the newsletter introduced the work of François Ewald to its audience and reviewed, not entirely uncritically, his major work on the welfare state.[58] As we have seen, Ewald is a key figure not simply for his editorship of Foucault's lectures and minor works but for his national role in the intellectual advocacy of welfare and labour market reform (*refondation sociale*) on behalf of the employer's association, MEDEF, in the late 1990s.[59] With Ewald and Bono, we can say that the California Foucault brought American intellectual radicals into contact with influential figures in what Mirowski and Plehwe would call the 'neoliberal thought collective' in France.[60] It would be a bridge too far to suggest that Foucault himself was a member or representative of that collective. Closer to the mark would be the hypothesis that this encounter was the crucible for a certain 'thought style' which, while not self-consciously neoliberal, imagined itself as progressive and practical, on the one hand, while absolutely rejecting older socialist and social democratic approaches on the other. While distancing itself from the extreme state-phobia of radical libertarianism it would nonetheless emphasize the 'dangers' of welfare state interventions and their resemblance to the policies of fascism and Soviet socialism. It distinguished itself from the totalitarian model of the top-down intellectual speaking in the name of universal values and 'totalising' theory (Sartre), relocating itself in a 'transversal' relation to the inclusive everyday struggles of hitherto marginalized groups and social sectors based on race, gender and sexuality. And it would foreground certain topics such as those of risk and insurance, the social, capital punishment, pornography, lifestyles, etc. – all of which are discussed in the newsletter.

In its Anglo-American version, virulent anti-communism would not need to be emphasized, given the lack of organized

58 There is Ewald's piece, 'Biopower', *History of the Present* 2, 1986, and, in *History of the Present* 3, 1987, an interview with Ewald by Paul Rabinow and Keith Gandal, and a review of his *L'État Providence* by Rabinow.

59 Behrent, 'Accidents Happen', pp. 585–6.

60 Mirowski and Plehwe, *The Road from Mont Pèlerin*.

mass communist parties in the US and the UK. It would not so much propose (or be received as) a frontal attack on Marxism, existing socialist politics, or concerns around class and economic exploitation, as pluralize Marxism, distinguish Marx the historian from institutional Marxism, reframe class in terms of multiple power relations including discipline, and historically relativize struggles over economic exploitation in relation to new, and thus more present and relevant, struggles over subjectivity. The California Foucault was thus less a neoliberal deformation of a previously more radical Foucault than a kind of experimental crucible for a style of thinking and intervening in politics that would sideline the major concerns of conventional socialist politics, explore the 'deployment' of neoliberal technologies, and articulate the possibilities of self-transformation.

There is, then, a consistency in Foucault's normative orientation. Under the shadow of totalitarianism, conventional political organizational forms, state politics and juridical reform are rendered problematic and devalued in favour of innovation and experimentation with, on the one hand, lifestyles and movements as elements of everyday life, and, on the other, practices, ordeals and tests that offer the possibility of self-transformation. What is important are new kinds of friendships and relationships, and the fostering of individual and collective experiences and counter-conducts outside the subjectifying gaze of the therapeutic confessional that comprises the welfare state. For the intellectual, it is no longer a matter of producing a rational knowledge of social problems rooted in inequality and exploitation, but of investigating how such knowledge binds the individual to a certain subjectivity. The objective is not to develop new social structures and provisions but to open up spaces of tolerance in which individuals can begin to maximize choice in both the life they will lead and the way in which they are to be governed.

7
Rogue Neoliberalism and Liturgical Power

> I hope that the truth of my books is in the future.
>
> Michel Foucault, 1980[1]

At the end of the first chapter of what remains Michel Foucault's most famous work, he asked himself the question of why he had wanted to write a history of the prison. He responded: 'Simply because I am interested in the past? No, if one means by that writing a history of the past in terms of the present. Yes, if one means writing the history of the present.'[2] Later, on several occasions, he would strive to link this concern with the nature of the present to the Kantian question '*Was ist Aufklärung?*' in an effort to rethink the problematics of German critical theory and the Frankfurt School. In an important interview, published in 1983 in the prominent US critical theory journal, *Telos*, he considered whether

1 Foucault, 'Foucault étudie la raison d'État,' p. 860. English version is Foucault, 'Truth is in the Future', p. 301.

2 Michel Foucault, *Discipline and Punish: The Birth of the Prison*, trans. Alan Sheridan, London: Allen Lane, 1977, p. 31.

Kant's question 'might not be characterized by saying that the task of philosophy is to describe the nature of the present, and of "ourselves in the present" '.[3] Yet there is a tension evident even in this interview. On the one hand, he introduced the 'proviso' that we must be cautious about theatrical declarations, for the present 'is a time like any other, or rather a time which is never quite like any other'.[4] Yet, in recounting the recent history of the Left in France, he asserted that what had emerged was a

> Left thought which is not encrusted in the political and which is not traditional in its approach to Marxism . . . I think that one day, when we look at this episode in French history, we will see in it the growth of a new kind of Left thought which in its multiple and non-unified forms (perhaps one of its positive aspects) has completely transformed the horizon of contemporary Left movements.[5]

In this interview, with the Germanist Gérard Raulet, one dimension of Foucault's strategy was clear: he presented himself both as the unexpected but nonetheless legitimate heir to the critical theoretical tradition at the same time as he insulated that tradition from its sources in conventional Marxism – the Marxism that is a 'dogmatism of parties and institutions', and indulges in 'rhetorical excesses' about 'class struggles'.[6] No matter how equivocal Foucault was at various times in his reading of different texts of Marx and forms of Marxist theory, he remained throughout his life implacably opposed to Marxism as a form of political organization and action.

The 'Left thought' that Foucault appealed to in this interview is most definitely not that of parties and institutions and formal

---

3 Foucault, 'Critical Theory/Intellectual History', p. 36.
4 Ibid.
5 Ibid., p. 43.
6 Ibid., pp. 19, 40.

organization. Rather, it occurred around issues such as the anti-colonial war of independence of Algeria and the multiple and decentred nodes of cultural change in contemporary France itself. Thus, in the same interview, Foucault discussed the role of the Second Left within the Socialist Party as being one of creating an opening to new struggles based in everyday life, 'to questions concerning daily life, sexual life, couples, women's issues . . . to the problem of self-management'.[7] He thus endorsed Michel Rocard and his circle in very clear terms when he noted 'that the light of Rocard and his group, and of the Rocard current in the Socialist Party, is (sic) now hidden under a bushel, has had a major effect'.[8] So – and this is another paradox – Foucault endorsed a strand of formal political organization precisely because it was one that fostered multiple, local and informal forms of political action. Foucault's position was not only a rejection of the politics of the old social-statist wing of the Socialist Party and of communism in general, but a rejection of the 'political' and of conventional formal organizations as such. Nevertheless, the rejection of the political, here and elsewhere, must strive to locate itself within the political spectrum. If Foucault's claiming of the critical theory tradition looked backward, the claiming of an informal sphere for a kind of formal politics looked forward – toward the centre-left project that will sweep liberal democracies over the coming decades.

While our own present attests to the durability of many of these kinds of informal and grassroots politics, it is not lacking – to stick with Foucault's own language – in novel and alarming diagnoses of itself as a moment of 'total perdition' or an 'abyss of darkness':[9] of a post-truth politics and the spread of fake news; of the dark arts of the internet; of 'populism' as movement, politics and incompetent policy; of explicitly illiberal democracies and regimes; of collusions and meddling in high politics; of anti-globalism, trade wars

7 Ibid., p. 41.
8 Ibid., p. 42
9 Ibid., p. 36.

and the making and remaking of state enemies such as Russia and China. Even the politics of everyday life and intimacy have taken on a theatrical character and a new essentialism: on the one hand, large corporations, universities and sporting bodies, among others, have a mandatory, almost religious obeisance to the values of 'diversity'; on the other hand, class, on the occasions when it is recognized, becomes merely one more feature of personal identity, or is recycled in the discourse of the nativist and xenophobic extreme right. Indeed, in the midst of mass anti-racist protests and public health and economic catastrophe, it would be tempting to imagine that our present is a time like no other, a hinge moment of epochal significance. Above all, it would be easy, and all too careless, to imagine that liberal democracies have made a sudden and unexpected turn toward an anti-liberal authoritarianism, thus unleashing unforeseeable potentials.[10]

While we take this opportunity to address our present, if such a fleeting entity can ever be truly identified, it is incumbent on us to offer some sense of how this study of what was produced in the recent past – Foucault's thought – remains a component of that present. To do this we will follow two intertwined narratives concerning neoliberalism and the apparent authoritarian and confrontational turn in liberal democracies. The first extends the story this book has been telling: moving from Foucault's encounter with neoliberalism and the relation to self as the privileged point of resistance and 'counter-conduct' to his influence on what Michel Sennelart has called 'governmentality studies',[11] and his unexpected affinities with later forms of social and political thought. The second is the story of a different scale: of frameworks of

10 There is the recent proliferation of books about 'the end of democracy': see, among others, Yascha Mounk, *The People vs Democracy*, Cambridge MA: Harvard University Press, 2018; David Runciman, *How Democracy Ends*, London: Profile Books, 2018; Steven Levitsky and Daniel Ziblatt, *How Democracies Die*, New York: Penguin, 2018.

11 Sennelart, 'Course Context', in Foucault, *Security, Territory, Population*, p. 390.

governing and politics in contemporary liberal democracies, with a particular emphasis on the extent to which these forms of governing claim to have been liberal, in the sense that they operate primarily in relation to the freedom of the governed and only occasionally resort to measures that are coercive or illiberal. At stake in the latter is the question of sovereign power, the nation, the state and the territory. One way of putting this is in the Weberian terms that both the critical theorists and Foucault would understand. For some time, those who practise governmentality studies, among others, have been exercised by the problem of the 'irrationality' of the rationalities of neoliberal *government* – for example, the way the homage to individual freedom requires stringent governmental interventions, disciplinary and coercive measures, and entails a host of paradoxes and aporias, including the possible suspension of democracy to institute a neoliberal order, as documented by Philip Mirowski and his colleagues.[12] Today – as we shall see below – we are forced to turn to the rationality of irrational neoliberal *politics*, to make intelligible, once again, the liturgical and theological character of a politics that Foucault and the Frankfurt School would regard as increasingly rationalized and governmentalized.

These stories are linked in that the former – concerning Foucault, governmentality studies and their aftermath – has been one influential way of understanding the latter, the actuality of forms of governing in contemporary liberal democracies. But it is also possible that the governmentality studies that examined the rationalities by which rule takes place in these societies were not entirely immune to the features of such rationalities and were thus hampered in their express (but impossible) aim of finding a non-normative mode of analysis of the rationalities and technologies of liberal, and neoliberal, government. Our thesis is that the current conjuncture can be understood as a result of two contingent events: the ultimate failure of what we have called the search for a 'left governmentality',

12 Mirowski, 'Postface'.

and the transformation of the basis of legitimacy from the public opinion fostered in the mass media to the evanescent and volatile fluctuations of public mood as revealed by social media, with a concomitant renewal of the public assembly and a dispersion and multiplication of publics.[13] Both public assembly and social media enact political liturgy or 'liturgical power', as Nicholas Heron has called it.[14] We might speak of a shift from liberal democracy, which at least ideally rested on the publicity of an arrived-at, objective truth-narrative, to an *acclamatory democracy* based on the publicity of multiple subjective truth-expressions.

As we have seen with Foucault, one of the key elements in the search for a left governmentality was a suspicion of the kind of public deliberation organized by institutions, parties, unions, and so on, and an embrace of the local 'experiments' of everyday life. The problem for such an anti-formal politics is that it must locate itself somewhere on the formal political spectrum – in Foucault's case, during his particular conjuncture in the early 1980s, this was on the right wing of the Socialist Party and the faction of Michel Rocard. But a deeper paradox is perhaps the way such an openness to diverse experiments in everyday life transforms the public sphere from a space for the formation of solidarities and a collective voice into Foucault's desired 'great proliferation of discourse', a 'great incessant', 'violent, discontinuous, pugnacious' and 'disorderly' 'buzzing of discourse'. Neoliberalism would in fact entail what Foucault had described as the 'great logophobia' of our civilization.[15] But these multiple atomized voices would finally express nothing more than the diverse individual preferences of the sovereign political consumer, transforming the public sphere into another version of the market. Is it any wonder, given the abstention of the 'centre left' after 1980 from the political, that politics has

---

13 Mitchell Dean, 'Political Acclamation, Social Media and Public Mood', *European Journal of Social Theory* 20:3, 2017, pp. 417–34.

14 Nicholas Heron, *Liturgical Power: Between Economic and Political Theology*, New York: Fordham University Press, 2018.

15 Foucault, 'The Order of Discourse', p. 66.

since been transformed by the techniques of marketing and, in recent years, by digital marketing that utilizes the multiple, diverse and privatized self-expressions, acclamations and opinions of the members of a virtual public sphere?

The story is told through three snapshots, or three 'presents', as the Foucauldian critical historian would say: first, that of the late 1970s and early 1980s, when Foucault delivered his celebrated lectures on the subject, but prior to neoliberalism entering the mainstream of public policy in liberal democracies on a global scale; second, that of the adoption of neoliberal technologies by social democratic parties in the 1980s and 1990s, which was also the high period of governmentality studies and sociological accounts of individualization; and, third, that of today, when Foucauldian perspectives have moved into a full-blown scholasticism and academicism, but with a particular kind of legacy in the humanities and social sciences, and when multiple forms of neoliberalism persist despite the damage to their credibility inflicted by the previous decade's financial crisis and the rise of political movements – often on the Right but also on the Left – explicitly targeting its neglect, abandonment and depredations.

This is a rogue neoliberalism, unanchored from the bases of its own legitimacy by financial crises, inequality and rapacity, but drawing upon a well of deep theological resources. In the process, it has unmoored its own various centre-left, cosmopolitan and globalist manifestations. It can reside both in the authoritarian re-sacralization of the market and the national economy and the purification of the nation itself from foreign, ethnic and racial contaminants, but also in the liberal-progressive identity and 'life-style politics' that claims to oppose it, and in the pieties of the 'rule of law' liberalism that seeks to keep it in check. In terms of cultural diagnostics and imagery, the Weberian 'soulnessness' of the Fordist industrial welfare state has been replaced by a low-level confessional civil war between progressivist and fundamentalist neoliberalisms, from which the political Left has either largely absented itself or joined the former. At the same time, a surplus of both political acclamation and capital accumulation is produced by social media companies, leading to a new kind of liturgical power that can be acted on, manipulated and controlled with the same ruthlessness that an earlier generation of spin doctors sought to act on the public opinion produced in the mass media. The manufacture of contempt has replaced the manufacture of consent.

The 1970s: coming down

We started this book by noting the significance – personal, intellectual and ultimately political – of the episode in May 1975 when Foucault took LSD with two younger men at Zabriskie Point in Death Valley, California. We have discussed his experiments with Zen Buddhism in Japan and with S/M practices and the leather scene in New York and San Francisco. We have noted his near-death car accident outside his home and the pleasures it brought him. We have also explored his understanding of the Iranian revolution in terms of death, sacrifice and the individual and collective forms of ascetic self-transformation it entailed. In these and other cases, Foucault stressed that politics had become a question of subjectivity and its transformation through limit-experiences, transgressions and ordeals, and that the core of resistance would henceforth be found in the relation of self to itself.

In these experiences and the conclusions he drew from them, Foucault was certainly not alone. The mid-1970s were, in many ways, transitional years, moving away from the more explicitly political collective actions that had followed May 1968 and the global anti-Vietnam War protests, toward a different kind of rebellion concerned with self-stylization. This entailed the assertion of the rights of groups engaged in such practices, rather than what Foucault himself would have regarded as an old-style revolutionary project. Like similar challenges to the formal political spectrum, these cultural transformations had among their conditions the end of the post-war settlement and of the Long

Boom (*les trentes glorieuses*), the emergence of 'stagflation', the resultant problematization of Keynesian macroeconomic policy, and the re-emergence of mass unemployment, particularly among the young.

At the same time, what would become the most influential political-intellectual movement, or 'thought collective', was – not before conducting its own experiments in Latin America and particularly with the Pinochet regime in Chile[16] – preparing to move out of the shadows and shape the policy prescriptions of liberal democracies. The most exemplary cases (though not the only ones – witness New Zealand from a very early stage) were the Thatcher government in the United Kingdom and the Reagan administration in the United States. The explicit focus of this movement, a distributed network with a key node at the University of Chicago, was not the intensification of experience and the capacities for autonomous self-sculpture, but the limitation of the welfare state by various forms of market liberalization and the unleashing or extension of new kinds of freedom of choice. In this sense, while they did not become widely available for another two decades, Foucault's lectures on governmentality and liberalism in 1978–79 were both pivotal and unique in that they underlined most clearly the intersection of this new concern for experimental self-creation with a recognition of the significance of the emergent neoliberal movement.

Foucault framed neoliberalism within his idea of 'governmentality' as a rationality of government, the latter understood as encompassing all the different ways in which human conduct would be tethered by various means (or 'technologies') to specific ends with uncertain effectivity and results. Neoliberalism was not to be understood as the philosophy or ideology of 'late capitalism' but as the most recent iteration of a liberal art of government, that is, as a critique, a method, or a test of how we are governed, of

16 Karin Fischer, 'The Influence of Neoliberals in Chile Before, During and After Pinochet', in Mirowski and Plehwe, *The Road from Mont Pèlerin*, pp. 305–36.

whether we are governing too much, of who or what is governing, and especially of the state.[17] As Foucault observed:

> Governmentality should not be exercised without a 'critique' far more radical than a test of optimization. It should not only question itself about the best (or least costly) means for achieving its effects, but also about the possibility and even legitimacy of its project for achieving effects. The question behind the suspicion that there is always the risk of governing too much is: Why, after all, is it necessary to govern?[18]

In the French original of this passage, Foucault uses the word *épreuve*, rendered in English here as 'test' – '*une épreuve d'optimisation*'. Later on in the same text, he becomes somewhat more reticent and himself uses the English word 'test' in quotation marks.[19] But despite such coyness, it is clear that liberalism and neoliberalism themselves are best regarded as *épreuves* that operate through the truth manifest in the market – the 'site', 'regime' or 'principle' of veridiction (or truth-telling) of the market, as Foucault put it in these lectures. Moreover, there is more than a simple verbal or even conceptual continuity here. The individual *épreuve* and the liberal political *épreuve* both take aim at those pastoral practices that form the individual as a subject inherited by the welfare state from the dominant form of Western confessional Christian culture.

It is thus striking how Foucault chose to use this term, *épreuve*, to describe both limit-experiences undertaken by the subject and the practices and procedures of liberal government. It suggests that liberalism is anything but a gentle critique of government and that the modes of rationalization of governing by political economy and modern economics are more akin to the heterogeneous

17 Foucault, *The Birth of Biopolitics*, pp. 317–25.

18 Ibid., p. 319.

19 See Michel Foucault, *Naissance de la biopolitique: Cours au Collège de France 1978–1979*. Paris: Gaillmard Seuil, pp. 324, 326.

range of experiences and events that encompass *l'épreuve* than they are to scientific inquiry, or *l'enquête*. Elsewhere, Foucault conceived of practices as diverse as Socrates' testing of the soul, Saint Anthony's writing as combat with the Devil, medieval medicine's notion of crisis, the ancient art of torture, and ritual and ceremonial combat, as elements in a series constituting an alternative 'technology of truth' repugnant to, but covered over and colonized by, modern science and philosophy.[20] As Foucault put it, the 'truth here does not belong to the order of that which is, but rather of that which happens. It is an event: it is not recorded, but aroused: a production in the place of apophantics.'[21] In this sense, one can never know the truth of the market through rational inquiry – a point of concordance with Hayek. That truth can only manifest itself as a continual test, even an ordeal, for how we govern. For neoliberalism, the true test of the art of government will be how it responds to crisis; this is perhaps why the 'correct' response, austerity, takes the form of *une épreuve*. 'Austerity' itself is a term that can be used not only for the forms of moderation in ancient sexual ethics (as we know Foucault did) but also for the collective moderation called for in response to economic crisis.

Foucault focused on the statecraft embodied by neoliberalism rather than regarding it principally as a philosophy that somehow has implications for the form of governing by the state. *Avant la lettre*, he produced the first account of neoliberalism as a 'thought collective' and 'thought style', and offered his audience in Paris one of the first expositions of the nature of, and differences between,

20 For discussion of medical notions of crisis prior to the eighteenth century, and their relation to juridical inquisition and alchemical practice, see the 'parenthetical' section of the lecture of 23 January 1974, in Foucault, *Psychiatric Power*, pp. 235–47. On Socrates' testing of souls and his investigation of the oracle at Delphi, see the lecture of 15 February 1984, first hour, in Foucault, *Courage of Truth*, pp. 73–92; on Athanasius's *Life of Saint Anthony* and his view of writing as a weapon of spiritual combat, see Foucault, 'Self-writing', in *Ethics, Subjectivity and Truth*, pp. 207–8.

21 Miller, *Passion*, p. 271, citing an extract from Foucault, *Psychiatric Power*, p. 237.

German Ordoliberalism and American Chicago School neoliberalism. We can say that Foucault gained a deep insight into neoliberalism precisely because he allowed himself to come so very close to it. And this insight is embedded in several themes that are relevant to our understanding of the relation between neoliberalism and a supposed authoritarian and antagonistic turn.

First, Foucault noted that neoliberalism actively seeks to construct forms of freedom rather than assume it to be a natural feature of unconstrained individuals pursuing their interests in the market, as had the more classical forms of economic liberalism such as that of Adam Smith. Second, the market itself is denaturalized, so that its construction becomes the principle of legitimation of the state, and only so under definite legal and political conditions, as in the case of the Ordoliberals, or a technique through which formerly public services and policy domains can be reconstructed – for example, drug policy or the entire field of crime and justice – as in the Chicago School. Neoliberalism thus entails less a rollback of the state, although at times it takes on such a character, than a mode of 'veridiction' for an art of government. Government is not simply reduced to a market or economic rationality (a common but basic mistake) but enters into a *tête-à-tête* with it. The market is a form of the manifestation of truth, and special authority thus goes to its truth-tellers, the economists. This manifestation of truth, or mode of veridiction, is not, however, that of *l'enquête*, from which will be derived the idea of truth in science and modern philosophy, but that of *l'épreuve*.

Third, for Foucault, neoliberalism presented a new understanding of subjectivity. Unlike the disciplinary and biopolitical forms of power he had analysed earlier, it no longer sought to 'make up people' through the normalizing techniques of the human sciences. Previous health, welfare and education systems sought to produce particular kinds of subjects. Domination had not proceeded through the objectification of what was truly human, as the Frankfurt School had contended, but through the creation of a certain kind of subject – docile, useful and self-responsible. Social work, criminal anthropology and child psychology, among the other disciplines of the human sciences, had conspired in the production of the 'modern soul'. Neoliberalism, in direct contrast, would take the side of the subject and its choices and seek to govern conduct not through the oppressive imposition of subjectivities but by acting on the conditions of choice, with the minimal supposition that choice was simply an individual's non-random reaction to the modification of variables in their environment.[22] Neoliberalism thus aimed not so much to produce subjects as to cultivate the desirable attributes of enterprise and competition by acting on the environment of individuals and their field of choice.

In this respect, as we have seen, neoliberalism, at least as an ideal or a political imaginary, marked for Foucault a rupture with the earlier forms of power that he had analysed and which had come to be embodied in the institutional and juridical structures of the modern welfare state. It was a way of governing that sought to maximize the autonomy of individuals in their own self-definition and self-creation and resist the subjection/subjectification of the welfare state and human sciences. This is not to say that Foucault saw no dangers in neoliberalism, as we have noted, but these should be weighed against the considerable potentials he found in it. However, in expressing the view that the Left would have to draw on liberalism, given 'the absence of a socialist art of government', Foucault set the course for what we have called the search for a left governmentality.[23] At the same time, the most famous names in the neoliberal thought collective were enunciating the principles of neoliberalism's relation to authoritarianism in the context of their involvement in the Pinochet regime in Chile and the apartheid regime in South Africa. Friedrich Hayek seemed to surprise even himself during an interview in Santiago when he found himself preferring a 'liberal dictator' to a 'democracy lacking liberalism', and arguing that sometimes 'democracy needs the

22 Foucault, *The Birth of Biopolitics*, p. 269.

23 Ibid., pp. 94 and 92: 'But I do not think there is an autonomous social governmentality. There is no governmental rationality of socialism.'

broom of strong government'.[24] More concisely, for Hayek, liberalism and democracy were not the same thing; the opposite of liberalism was not authoritarianism but totalitarianism, and 'an authoritarian government may act on liberal principles'.[25] Contrary to the supposition of a recent authoritarian turn, even at this early stage neoliberalism as an intellectual and political project was prepared to sacrifice, at least temporarily, democratic procedures and rights for an authoritarian state willing to implement the conditions for a 'free market'. In this respect, it had learned the lessons of the 'commissarial dictatorship' that Carl Schmitt had identified just after the First World War, and of the 'constitutional dictatorship' Clinton Rossiter had theorized after the Second.[26] That is to say, it is sometimes necessary, in order to preserve or correctly apply a liberal constitutional order that establishes a free market, to suspend for a time the very rules of that order itself, including democracy and the rule of law.

Towards a left governmentality

By the early 1990s neoliberalism had become the dominant project of public governance in the Anglophone world and certainly a vigorous challenger to the previous 'path dependencies' of the Nordic social democratic welfare states and of Western European forms of corporatism. It was exported and either welcomed or violently imposed in many parts of the world from Latin America to the former Soviet Union. After the first decade of forms of neoliberalism that emphasized the rollback of the state through the privatization of public services, fiscal austerity and

24 Friedrich Hayek, 'Interview', *El Mercurio*, 12 April 1981.

25 F.A. Hayek, 'The Principles of a Liberal Social Order', in *Studies in Philosophy, Politics and Economics*, London: Routledge and Kegan Paul, 1967, p. 161.

26 Carl Schmitt, *Dictatorship*, trans. Michael Hoezl and Graham Ward, Cambridge: Polity, 2014; Clinton Rossiter, *Constitutional Dictatorship*, Princeton: Princeton University Press, 1948.

anti-inflationary monetary policies, the Left, or what styled itself as the 'centre-left', began to search out what lessons it could learn from neoliberalism. By the mid-1990s, it was labour and social democratic parties, and international organizations such as the Organization for Economic Cooperation and Development (OECD), that would be instrumental in carrying out a comprehensive reform of institutions and institutional practices, particularly in regard to welfare, social security, health care and education, in accordance with the principles of competition and enterprise. This 'new public management' programme set out to re-compose the public sector so that it would act more and more like a series of 'quasi' or constructed markets. 'Precarity' was now a firmly entrenched feature of liberal democracies, and the occasion for ever new cultural problematizations and 'culture wars', as well as demands for the reformation of governmental practices under the Orwellian newspeak term 'welfare reform'. This was a term especially associated with the Clinton-era Personal Responsibility and Work Opportunity Reconciliation Act of 1996, and with the new welfare discourse more generally.[27]

Foucault's lectures on neoliberalism had ended a month before the signal election of the Thatcher government in the United Kingdom. In 1983, he promised to deliver a book on the socialist art of government as a consequence of his diagnosis of its absence.[28] He had made two points that are salient here, in relation both to the course of social theory and philosophy and to the search for a left governmentality. First, while there was no autonomous socialist governmentality, socialism could, and in its historical forms did, borrow from other forms of governmentality. While the socialism of the communist parties had borrowed from the governmental techniques of the police state and tied itself to a

27 Sanford S. Schram, *After Welfare: The Culture of Postindustrial Social Policy*, New York: New York University Press, 2000.

28 Foucault, *The Birth of Biopolitics*, p. 100n. Didier Eribon notes in his biography that Foucault thought of publishing such a book under the title 'la tête des socialistes'. See Eribon, *Michel Foucault* (English edition), p. 495.

'governmentality of the party', the post-war German Social Democrats, after the Bad Godesberg Congress of 1959, had effectively abandoned socialist precepts and Marxist theory and embraced the consensus of a liberal governmentality associated with the Ordoliberals.[29] Foucault seemed to suggest a version of Thatcher's TINA (There Is No Alternative) principle: leftist and socialist parties would be forced to decide on the art of government available to them, and that choice would be between the dark arts and heavy hand of totalitarianism and the enlightened and light techniques of economic liberalism.

The second point concerned the shift of the focus of politics from the question of exploitation to that of subjectivity, and the implications of this for public policy. For Foucault, as we have seen, American neoliberalism, at least as an ideal programme, works through constructing choice, not through the production of subjectivity, as did the Christian-pastoral welfare state.[30] This difference is also played out on the register of practical policies. Criminal justice will not be organized according to the truth of various forms of subjectivity but according to the 'negative demand' for crime and a calibration of the risks of the individual subject considered not as a criminal, but as a rational subject of choice.[31] In proposals for a negative tax during the Giscard presidency, the question of the unemployed person was no longer one of disciplinary, bureaucratic or inquisitorial practice but of the choices of the individual in a game of competition. It was to be up to individuals whether they wanted to work or not, in the knowledge that they could be sure of a minimal subsistence, saved from absolute but not relative poverty.[32]

---

29 Foucault, *The Birth of Biopolitics*, pp. 90–2, p. 191. For Foucault, 'the famous Bad Godesberg congress with its absolute renunciation of the most traditional themes of social democracy certainly was the break with Marxist theory, with Marxist socialism' (p. 90).

30 Ibid., pp. 259–60.

31 Ibid., p. 255.

32 Ibid., pp. 205–7.

In the interview we have already cited with the chief of the CFDT, Robert Bono, for a volume of Second Left policy concerns entitled *Social Security: The Challenge*, Foucault began to sketch out what this left governmentality would look like. While the problem of the welfare state had always been one of a trade-off between security and autonomy, now its pathology was not simply the possibility of marginalization from society through exclusion but also the integration of the subject into the mechanisms of social security themselves and the resulting dependency that entailed. 'I believe there is a need to resist the phenomenon of integration,'[33] Foucault said, suggesting that it is necessary to defer to what he calls the 'political, economic and political rationality of modern societies', namely the policy prescriptions he discusses in his analysis of neoliberalism.[34] Such a rationality was consistent with his answers to these problems framed in terms of a 'way of life' and 'lifestyles' and with the focus on the 'relation of self to self' not as a handle for power but as a mode of resistance to it.[35] Thus, in keeping with the social movements of everyday resistance to institutional, disciplinary and patriarchal power, social security would now be founded on the relation with oneself and one's environment and guarantee the principle of autonomy. Foucault thus sought to combat welfare dependency by means of the technologies of the 'relation of self to self', rather than analyse how the neoliberal reform of the welfare state utilizes those relations. This had undoubted implications for the management of the welfare state, such that it would become a 'vast experimental field' that entailed not a piecemeal but a complete restructuring.[36] Just as the subject in its everyday life and its relation to self remakes itself through intense ordeals (*épreuves*) and the new kinds of truth they make possible, so the entire welfare state would be put to the test

33 Foucault, 'Social Security', in *Politics, Philosophy, Culture*, p. 162.
34 Ibid., p. 160.
35 Ibid., pp. 162–3.
36 Ibid., p. 165.

in relation to a new regime of the truth of the market. Unfortunately, and surprisingly, the Foucault who wrote so eloquently on discipline did not anticipate that this vast experimental field would be less one of light-touch interventions to encourage entrepreneurial identities than one that put the welfare recipient through the mandatory ordeals of workfare, compulsory job applications, psychological testing, management as a case and permanent retraining. He did, however, foresee that in this approach to the liberal arts of government, the mode of veridiction would be that of the market. While Foucault anticipated the relation to self as a liberating counter-conduct to the disciplinary dispositive of the welfare state, the neoliberal reform of that state would target precisely that relation as its mode of operation and legitimation.

By the 1990s the restructuring of the welfare state from top to bottom was a real and pressing concern and no longer simply a matter of the observations of theorists. The idea of social rights was displaced by the mutual obligation of individuals and government, in which the latter would ensure, but not necessarily provide, some kind of social provision in exchange for social beneficiaries remaking themselves in particular ways, learning to plan their own lives, combatting the ill effects of their risk of welfare dependency, undertaking training and retraining as required, undergoing therapy and being case-managed, and learning to act more and more like an enterprise. Key themes would include the *telos* of an 'active society', with flexible and agile populations equipped by 'lifelong learning' and able to grasp the changing opportunities of the market, now projected on a global scale rather than remaining at a national one, and made competitive by investments in human capital and the enterprise of the individuals that composed it.[37] As Foucault foreshadowed, the individual, undergoing a perpetual series of tests and ordeals, would be promised the pleasures of life as an enterprise.

---

37 Mitchell Dean, 'Governing the Unemployed Self in an Active Society', *Economy and Society* 24:4, 1995, pp. 559–83.

While Foucault would look to Greco-Roman Antiquity for examples of an autonomous practice of the care of the self, other theorists of left governmentality would find an easier route through the sociological supposition of changing forms of subjectivity. Social theorists such as Ulrich Beck in Germany and Anthony Giddens in the United Kingdom argued that, under conditions of late modernity, the individual would no longer be bound by the ascribed characteristics of class, race, ethnicity, gender and sexuality that had been transmitted by traditional, patriarchal, familial and religious forms of socialization.[38] Rather, individuals were now capable of remaking themselves, with or without the help of the armies of therapists and self-help experts; of examining the contents of their given identities, including those of class; of challenging them and making new choices for themselves. Where once you were born into a class, now you could reinvent your way out of it. Where once you were assigned a gender on the basis of your anatomy, now you could discover your true gender and sculpt your anatomy accordingly – for the Foucauldian theorist Nikolas Rose, biopolitics had become an 'ethopolitics' focused on one's 'somatic individuality'.[39] Individuals would be capable of narrating and re-narrating their own lives, choosing their own personal and sexual identities, and entering into intimate relations on a new ground of equality rather than being constrained by conventional patriarchal and traditional hierarchical relations, including those of class. At its best, this 'reflexive project of the self' would lead to a new 'cosmopolitan' identity capable of understanding and empathizing with the trajectory of other very diverse pathways to this reflexive identity. As class solidarities loosened and lost their defining significance, the presence and impact of the class politics of mass labour parties and trade unions would diminish and

---

38 Ulrich Beck, *Risk Society: Towards a New Modernity*, trans. Mark Ritter, London: Sage, 1992; Anthony Giddens, *Modernity and Self-Identity: Self and Society in the Late Modern Age*, Cambridge: Polity, 1991.

39 Nikolas Rose, 'The Politics of Life Itself', *Theory, Culture and Society* 18:6, 2001, pp. 1–30.

eventually disappear. Reflexive, self-making individuals would identify with the different communities and forms of political association around these new identifications. The autonomy, vibrancy and vitality of civil society or community would be rediscovered. Civil society would not only be the place for the experimentations made possible by these new diverse collective identifications, it would also become the means by which the fiscal problems and bureaucratic sclerosis of the welfare state would be attenuated, if not fully solved, and, on a global scale, the problems of war, poverty and the environment would be addressed.[40]

The diagnostic moment for such social theory comes when we turn to public policy. Because the truth of the subject was changing, and the potential of a new self-making or reflexive individual was emerging in a 'second modernity', it was no longer possible to provide governmental programmes and politics based on the old solidarities of class and family. Rather than being the recipient of a right, the individual had to become a certain type of subject, with the help of a range of experts, but no longer under their tutelage and as a full and equal partner with a maximum of autonomy, as Foucault might have said. The vertical relations of state, authority and expertise were to be replaced by horizontal and reciprocal ones that enlisted the subject's own capacities, lifestyle, forms of freedom and 'relations to self' in the process. Life had become a 'planning project'.[41] As Giddens put it, 'We have to make our lives in a more active way than was true of previous generations, and we need more actively to accept responsibility for the consequences of what we do and the life habits we adopt.'[42] Or, even more bluntly, this from Ulrich Beck: 'In the individualized society, the individual must learn, on pain of permanent

40 See, for example, Mary Kaldor, *Global Civil Society: An Answer to War*, Cambridge: Polity, 2003.

41 Elisabeth Beck-Gernsheim, 'Life as a Planning Project', in Scott Lash, Bronislaw Szerszinski and Brian Wynne (eds), *Risk, Environment, Modernity: Towards a New Ecology*, London: Sage, 1996, pp. 139–53.

42 Anthony Giddens, *The Third Way: The Renewal of Social Democracy*, Cambridge: Polity, 1998, pp. 36–7.

disadvantage, to conceive of himself or herself as the center of activity, as the planning office with respect to his or her own biography, abilities, orientations, relationships and so on.'[43]

Such was the universal lesson of this 'second modernity' for rich and poor, for S/M-practising philosophers and dope-smoking unemployed youth, for Cambridge dons and black American teenage moms alike: no longer *cuius regio, eius religio* (whose realm, his religion), as it was in the formation of the early modern European state, but, in the formation of the late modern neoliberal subject that has displaced that state, *cuius societas, eius forma vitae* (whose society, his form of life). Central to the neoliberal form of life were *les épreuves* by which we confront the selves given to us and which we must go beyond. These ordeals would not only be the province of cosmopolitan intellectuals, sexual libertines and bohemians but also of the unemployed older worker, the precarious youth and the single mother. The social state would be put on trial by the market as 'a privileged site of experimentation in which one can pinpoint the effects of excessive governmentality and take their measure',[44] as Foucault put it when paying homage to the Second Left theorist, Pierre Rosanvallon, in the course summary of his lectures on neoliberalism.

There was then a direct link between sociological theories of the individualization processes of late modernity and the programmes of government that sought to elicit such self-transformational capacities from the individual. This was the key lesson of the Third Way politics in which Anthony – later Lord – Giddens would play the 'crown theorist' to Tony Blair's New Labour. But the aporias of turning a general sociological theory of the subject into a normative governmental one would soon multiply, with devastating consequences for those who would meet the newly privatized, marketized and individualized service provision amid the ruins of the welfare state – Foucault's 'vast experimental field'. The categorization of

43 Beck, *Risk Society*, p. 135.
44 Foucault, *The Birth of Biopolitics*, p. 320.

individuals according to such individualizing capacities leads to a particular hierarchy in terms of their capability of exercising autonomy, and so to the emergence of multiple categories of those 'at high risk of welfare dependency', who should then be subject to a range of educational, training and therapeutic practices to assist them in the forming of capabilities and making the correct choices. According to Tom Boland and Ray Griffin, the welfare dependent is thereby placed in a permanent purgatory, awaiting an ever deferred entry into the paradise of the market, the enterprise and entrepreneurship.[45] Because they do not have, or have yet to develop, capacities for rational choice, they need to be encouraged, enticed and subject to trials, ordeals and tests; hence the long deliberation on and experimentation with the relationship between liberalism and paternalism, first with the New Paternalism[46] and later with the advocacy of a libertarian paternalism and nudge theory.[47]

During the 1970s, neoliberal policy prescriptions had been revealed not only to be entirely compatible with authoritarian and dictatorial regimes at national levels but, in many instances, to require them. By the 1990s, it was becoming clear that neoliberal prescriptions for the shaping of choice and freedom were necessarily connected to the instantiation of systems of obligation and coupled with more or less disciplinary, coercive and sovereign instruments. Combining these in an ordeal or trial, the widespread use of workfare programmes simulated employment for social welfare beneficiaries and made participation in them a condition for receiving benefits.[48] The limits of the governmentality of the welfare recipient are revealed by the increasing use of the removal

45 Tom Boland, and Ray Griffin, 'The Purgatorial Ethic and the Spirit of Welfare', *Journal of Classical Sociology* 18:2, 2017, pp. 87–103.

46 Lawrence M. Mead, *The New Paternalism: Supervisory Approaches to Poverty*, Washington DC: The Brookings Institution Press, 1997.

47 Richard H. Thaler and Cass R. Sunstein, 'Libertarian Paternalism Is Not an Oxymoron', University of Chicago Public Law & Legal Theory Working Paper No. 43, 2003.

48 Jamie Peck, 'Workfare: A Geopolitical Etymology', *Environment and Planning D, Society and Space* 16, 1998, pp. 133–61.

of benefits from the individual for failing to participate in these programmes or to apply for enough jobs, and the mandating of what benefits can be spent on. The net effect of this conditionality is the deterrence of the use of social welfare by large sections of the population, leaving them to the vagaries of the precarious and minimum-wage employment market, 'zero-hour' contracts, the 'gig economy', the support of their families and friends, the empty promises of entrepreneurship and start-ups, or, worse still, grifting and less socially acceptable ways of eking out a living. There is little choice between the ordeals required to remake oneself as an enterprise and the quotidian ordeals of a deconstructed labour market. The neoliberal celebration of identity and self-making is mired in the confrontations it generates in its experimentations within what was once the welfare state.[49] The model of *l'épreuve*, of the trial and of putting oneself to the test, of the infinitesimal calibrations of pleasure and pain, of the emergence of new identities and subjectivities, was no longer the preserve of the S/M club and its transgressive excitements, but had come to pervade the social sector entirely.

Confessional civil war

The cultural diagnosis most appropriate to the Fordist, industrial welfare state was perhaps Max Weber's 'iron cage', in which the individual was reduced to the compulsory pursuit of a career, or at least the performance of a job, within the industrial and bureaucratic divisions of labour of large corporations and government departments.[50] The fate of modernity appeared to be one of soullessness and alienation. Recently, in Europe and the United States,

49 Mitchell Dean, 'Liberal Government and Authoritarianism', *Economy and Society* 31:1, 2002, pp. 37–61.

50 Max Weber, *The Protestant Ethic and the Spirit of Capitalism*, trans. Talcott Parsons, London: Unwin, 1985, p. 181.

another trope has appeared: that of civil war. Emmanuel Macron, president of France, has used the term to describe the relationship between the European Union and self-proclaimed 'illiberal democracies' such as Viktor Orbán's Hungary and those following in its wake.[51] Many commentators in the United States have taken up the theme of civil war, for instance to describe the relation between the unpredictable authoritarian decisionism of the Trump administration that undermined the 'rule of law', and the legal protection of the autonomy of the states of the Union.[52] In this way, the cultural-political diagnostic of the present seems much closer to Carl Schmitt's analyses during the Weimar Republic than to those of Weber's *Protestant Ethic*, as a continuation of confessional civil war by other means.[53] Indeed, after the full flush of the alignment between liberalism and cosmopolitan globalism in the 1990s, we have witnessed the re-emergence of deadly antagonisms taking several forms: from the civilizational clashes theorized by Samuel Huntington, to the discovery of non-state enemies of humanity in the 'war on terror' during George W. Bush's administration, to the revival of state enemies such as Russia (condemned largely by progressive liberals) or the mass media and China (attacked by the alt-right). Today, these antagonisms take the form of a kind of low-intensity confessional civil war within liberal democracies themselves. This is especially exacerbated by the success of the liberal-progressive hashtag politics of the #MeToo and #BlackLivesMatter movements, on the one hand, and new points of social media articulation of the white supremacist far-right on the other.

On occasion, this confessional civil war manifests itself in the speeches of politicians during the hurly-burly of political campaigns. In the United States, a finance-friendly progressivist

51 Steven Erlanger, 'Fight Over Values Risks a "European Civil War", Macron Says', *New York Times*, 17 April 2018.

52 Linda Greenhouse, 'The Supreme Court and the New Civil War', *New York Times*, 26 April 2018.

53 Gary L. Ulmen, 'The Sociology of the State: Carl Schmitt and Max Weber', *State, Culture, and Society* 1:2, 1985, pp. 3–57.

neoliberalism has fought the alliance of a literally armed 'white working class' with Christian fundamentalists and evangelicals. Before Hillary Clinton's characterization at an 'LGBTQ gala' fundraiser of half of Trump's supporters as being in 'a basket of deplorables' – who were also, with a more theologically resonant accent, 'irredeemable' – there was the then senator Barack Obama's 2008 view of the 'white working class' who, due to economic hardship, become bitter and 'cling to guns and religion'.[54] In Europe during the debt crisis, the confessional civil war took place between the Protestant Northwest and its institutions – such as the Ordoliberal-inspired European Union, the European Central Bank and the German government and finance ministry – and the countries of the Orthodox and Catholic South and East. In the language of the German finance minister Wolfgang Schäuble, the latter lacked the 'solidity' of character and the regularized and self-responsible life conduct required for necessary European 'solidarity'.[55] In even more blunt terms, the head of the eurozone's finance ministers, Jeroen Dijsselbloem, questioned the idea of solidarity with those who 'spend all the money on drinks and women and then ask for help'.[56]

One does not have to accede to Macron's diagnosis to grant that civil war acts as an effective political imaginary in the present. From Macron's perspective, there is an identity between liberalism and democracy. In a speech to the European Parliament in April 2018, he warned that 'a sort of European civil war is reappearing' and the 'fascination with illiberalism is growing every day'.[57] While he allows for another type of democracy, 'authoritarian

---

54 Amy Chozick, 'Hillary Clinton Calls Many Trump Backers "Deplorables", and G.O.P. Pounces', *New York Times*, 10 September 2016.

55 Josef Hien, 'The Religious Foundations of the European Crisis', *Journal of Common Market Studies* 57:2, 2019. See the analysis of Schäuble's speeches on pp. 188–9.

56 Mehreen Khan and Paul McClean, 'Dijsselbloem Under Fire After Saying Eurozone Countries Wasted Money on "Alcohol and Women"', *Financial Times*, 21 March 2017.

57 Emmanuel Macron, Speech to the European Parliament, 20 April 2018.

democracy', he insists that only liberal democracy can truly secure the 'authority of democracy'. In doing so, he makes liberalism the saviour of democracy and a despotic or authoritarian liberalism a contradiction in terms. What has been called the 'rubber-bullet liberalism' of the police response to the *gilets jaunes* protests would appear to demonstrate otherwise.[58]

More broadly, the Macron view suppresses the different levels of the relationship between neoliberal rule and authoritarianism, whether at the scale of national regimes in relation to the international order or of the techniques of management of various populations and individuals. This perspective also fails to recognize how much of the neoliberal policy agenda is being implemented by that which it posits as its opposite. Rather than two opposed ideologies and contrasting worldviews, as in the Cold War binary of communism and capitalism, progressive financial neoliberalism finds a distorted version of itself in its Other. The nativist and racist expulsion from the body of the nation of undesirable populations is tightly coupled with the expulsion from the market of unnecessary regulation. Populism clings like mud shaped by neoliberalism's anti-statist and anti-bureaucracy tyre tracks, from Trump's 'drain the swamp' variety in the United States to the leader of Italy's La Lega party, Matteo Salvini, characterizing the then prime minister designate, Giuseppe Conte, as an 'expert in simplification and de-bureaucratization'.[59]

So what has happened? Neoliberalism as a thought collective and path dependency has largely succeeded in the economic 'neutralization' of the political left in the first two decades of the twenty-first century. The search for a left governmentality, or the making of the welfare state a 'vast experimental field' by centre-left parties, together with a widespread intellectual anti-statism and rejection of formal politics in favour of local social movements

58 Jane H. Caelinnan, 'Rubber-Bullet Liberalism', *Jacobin*, 1 February 2019.

59 Jason Horowitz, 'Italy's Populists Offer Giuseppe Conte for Prime Minister, NYU Claim in Question', *New York Times*, 21 May 2018.

and the vitality of civil society, has undermined labour and social democratic parties' organic concerns with the conditions of the working and precarious populations, leaving little effective voice of discontent other than anti-globalist appeals to a 'walled sovereignty'.[60] Instead, as exemplified by the Hillary Clinton campaign in 2016, the centre-left has become – or at least can be readily portrayed by its opponents as – the party of diversity and 'politically correct' identity politics disconnected from fundamental concerns around economic exploitation, widening inequality, narrowing life chances and falling life expectancy for a sizable segment of its traditional constituency. Even #MeToo, a movement which began as an important collective fight against sexual harassment and sexual exploitation, has been appropriated by a neoliberal individualist agenda focused on the number of women gaining entry to Harvard or becoming CEOs of major corporations, or on the relative size of Hollywood stars' pay cheques. As a consequence of this, it becomes possible to articulate economic grievance and disappointment by attacking the cultural as well as economic 'elites' of contemporary capitalism. It also becomes possible to articulate a kind of inverse identity politics for those left out of it. Thus, groups that include many who would be conventionally defined through ascribed characteristics as white, male and working-class demand to be heard not in terms of their class position but as yet another identity group with their own activities, needs and rights. Is not gun ownership simply another lifestyle choice for people in rural areas? In an age where sexual minorities discover the truth about themselves and assert their rights through the overcoming of ordeals, should the same not apply to the ordeals of involuntarily celibate men, as the 'incel' movement argues? As Walter Benn Michaels has recently noted, this dynamic is now leading an increasing number of white people to represent their own problems in terms of discrimination. In a society where the

60 Wendy Brown, *Walled Sovereignty, Waning States*, New York: Zone Books, 2010.

gap between the wealthiest 10 per cent and the rest is widening, a growing number of them, feeling themselves losing ground, think they are not victims of exploitation but of positive discrimination. As Benn Michaels notes, 'while Trumpists tell them they're the victims of racism', 'liberals tell them they're racists'.[61] The very way in which social injustice is understood has been profoundly affected as a result. The abandonment by the Left of traditional concerns with exploitation has opened the way for populism and a new identity politics on the Right, duly turned into a therapeutics with its own 'technologies of the self' offered by celebrity intellectuals – such as the Canadian psychologist, Jordan B. Peterson – who, in another time, might simply have been regarded as flaky or nutcases.

A parallel development has occurred in 'progressive' politics in general. It too has turned from the formal political domain of parties focused on state power to the question of subjectivity, as Foucault had forecast. If for Foucault, and Deleuze and Guattari, the main enemy of transversal politics was the fascism within each of us and the micro-fascisms in our daily lives and experiences, and particularly in the bearers of formal authority of all types,[62] today progressive politics, particularly in the United States, exhorts (and indeed trains through corporate 'diversity management' programmes) whites to confront their inner racism, and, in doing so, overcome what Robin DiAngelo has called their 'white fragility'.[63] Alongside the protests that erupted in the United States in 2020 against police killings of Black people, we find a renewed confessional politics that is closer to the self-mortification practices of *exomologesis* identified by Foucault than to the private confessionals of the experts of the welfare state he traced to the institutionalized Catholic Church. As

61 Walter Benn Michaels, 'The Political Economy of Anti-Racism', nonsite.org, Issue 23, 11 February 2018.

62 See, as the key exemplar, Foucault's 'Preface' to Deleuze and Guattari's *Anti-Oedipus*, pp. xi–xiv.

63 Robin DiAngelo, *White Fragility: Why It's So Hard for White People to Talk About Racism*, Boston: Beacon Press, 2018.

the warring sects of the seventeenth-century confessional conflicts in Europe illustrated, one of the problems with confronting the enemy within – in a process of 'lifelong self-transformation' that will allow entry into the charismatic community of believers – is that it is all too easy to identify those still possessed by such an inner enemy as your own deadly enemy. The 'civil religion of America', as Robert Bellah called it in the 1960s[64] – which allowed a degree of civility between conflicting groups with different interests and viewpoints and encompassed those without strong beliefs – can all too readily give way to a kind of sectarian violence between those passionately committed to diametrically opposed value systems. For us, the main lesson concerning the practice of confession lies not in the 'subjectification' machinery of the bureaucratic welfare state and the human sciences, as it did for Foucault, but in the new collective self-confrontations and experimentations, expiations of guilt and ordeals, that occur in public spaces and practices: in the workplace, on the streets, and in the stadium.

At the same time, and amplifying this, the kind of developments that undermined the Fordist system of industrial production and the welfare state have utterly transformed the previous hegemony of the capitalist media corporations and the form of public sphere and public narratives they sustained. Social media, and the forms of participation it has engendered, have not only multiplied sources of knowledge and opinion and increased opportunities for political participation and identification, they have also unravelled the regimes of truth characteristic of the mass media.[65] The 'objective' voice of the narration formed through the mass media is displaced by the more volatile swings of the public mood registered and almost immediately legible on social media, and by the tribal truths of those who make specific identifications through that media. The latter, of course, has become a new domain of

64 Robert N. Bellah, 'Civil Religion in America', *Daedalus: Journal of the American Academy of Arts and Sciences* 96, 1967, pp. 1–21.

65 Dean, 'Political Acclamation'.

political manipulation and control, much to the surprise of the peddlers of liberal teleologies promising the progressive expansion of civil society. Yet the relations of power and the possibilities of manipulation run much deeper than the surveillance society or 'algorithmic governmentality' can allow. While there is much hyperbolic talk of a 'politics of untruth' or of 'post-truth politics', we can at least say that the mass media, like science, has lost its monopoly on truth. Indeed, the demand for the regulation of social media in the name of individual privacy and truthful public discourse, and the protests in defence of science, can be understood as belated and parallel attempts by the mass media and institutionalized science to reclaim their monopolies on certain manifestations of truth. What is paradoxical is that those who might once have criticized the mass media as purveyors of ideology and science as reductionist and positivist now find themselves aligned with both.

When the alt-right emerged as an actor in the 2016 US election, it may have appeared as little more than white supremacism mixed with wounded masculine aggression.[66] However, at least publicly, it succeeded in representing itself as a conjunction of social media savvy with the appropriation of identity politics on behalf of the 'forgotten' populations laid to waste by global capitalist competition and the deconstructed welfare state. It demonstrated how the political manipulation of the public sphere could now be extended from the dispositive of public opinion associated with the mass media to the dispositive of the 'public mood' formed through social media.

While it is easy, if somewhat facile, to regard this latter shift as a seismic catastrophe for liberal democracy, one could argue that it was founded on an extension of one of the oldest elements of democracy: acclamation, the shouts and cries accompanied by hand gestures and flag waving, that were at the core of both the

66 Joshua Green, *Devil's Bargain: Steve Bannon, Donald Trump and the Storming of the Presidency*, New York: Penguin Press, 2017.

liturgical power of the Christian church and the mass identifications of authoritarian and direct democracies.[67] The acclamations of the public assembly, which had been displaced by the kind of acclamation produced by the corporate mass media, was now being renewed, not least by the 2016 Trump campaign itself, in tandem with the likes, posts and 'friending' of social media. These 'digital marketing' techniques that had formed the basis of the business model of social media platforms now found their way into the marketing of political candidates. Insofar as both populist politics and social media posts are versions of acclamatory will and affect, they share a previously unacknowledged affinity. While the Trump campaign exemplified the links between the acclamations of the political rally and those of social media,[68] it is not without note that both parties in Italy's populist government of 2018 were adept in social media mobilization, with Five Star beginning as a digital movement. The Tories in the UK were quick to learn these lessons in relation to the 2019 election campaign. The ensuing scandals (notably Cambridge Analytica's use of Facebook profiles in the case of Brexit) were nothing more than the surface ripples of a deeper break in the transformation of the form of political acclamation that has provided legitimation within liberal democracies. Political acclamation has gone viral. It has jumped not only platforms, but also forms of media and kinds of social and political collectivity.

It is remarkable that this shift in liberal democratic politics under Trump was articulated in a similar fashion to the rollback phase of neoliberalism in the 1980s. Deregulation occured in relation to environmental and financial areas (on the latter, witness the fate of Dodd–Frank). There was the abandonment of international agreements that impose regulatory standards and frameworks, for example, the Paris Accords on climate change. For the first time in

67 See Heron, *Liturgical Power*.

68 Mitchell Dean, 'The dark arts reach the internet', *TELOSscope*, 27 March 2018.

a quarter century, there was a disarticulation of neoliberalism and globalism, manifest in the withdrawal or threatened withdrawal from international trade agreements or the demand for a renegotiation of their terms. Given the success of the Left takeover of neoliberal forms of governmentality, the response was less a form of governmentality than an anti-governmentality, a search for a pure and virtuous market or national economy, no longer tethered by governmental regulation. In the US Executive Order of 10 April 2018, 'welfare reform' became equivalent to enforcing a requirement of work for those seeking assistance of any kind, thus strengthening the 'purgatorial ethic' that has animated it.[69] In the demand for a removal of those vestiges of the welfare state that distort human virtue and proper conduct, there are deep layers of differential treatment of populations according to race and place. Nevertheless, the governmentality of the sophisticated social democratic activation machine proved as dispensable in the Trump era as the Art Deco friezes of the demolished Bonwit building were that made way for Trump Tower.

One should not underestimate how attitudes and most importantly affects toward race, migration and Muslims played a significant role in the electoral behaviour of white voters in the United States. However, a key question remains unanswered. It concerns how such attitudes and affects are mobilized and manipulated today. Here, the need for rethinking the formation of the public sphere and the role of social and digital media is apparent, as too is the need for asking hard questions about the nature of political identification and the form that political acclamation takes today. The assertion of the presence of a new sphere of political manipulability is something to be explained, rather than itself being the explanation it is often claimed to be. If at the core of these political identifications are affects such as resentments toward others, then how have these resentments become central to the political behaviour of large numbers of people? While we should not ignore the

69 Boland and Griffin, 'The Purgatorial Ethic and the Spirit of Welfare'.

complex history of racial and ethnic domination and exclusion in formerly colonial powers and current imperial ones, the neoliberal erosion of the welfare state and its transformation into a sphere akin to purgatory for welfare recipients and those rendered jobless only intensifies the personal experience of precarity, the resentment of those who must have recourse to welfare, and the 'demonization' of those who have no other option.[70]

Contemporary neoliberalism is rogue in the sense that it has lost its identification with a unified political movement providing it with some kind of legitimacy. Broadly, it first entered the public political domain in the guise of a conservatism during its rollback phase, and then turned to labour and social democratic parties during its rollout, or implementation phase. Today, a rogue neoliberalism belongs to no one side and attaches itself to diverse political and economic formations: fundamentalist Christians and diversity advocates, finance and real estate capital, progressive liberals and conservative authoritarians, sovereign decisionism and the rule of law. Anti-bureaucratic advocacy for businesses, the belief in market-based solutions, even for climate change, the vociferous boosterism of entrepreneurship and innovation, and the mantra of individual responsibility and self-help are shared across progressive and reactive neoliberalism. With a few noble exceptions, the Left has dealt itself out of the political game or joined on the side of progressivist neoliberalism. If there is a civil war, it is like the conflict between various kinds of Catholics and Protestants four centuries ago, not a war between different religions but between different confessions of the same religion. Neoliberalism, in seeking an economic neutralization of the political through the reconstruction of the state and the public domain as a set of markets, has displaced the political into the realm of affective identity and identification: diverse and inclusive on the one hand; supremacist and nativist on the other. The opportunities

70 Adam Kotsko, *Neoliberalism's Demons*, Stanford: Stanford University Press, 2018.

for the expression of and participation in such a form of politics have multiplied with the internet; the key mechanisms of identification are the acclamations (and narcissistic self-acclamations) that define social media. Neoliberalism has become a series of rogue affects, of tribal identifications formed through the ordeals and tests that mark, tattoo, mould and dress bodies in the pleasures of the enterprise, paraded in its different paradigms by a series of families that cross political divides: the Trumps, the Clintons, the Obamas, the Macrons, the Kardashians. The search for a left governmentality marked the abandonment of the traditional core constituencies of labour and social democracy who, if they can still be bothered to vote, might now declaim (give a 'thumbs down' to) the system itself, as in Brexit, or acclaim (give a 'thumbs up' to) those who are the most entertaining ('BoJo', 'the Donald'). The art of digital political marketing is to encourage such affects at the moment closest to the entry to the voting booth, itself now a moment of privatized acclamation or consumer choice rather than of thoughtfulness and careful deliberation.

The present moment is also a crucial one for the humanities and social sciences, which are undergoing their own transformations with the reconstruction of the university space of research and teaching as one of competition and performance. They have the tools, the methods, the heritage and the historical sense to make the present intelligible. However, they are hampered by the inherited and now quite dominant critical traditions following post-structuralism and the turn to understanding power as a purely immanent phenomenon that have, among other things, reduced the political to a debate over forms of governance, displayed and encouraged an analytical anti-statism, and absolutely neglected the problem of the formation of publics through the acclamations, ceremonies, protocols and liturgies of politics and political communication. If, in the 1970s, the external enemy of totalitarianism presented a barrier to critical thought concerning liberal democratic capitalism, today the internal enemy of populism plays a similar and additional role.

One way out of these analytical shortcomings has, for the past few years at least, been the radical problematizations made available by first a political and then an economic theology.[71] In the latter, we find the broadest and most compelling attempt to rethink – using the history not only of discourses of civil government but also those of divine government – the relationship between the mundane governance and economic management of life and the sovereign power that is constituted as its foundation and source of authority. In this respect, contemporary critical thought is slowly finding a way to pose the questions of sovereignty, law and the state, of the basis of legitimation of social and political orders, and of the sources and origins of power and authority, that were systematically occluded in the political thought of Michel Foucault. If his thought maintains a relevance today, it is for what it fails to observe, and for what it perversely anticipates, particularly in the course of a Left politics underscored by the anti-statist and anti-bureaucratic valorizations of civil society, social movements and identity politics. Chief among these are the continued pertinence of the search for a supreme power and its foundations even within economic forms of rule, and the way the relation of self to self is not simply a source of resistance to power, a modality of counter-conduct to the hegemonic forms of the government of conduct, but will become the essential weapon of neoliberal governing and politics.

We know we place ourselves at risk by making the arguments in this book. It will be said that Foucault's work was more nuanced, complicated and subtle than any attempt to give his work the coherence we have found can encompass, that we have failed to

71 See, for example, Elettra Stimilli, *The Debt of the Living: Ascesis and Capitalism*, trans. Arianna Bove, Albany: SUNY Press, 2017; Dotan Leshem, *The Origins of Neoliberalism: Modeling the Economy from Jesus to Foucault*, New York: Columbia University Press, 2016; Devin Singh, *Divine Currency: The Theological Power of Money in the West*, Stanford: Stanford University Press, 2018; and Heron, *Liturgical Power*.

read him properly by attributing value positions to him where there were none. But, by placing his work in its historical, political and social context, we have sought to understand the relation between the analyses found in his major texts and lectures and the occasions on which he did, quite explicitly, align himself with and support particular political actions and organizations, whether in France or abroad. In general, Foucault tended to perform a kind of normativity rather than explicate a value-based one – and it is this performing of positions within a definite context, in relationship to particular interlocutors and a specific political conjuncture, that we have sought to make intelligible here. In this chapter, by tracing some of the effects within contemporary thought and practice, we have sought to pose very fundamental questions, far from alien to those of Foucault himself. Our reflections on Foucault were not intended to capture every equivocation of the author in his work, every hesitation between his intention and the expression of his thought, every advance toward and retreat from the full implications of his claims, every movement of his mind, every paradox with which he teased us, or every felicitous and illuminating indecision that troubled his intelligence. We have tried instead to discover the inner logic and trajectory of Foucault's thought, so that we can decide what its effects are today, what parts of it might still illuminate the dilemmas of our time, our present and our struggles, and what parts of it can now join the dusty shelves full of the ideas of eminent thinkers given every due consideration but now significant only as elements of our intellectual pre-history or of the eternal Academy.

Epilogue

When we use Foucault today, we can no longer imagine that we have entered a safe haven or that his name invokes an intellectual insurance policy against analytical missteps or political enthusiasms. Certainly, his pronouncements on rape or the age of consent would appear naive and unreflective to us, and his lack of attention to inequality, both at a structural level and in regard to interpersonal morality, would diminish his relevance to our present. The case of Iran can serve as a salutary warning in itself. There are, no doubt, keen insights in his writings about and anticipation of the world-changing impacts of Islamic movements. But his support for the mullahs and failure to appreciate the political complexity of the uprising and its different elements contributed to shaping public opinion in Europe while underestimating the immediately violent and oppressive consequences of the installation of a Shi'ite theocracy there. It is true that he discovered in the Iranian revolution a series of elements often overlooked in conventional political analysis, in particular the ceremonial and liturgical character of mass politics and the acclamatory relation between the charismatic leader and his followers. But there is a double misstep in this observation. First, Foucault disconnects his analysis of political spirituality from the more mundane political analysis of factional rivalries and alliances, and thus ignores the multiple actors with different objectives at play in the Iranian uprising. This gives his own analysis a strangely populist and celebratory cast in terms of the relation between the charismatic leader and the movement. Second, he projects this political spirituality onto the Orient and claims that none of these elements of sovereignty, including liturgy and acclamation, continue to be in play in Europe and the West. Given the recent recharging of nationalist and sovereigntist politics and powers, and the emergence of charismatic, strong leaders capable of eliciting popular acclamations and identifications, this judgement too would seem to reveal the limits of his thought in our present.

We must also be aware that his legacy is now the subject of a struggle, involving in particular those who consider the final Foucault to be entirely compatible with what Nancy Fraser called 'progressive neoliberalism': this 'real and powerful' if unlikely alliance between, 'on the one hand, mainstream liberal currents of the new social movements (feminism, antiracism, multiculturalism, environmentalism, and LGBTQ rights)' and, 'on the other hand, the most dynamic, high-end "symbolic" and financial sectors of the U.S. economy (Wall Street, Silicon Valley, and Hollywood)', temporarily uniting 'a distinctive combination of points of view on distribution and recognition'.[1] We do not doubt the importance of these social movements and do not underestimate their emancipatory goals or the stress they place on personal fulfilment and transformation. However, if the 1980s posed the question of the articulation between working-class politics and these new social movements, then that articulation was not helped by Foucault's relentless bifurcation of the old class politics from the politics of the transformation of subjectivity in new lifestyles, downplaying of the importance of the state and the juridical order in favour of

1 Nancy Fraser, 'From Progressive Neoliberalism to Trump – and Beyond', *American Affairs* 1:4, 2017.

local experimentations, and somewhat bizarre valorization of the 'ordeal' over the inquiry. Indeed, as we have seen, by conceiving liberal governmental measures in relation to the veridiction of the market as *épreuves*, he suggested a fundamental relation between the forms of personal and political austerity that would characterize the neoliberal subject.

Moreover, his enduring suspicion of conventional state-centred politics, rooted in French anti-totalitarianism, and his opposition to any organized socialist or social democratic project, do not serve us well in engaging with the consequences of the most effective political thought collective of the last forty years – a collective that has contributed to rising inequality, austerity and public debt, accelerated the corrosion of public services, public office and public trust, and reduced the capacity of actual existing democracies to address the problems of economy, health, security and environment that confront them. It is this anti-statism that has led to a widespread implosion of the parliamentary Left. What has replaced it is not a left governmentality but a recharged sovereignty that Foucault imagined had been displaced in the West, replete with the rituals of public assembly and charismatic acclamation he had found only in Iran and in the European past. Yet today, the clear and present danger of totalitarianism manifests itself not in the sclerotic hierarchies of communist parties or in the bureaucracies of the welfare state, but in the failure of the political system to address questions of inequality and exploitation and the capillary proliferation of neo-fascist movements.

Perhaps, to some extent, Foucault both foresaw and participated in the formation of a certain alliance between two critiques of the welfare state: one that would seek a transformation of the public sector through the generalization of a market rationality, and one that sought a maximization of autonomy, self-government and difference outside of institutional knowledge and practices. While closer to the latter, he came to recognize both as critiques of the state of the 1970s. While neoliberalism is often imagined as an ideology imposed by the Right, its most effective agents have often been precisely those intellectual elements and parties of the Left that managed to articulate the desire for autonomy against the disciplinary forces of the welfare state with the new forms of regulation rooted in a market rationality. It is perhaps up to us, in an era in which inequality and public austerity are at the centre of the political agenda, to prise these two critiques apart, to demonstrate the socially destructive effects of neoliberal policies and to rearticulate a liberatory ethos along with policies that curtail the growth of inequality while strengthening social rights and protections. As a first step, we must recognize the extent to which those ways of thinking we have made our own have played their own small part in our pervasive and disabling contemporary anti-statism.

We find the reality of Foucault's story more incredible even than anything imagined by the novelist Laurent Binet. While Binet's *The Seventh Function of Language* is a classic *roman policier* populated by well-known intellectuals of the 1980s (including Foucault), the release in 2011 of a redacted 1985 CIA report on French intellectuals suggests that Foucault's life had already become part of a spy thriller. Viewing the situation through their concern with America's status in French public opinion and political discourse, the CIA intelligence gatherers got quite a lot right about changes in the French intellectual and political scene: the shift to an interest in economic liberalism across the political spectrum that would displace the old Right tainted by collaboration and fascism; the effects of anti-Sovietism and anti-totalitarianism on French domestic politics and the perception of the US; the emergence of a new centre-left within the Socialist Party and the schisms of the Left; the centrality of the New Philosophers, and their use of media and publishing houses as weapons in struggles. Foucault would play a role in each of these shifts. The report concludes by granting him the highest position in the French intellectual pantheon and noting, not without subtlety, his favourable disposition toward the New Philosophers:

> the New Right can point to kudos from Michel Foucault, France's most profound and influential thinker. Foucault has praised the upstarts for, among other things, reminding philosophers of the 'bloody' consequences that have flowed from the rationalist social theory of the 18th-century Enlightenment and the Revolutionary era.[2]

The release of this CIA report completes a strange circle that would be of interest to the novelist but for us can only remain in the realm of historical contingency. The CIA would notoriously conduct human experiments with LSD from the 1950s under its Project MKUltra. Indeed, the dismissed Harvard faculty member who conducted his own experiments at that university with mind-altering chemicals, Timothy Leary, would give the spy organization 'total credit for inspiring and sponsoring the entire consciousness movement and counter-culture events of the 1960s'.[3] Simeon Wade, one of the two men who gave Foucault LSD, and himself a proselytizer of the generative effects of hallucinogenic drugs, had known Leary while doing his PhD on intellectual history at Harvard.[4] Of course, none of this is to indicate some greater conspiracy, although one can certainly imagine an historical novel plotted around these small degrees of separation. Rather, it suggests that Foucault's own 'acid test', his own *épreuve* at Zabriskie Point in 1975, like his other limit-experiences in the sadomasochism clubs of New York and San Francisco, the Tokyo Zen temple or the Taoist communes in California, was not simply a matter of the 'relation of self to self'. The biographical facts of his life and his death from AIDS cannot be

2 Office of European Analysis, *France: Defection of the Leftist Intellectuals. A Research Paper*, Directorate of Intelligence, Central Intelligence Agency, 1985, p. 14.

3 'Timothy Leary Credits CIA for LSD', available on YouTube.

4 Dundas, 'Foreword' to Wade, *Foucault in California*, pp. x–xi.

dissociated from the characteristic but pervasive cultural, political, erotic, economic and even espionage experiments of his era. This 'true' story is so strange that it would be hard for a novelist to create it solely from their imagination, let alone construct a coherent narrative around it. Its implications for our present and our politics nevertheless remain hugely significant.

Index